THE FLEXIBILITY PARADOX

Why Flexible Working Leads to (Self-)Exploitation

Heejung Chung

First published in Great Britain in 2022 by

Policy Press, an imprint of
Bristol University Press
University of Bristol
1–9 Old Park Hill
Bristol
BS2 8BB
UK
t: +44 (0)117 954 5940
e: bup-info@bristol.ac.uk

Details of international sales and distribution partners are available at
policy.bristoluniversitypress.co.uk

British Library Cataloguing in Publication Data
A catalogue record for this book is available from the British Library

ISBN 978-1-4473-5477-2 hardcover
ISBN 978-1-4473-5481-9 ePub
ISBN 978-1-4473-5479-6 ePdf

Cover design: Nicky Borowiec
Image credit: AdobeStock
Bristol University Press and Policy Press use environmentally responsible print partners.
Printed and bound in Great Britain by CPI Group (UK) Ltd, Croydon, CR0 4YY

This book was written as a part of my lifelong goal to make our society one where everyone can work shorter, flexible, autonomous and thus more productive and socially meaningful hours.

Contents

List of figures, tables and box

Figures

Tables

Box

Acknowledgements

Writing a book is hard. Writing a book during a pandemic is even harder. Writing a book about flexible working during the pandemic where all of a sudden half the population was working from home seemed impossible. It felt like trying to measure a very fast-moving target. Although I hesitated, thinking that by the time the manuscript was published it would be outdated, I've decided it was time. It felt like more than ever people needed a book that talked about the potential negative consequences of the all-so-coveted flexible working, control over one's work. More importantly, it felt like people needed solutions, and quick. So here's my five cents on the issue.

The book was definitely a group effort. The book would not have been possible without the UK Economic and Social Research Council who funded much of the research presented in this book. I would like to thank all my co-authors and collaborators who have worked on different papers and projects over the years which I draw heavily from. This includes Mariska van der Horst, Tanja van der Lippe, Pia Schober (my BFF!), Hyojin Seo, Cara Booker, Clare Kelliher, Lonnie Golden, Steve Sweet, Deniz Yucel, Sarah Forbes, Holly Birkett and Pierre Walthery. I would like to especially thank Yvonne Lott, an amazing co-author and partner-in-crime in examining issues around flexible working and gender inequality who has given me detailed feedback on this book. I would also like to thank the RAs of the project, Jon Ward and Yeosun Yoon who made this project what it is. There are also people whom I consider the flexible working and work-family research all-stars, who have helped me grow as a researcher over the years. Their work influenced me greatly as you will see their names being frequented in the reference list. This includes Erin Kelly, Hans Pongratz, Jennifer Glass, Laura Den Dulk, Jaesung Kim, Anna Kurowska, Clare Lyonette, Pascale Peters, Peter Berg, Scott Schieman, Mara Yerkes and others in the Work and Family Researchers Network and the European Social Policy Analysis Network. Thank you all for those exciting discussions, many of which over dinner and wine. There are editors of journals and books, and the anonymous reviewers of this book and articles I've published. I would especially like to thank Jana Javornik, Jennifer Tomlinson, Emmanuele Pavolini and Martin Seeleib-Kaiser.

There are practitioners, journalists and book authors whose work has shaped me greatly, people fighting the same good fight as myself, and through numerous discussions with them my thoughts became much clearer. These include Christine Armstrong, Mandy Garner, Josie Cox, Emma Jacobs, Alexandra Topping, Rebecca Seal, David D'Souza, Gem Dale, those at Radio Kent and others. I would especially like to thank Brigid Schulte (and others at the Better Life Lab), a real champion of my work, who has helped me throughout my project. Alex Soo-jung Kim Pang has been an incredible ally of good working practices, whose work always inspires me. There are policy organisations I would like to thank, and people, many of whom have moved onto other jobs! This includes the UK Government Equalities Office (Francine Hudson), BEIS (Rebecca Jones-Mahmut), DWP (Damien Smith), TUC (Scarlet Harris), Working Families, the ILO (Jon Messenger), Chartered Management Institute, Chartered Institute for Personnel Development, Time Wise, the Fatherhood Institute, Workingmums, the European Foundation, COFACE (Liz Gosme and Paola Panzeri), Business Europe, ETUC, the European Commission – DG Justice (Greet Vermeylen) the Korean Labor Institute, and the Korean Confederation of Trade Unions (Lee JooHo), and many others. Thank you to those at Policy Press, especially Laura Vickers-Rendall, who made this book possible. Thank you to Adam J. Kurtz for allowing me to use his artwork.

Now to those who made life fun and enabled me to detach away from work, helping me to stop the flexibility paradox from happening to me! Trude Sundberg and Tina Haux who were always there and gave me feedback for this book. Beth Breeze did her magic to help me get the grant. I also want to thank Lindsey Cameron, Kate Matthews, Harmonie Toros, Caroline Chatwin, Anke Plagnol, Alex Afonso, Teresa Kao, Jongwoo Kim, Youngjun Choi, Vince Miller, Jess and Ashley Littlewood, colleagues at the University of Kent, my band Melzebra and the Buffalos, my football club The Canterbury Old Bags, the neighbourhood gang the Hillywoods and many others across the world (Seoul, Amsterdam, Berlin and so on). I want to thank those, especially women, whose support in carrying out much of the unpaid domestic labour enabled me to have the time and space to carry out this work. This book is also the fruits of their labour. Finally, I would like to thank my family in Korea, Germany, across the world. I would especially like to thank my grandma, my number-one fan, who sadly passed away in 2018. She would have been overjoyed to see this book come out. I want to thank those who have to deal with me on a day-to-day basis – Marcel, Hannah, Buttercup and Sparky. You guys drive me nuts and keep me sane. I will always bask in your love. I want to finally dedicate this book to the flexible worker. Writing this book has provided me with an opportunity for reflection on my own ways of working and living as an 'autonomous' worker. I hope this book enables many others to do the same.

Introduction: The flexibility paradox and contexts

Introduction

Who doesn't want to have the freedom to choose where to work and when to work? This seems like a no-brainer. As human beings, most, if not all of us, are naturally inclined to love having more control over our lives. Control over our work is bound to let us shape work around other demands of our lives, our family lives, our hobbies and other pursuits. It should potentially expand our leisure and let us enjoy our lives outside of work more. Right? Then why is it that the groups with the most control over their work, such as academics or software programmers, who are given the freedom to work whenever and wherever they wish, end up working excessive hours (Bothwell, 2018)?[1] This book is about exactly this – the flexibility paradox – why freedom leads to even more self-exploitation – or to quote Orwell, 'Freedom is Slavery'. Why when workers have more control over their work, they end up working all the time and everywhere. Why when workers get access to unlimited holidays, they end up taking less. Why despite the myth of academics getting three months off in summer, many academics end up struggling to spend even a fortnight on vacation.

This isn't just about academics. As the later chapters (Chapter 5 to 7) will show, this is a phenomenon that cuts across a larger group of the population and resonate with many people. I've realised how much this is the case when my think piece – 'Flexible working is making us work longer' – gained an incredible amount of attention in 2016,[2] with many people commenting on how the story I wrote reflected their own experience of working flexibly, regardless of what they did and where they lived. So why does this happen? To better understand the flexibility paradox, why more control over our work leads to more self-exploitation, it is important to understand the larger societal context in which flexible working was/is being introduced. What this book sets out to explain is that the freedom and control over your work isn't really freedom away from work largely due to the context in which we live in, namely, a work-centric society, where passion at work is expected and where traditional gender norms prevail. Flexible working is merely an amplifier – whatever problems your work/gender culture are likely to produce, it will amplify these problems to the max – which obviously means different things for men and women. In this book, for the sake of simplicity and data restrictions, gender is divided into men and women. However, it is important to note and accept the wide range of gender identities that spans the two spectrums.

The contexts

In this section, I will very briefly discuss some key trends that have driven the rise in flexible working in recent times; including the rise in female labour market participation, increased demand for work–life balance from all workers including fathers, and the developments we see in digital technologies. The need to improve productivity and cut costs, including real estate costs especially in central locations in major cities, environmental issues, and the COVID-19 pandemic and the lockdown measures that followed are also crucial factors that have driven the debates around flexible working. I will also explore some key contexts that help us understand why the flexibility paradox phenomenon happens. There are many, but I will focus on work-centred cultures and the rise in passion at work, the rise in insecurity among workers, and the decline in workers' negotiation powers. Contexts such as work culture, gender normative culture, and institutional contexts are examined more closely in Chapter 9.

Contexts of the increase in flexible working

Increase in female employment and demand for better work–life balance

Since the 1970s there has been an increase in women's participation in the labour market. For example, in the UK in 1971, 53 per cent of women between the age of 16 and 64 were employed, while by 2020, this number rose to 73 per cent (ONS, 2021b). One of the biggest growths in female employment rates was found among mothers with dependent children – for example, 75 per cent of women with dependent children were employed in 2019, outnumbering that of women without children (ONS, 2019). Similar trends have been found all over the world, where mothers' employment rates have risen significantly, especially among those with tertiary education levels (OECD). This has led to an increase in the demand for a better work–life balance from both men and women. Even up to the 1960s, although large variations exist, the societal norm was that of the male-breadwinner and the female-caregiver. Fathers were perceived to be responsible for the breadwinning for the entire (nuclear or sometime extended) family while wives or mothers were expected to stay at home and tend to the housework and childcare. According to the British Social Attitude survey, even in the late 1980s, half of all respondents agreed with the statement 'a man's job is to earn money; a woman's job is to look after the home and family' (Scott and Clery, 2013). By 2017, this dropped to 8 per cent of the population (Taylor and Scott, 2018).

Once this traditional division of labour was disrupted, a large number of workers needed changes in work arrangements that enables a better balance between work and family life. This was mostly demanded by women, who still carried out the bulk of the housework and care (Hochschild and Machung, 1989; Bianchi et al, 2012; Dotti Sani and Treas, 2016). However, this demand for better work-life balance has also increased among men, especially of younger generations (Deloitte, 2018; Franklin, 2019). For example, in a survey of fathers in the UK in 2017, 69 per cent said they would consider their childcare arrangements before they took a new job or promotion, close to half (47 per cent) wanted to downshift into a less stressful job due to family and care reasons, and more than a third (38 per cent) said they would be willing to take a pay cut to achieve a better work-life balance (Working Families, 2017). For many companies, there is now an increasing pressure to provide flexible working policies for their employees especially if they want to recruit and retain the best skilled staff. This is especially the case for companies where their target workforce is spread across the world – where in some cases, as we will show later, companies opt out of any real physical office space at all. Ironically, however, this increase in demand for work-life balance happened when in countries like the US, working hours for full-time workers steadily increased (Schor, 2008) and when developments in technologies made the blurring of boundaries easier (Working Families, 2021).

Developments in digital technologies

Another driver of flexible working, especially in relation to remote working/working from home is the development of technology. In the past few decades we have seen an accelerated speed in the development of technologies that allows us to work anywhere and everywhere. According to the report by the European Foundation and the International Labour Office (Eurofound and the International Labour Office, 2017), in 2015, around 60 per cent of all workers in Europe used some sort of technological/information devices such as computers, laptops, smartphones, tablets or other portable devices at work. Furthermore, 98 per cent of companies, excluding micro companies of ten or less employees, used computers in their work and 97 per cent used internet access for their work. Similarly, in a report in 2016 (Muro et al, 2017) 23 per cent of all US jobs were seen to require high digital skills, up from 5 per cent in 2002, and an additional 48 per cent of all jobs were seen to require medium digital skills, again up from 40 per cent in 2002. The rise in the use of digital technology was especially the case for higher-paid/higher-skilled service occupations. However, what this report highlighted is that many other jobs that previously did not use any digital technology, such as warehouse workers, now make use of computers and other devices in their work. With such changes in modern-day workplaces, as well as a surge of different apps and software that allows workers to work remotely, the possibility of working from home has increased.

Commuting, and office and travel costs

Remote working has also increased due to the rise in rent/building costs, especially among companies based in large urban areas (Lyonette et al, 2016). Many companies are opting for smart working spaces – where desk space is shared – and increasingly, we are seeing (large) companies without any physical office spaces. For example, Automattic, a large multi-national company with more than 900 workers, does not have a real office space and the majority of the work is done online. They cited office costs as the main reason for going fully remote (Hannah, 2019). Having an all-remote work environment also means that organisations can save housing costs for employees, who do not have to pay for houses/rent in major cities such as New York and London. This can cut down on the business costs of having to supplement rental costs. Environmental issues are also a factor when it comes to the use of flexible working arrangements (Hook et al, 2020). Flexitime and staggered start and end times of work can help workers avoid peak congestion times of mass commutes, which in turn helps others who have no choice but to stick to a nine-to-five schedule. Enabling workers to work from home helps tackle environmental issues by reducing the carbon emissions and air pollution that would have been generated by the commute. A good example of the extent to which this can help is what happened in 2020 during the period of COVID-19 in parts of China during lockdown, where we saw a significant improvement in air quality (He et al, 2020), although not all of this can be purely down to working from home. Post-COVID-19, many companies, especially those who were targeted as some of the key drivers of climate change – for example oil industries – have mentioned the need to cut the carbon footprint of their offices as one of the key reasons why they were moving towards remote and other flexible working practices (Ambrose, 2021).

COVID-19

Possibly the largest factor that has driven and will drive the increase of flexible working practices in the future is the COVID-19 pandemic and the lockdown measures that were in place to contain the spread of the virus. We explore the changes that occurred during the COVID-19 pandemic in greater detail in Chapter 10. It is worth noting that despite the growing demand for homeworking, we did not see a remarkable growth in the past decade (for more see Chapter 2). However, in 2020 with the majority of industrialised countries being forced to go into national lockdowns due to the spread of the virus, we have seen a rapid increase in flexible working practice. For example, in the UK, half of the workforce was working from home during the pandemic (ONS, 2020d). For white-collar office workers, the proportion rises to up to 80–90 per cent (McKinsey, 2020a). We also see a rise in homeworking in sectors previously thought to be impossible to carry out work from home, such as education and health care sectors. The pandemic has given rise to a sharp uptake of software and digital platforms that have been developed in recent years (McKinsey, 2020a). In other words, COVID-19 has provided companies a kickstart in the implementation of systems that allow for more remote working. What is more, as the lockdown measures were prolonged, managers and workers are beginning to see the benefits of the new digitalised workplaces (CIPD, 2021). We are seeing several reports of companies now transforming the way they work with hybrid office and homeworking practices expected to be embedded in most companies in the future. We have also seen a change in workers' perception towards flexible working, where most workers want a hybrid combination of working from home two or three days a week, with full-time office-working becoming less of a norm (Alexander et al, 2021; Burgess and Goldman, 2021; CIPD, 2021) (more in Chapter 10).

Contexts of self-exploitation

Always-on culture

Due to developments in technology, we now have the ability to work anywhere though our various mobile devices. As Alex Soo-jung Kim Pang notes, "we now carry our offices around in our pockets".[3] In a study by a UK job search site (Nair, 2018), two thirds of all UK workers surveyed said they had sent work-related emails and made work-related calls outside of working hours, and a similar number agreed that mobile devices have blurred the lines between their work and their personal lives. This type of 'always-on' culture has resulted in poor sleep, stress, exhaustion and encroachment on family and leisure time. Many companies and countries are trying to tackle this – including the right to disconnect policies introduced by the French government in 2017 (Barrett, 2019), recently introduced in Ireland,[4] Portugal, and currently being discussed in the European Parliament (European Parliament, 2021). Other policies also exist, such as the one introduced by Daimler in Germany in 2014 where your emails were automatically deleted when you went on holiday (Gibson, 2014). However, despite these developments, we are entering a culture where workers are expected to be accessible at all times given that the technological developments we have seen over the years have enabled this to happen. This is not helped by the rise in insecurity and work–centred cultures.

Insecurity

The current context in which the majority of us operate is one of declining workers' negotiation power both collectively and individually, resulting in widespread insecurity. Union density has been declining since the 1970s/80s in most OECD countries. Currently in most countries, with the exception of some Northern European countries, less than a quarter of workers are unionised according to the most recent OECD data (see Figure 1.1). This, together with the rise of precarious contracts (Standing, 2011), has led to a large and growing number of workers feeling insecure about their employment and future income (van Oorschot and Chung, 2015). According to the European Social Survey in 2016/17, across the 23 European countries surveyed, more than one in five workers felt that it was likely or very likely that they would lose their job and would have to spend some time looking for another one in the near future (see Figure 1.2). This is especially worse for the younger generation, where a quarter of those under 30 felt that

Figure 1.1: Trends in trade union density across selected OECD countries from 1960 to most recent data

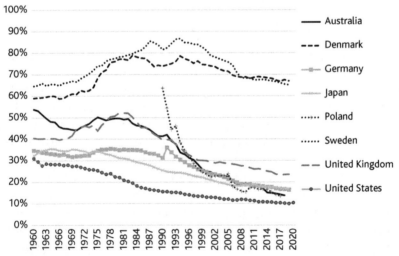

Source: OECD.stat

Note: Percentages are based on administrative data, with the exception of the United States from 1981 and some years for Australia and Sweden where survey data was used only when administrative data was not available. Some data points have been smoothed out across time when interim data points were not available.

Figure 1.2: Prevalence of income and employment insecurity across Europe in 2016/17

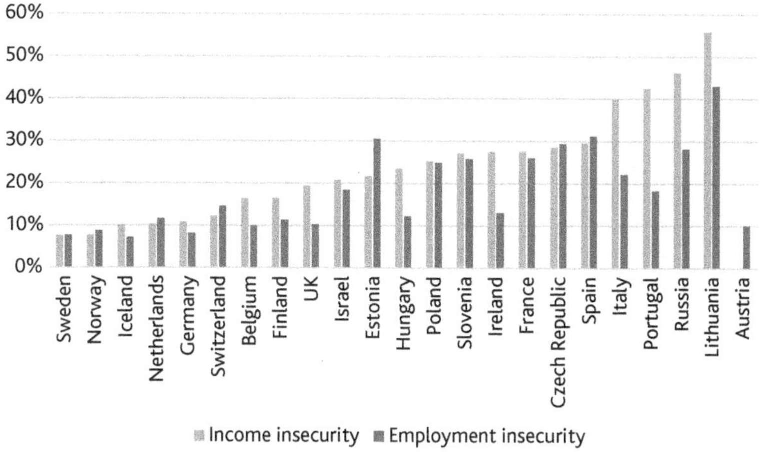

■ Income insecurity ■ Employment insecurity

Note: Austria does not have data for income insecurity.

Income insecurity: proportion of workers who state it is likely or very likely that their family will not have money for basic household necessities in the next 12 months.

Employment insecurity: proportion of workers who state it is likely or very likely that they will be unemployed and looking for work for at least four consecutive weeks in the next 12 months.

Source: European Social Survey 2016/17, weighted data, author's calculation

their employment status was insecure. This is likely to do with the rise in insecurity of both employment and income for younger workers without much opportunity for growth compared to previous generations, with increased levels of competition (Chung et al, 2012; Harris, 2017; TUC, 2020). The proportion of people who felt that their income is insecure is even higher, just under one third of all those surveyed felt they would have enough money for their household necessities in the next 12 months. Such insecurities will inevitably further reduce workers' negotiation power within the workplace and the labour market, leaving workers without much individual or collective bargaining powers. This can explain why workers are not able to rest or relax and pursue leisure interests when given freedom over their work, due to the potential consequence of job losses, and the reduced competitive edge in the more individualised labour market.

Work-centred society

In addition, or perhaps due to the heightened insecurity and lack of opportunities, many of our societies are becoming more work-centred than ever before (Frayne, 2015). Increasingly, we see that one's work takes precedence over other aspects of one's life, such as leisure. According to the European Value Study of 2017 (Figure 1.3), a large proportion of

Figure 1.3: Work orientation attitudes of individuals across four European countries

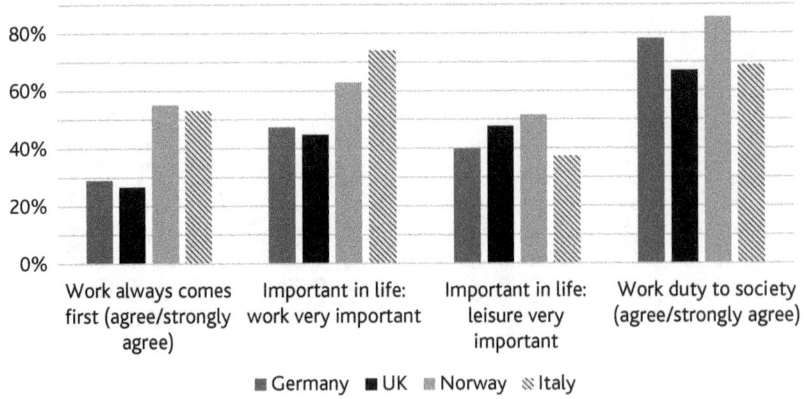

Note: Work always comes first: percentage of those who answered 'agree' or 'strongly agree' with the statement 'Work should always come first, even if it means less spare time'.

Important in life: percentage of those who answered 'very important' to question 'Please say, for each of the following how important it is in your life' (work and leisure).

Work duty to society: percentage of those who answered 'agree' or 'strongly agree' with the statement 'Work is a duty towards society'.

Source: European Value Study 2017, weighted data, author's own calculation

the population agree that work always comes first and work is a duty towards society. More people believe that work is very important in life, in comparison to those who say leisure is very important in life (with the exception of the UK, ironically). What these statistics show us is how much the notion of work is central to our lives in our current day societies, as well as the extent to which it is widely accepted that one's value is measured through what one produces at work.

These figures also evidence how our societal norm around work is based on the ideal worker model (Acker, 1990; Williams, 1999) – idolisation of workers who prioritise work above all else and have no other responsibilities outside of work. Here, commitment and productivity are measured through the number of hours one puts in, resulting in very long hours especially in professional or higher-status occupations (Reid, 2011; Glavin and Schieman, 2012). This ideal worker culture is linked to hegemonic masculine identities in the workplace (Anker, 1997; Berdahl et al, 2018). Here, long-hours work is considered brave, an enactment of masculinity, and the display of one's exhaustion, physically and verbally is done 'in order to convey the depth of one's commitment, stamina, and virility' (Williams, 2010: 87). Elon Musk, the CEO of Tesla, SpaceX and co-founder of PayPal, is the embodiment of such masculinist culture, especially in Silicon Valley, where working long hours equates to commitment and 'changing the world'. He boasts about 120-hour working weeks, noting that others should follow suit,[5] as depicted in a tweet – where he argues 'nobody ever changed the world on 40 hours a week' (Elon Musk, Twitter, 26 November 2018). Unfortunately, he is not alone and working excessively is something that is expected by many CEOs and business leaders, such as Jack Ma of Alibaba who promotes the 996 rule,[6] or the CEO of Goldman Sachs who expects physically harmful working hours to 'go the extra mile for our clients'.[7] Thus based on this context, it is no surprise that when we are told to choose the hours we want to work, we end up doing more and more. This behaviour is a way for workers to survive in a competitive market and/or to distinguish themselves from the rest of the pack, and adhere to the dominant work culture that exists in many of our societies, where if you do not make such sacrifices of yourself and your time, you are considered to be not serious or not passionate about your work.

Passion

One way these long-hours work devotion cultures play into our system is the way we talk about passion at work. Workers are expected to work very long hours, to pursue a passion, because your work now needs to be your passion. Our culture is one where increasingly we are expected to be passionate about our jobs and made to think that we are the curators of our own destinies – that is, entrepreneurs of our own careers (Bröckling, 2015). Even less than half a century ago, jobs were considered where one earns a wage, in order to enjoy other aspects of one's life (see Chapter 5 for more evidence). Now, there is an ever growing pressure on everyone to find one's true calling/passion.

Doing a job you love is great, right? Well, not necessarily when we consider the 'passion exploitation' theory (Kim et al, 2020) – the idea that passion is closely related to how easily others can exploit you (more in Chapter 5). Namely, when people think you love your job, they feel that fulfilling your passion is a big enough reward so they exploit you more easily (make you work harder without compensation). This combined with the individualisation of our working contracts means we end up being entrepreneurial selves – who should individually bear and respond to the risks that occur in our working lives. Again, this makes workers work all the time and everywhere when boundaries are blurred. This is nicely summed up in the picture by Adam Kurtz (see Figure 1.4).

The book

Flexibility paradox

What I argue in this book is that flexible working, and the control over your work in this climate, is unlikely to be used as a strategy to expand your leisure or enable you to focus on your life outside of work. The fact that flexible working leads to overwork, blurring of boundaries and the encroachment on your private life may not be new (see Chapter 5). However,

Figure 1.4: My book embodied in one picture

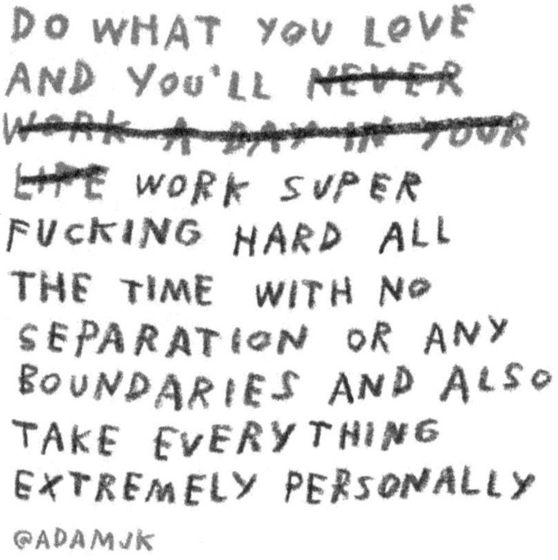

DO WHAT YOU LOVE
AND YOU'LL ~~NEVER~~
~~WORK A DAY IN YOUR~~
~~LIFE~~ WORK SUPER
FUCKING HARD ALL
THE TIME WITH NO
SEPARATION OR ANY
BOUNDARIES AND ALSO
TAKE EVERYTHING
EXTREMELY PERSONALLY

@ADAMJK

Source: picture courtesy of Adam J. Kurtz, https://shop.adamjk.com/

this book contributes to these debates in the following three ways. First, it aims to explain WHY the flexibility paradox happens. This is done by examining the larger structural changes happening in our society – such as the internalisation of capitalist ideals as one's own goal. The norms around work, work-life balance, gender norms as well as workers' negotiation powers and insecurities help shape attitudes towards flexible working, its outcomes and concurrently its access. This helps us know what to do to ensure that the flexibility paradox does NOT happen. Second, previous scholars have not devoted enough attention to how the paradox manifests itself differently for women and men under our given gender norms and parenting culture. I aim to address this gap in this book by theorising why we expect a gendered paradox and providing empirical evidence of this phenomenon. Third, the book explains and provides empirical evidence of how the stigmatised views around flexible working can be a key factor in the problems of flexible working and its gendered outcomes. What is more, I link the ideas of flexibility stigma back to work cultures, gender norms, parenting cultures, workers' bargaining power and institutions to evidence again why contexts matter.

The main argument of this book is as follows. Why do workers end up exploiting themselves, and exploiting themselves possibly more than what managers have/could have done when they have more 'freedom' and control their work? In many societies, workers are made to think that they are the managers of their own careers and labour market risks (Pongratz and Voß, 2003; Bröckling, 2015), and any other socio-economic risks one experiences is also one's own responsibility. This explains why flexible working, where workers have control over the boundaries of work, results in the encroachment of work on private life. This encroachment can be seen in terms of hours worked, that is, longer (unpaid) overtime hours, and workers working harder than before (for example without breaks) and through mental encroachment – namely thinking and worrying about work when not at work. This all can make workers feel higher levels of conflict between work and family life. However, the story doesn't end here. Self-exploitation takes different shapes and forms depending on your gender. Although gender normative views about men and women's role have progressed over the past decade, many of us still live in societies where men are expected to be the main breadwinner of the household and women are expected to be responsible for childcare and housework. This explains why we see gendered patterns of the flexibility paradox. Men expand their work – or self-exploit themselves more in the workplace when given the freedom to choose when and where to work. Women, on the other hand, especially due to the societal pressures of intensive parenting cultures (Hays, 1998), self-exploit themselves both at work and home by carrying out more childcare and housework. This results in flexible working potentially exacerbating gender inequalities patterns both in the labour market and within the household, that is, the division of labour. The increased involvement of women in housework and childcare through flexible working can also be explained by the subjectification of the self or internalised capitalism. Childcare is an investment into the household's potential for future income gains and reduction of labour market risks. All of this shapes the way we as society think about flexible workers, or more so the stigmatised views we hold against workers who deviate away from the 'ideal worker' type – again, where an ideal worker is someone who works very long hours in the office.

This book is not a self-help book nor can I promise to provide all the solutions to tackle the flexibility paradox and the self-exploitation problem. However, what I will attempt to do is to try to show how institutional and cultural contexts matter, and how shaping the contexts in which flexibility is enacted can shape the outcomes of flexible working for the better. This provides us with some empirical evidence of what changes we need to make to ensure that flexible working can be applied to meet the key challenges in the labour market without resulting in the unintended negative consequences I mentioned earlier.

Background

This book is based on what ended up as a five-year project funded by the UK's Economic and Social Research Council called Work Autonomy,

Flexibility and Work-Life Balance (www.wafproject.org). However, much of the work presented here also draws on my work prior to and during my PhD (Chung et al, 2007; Chung, 2009). The project aimed to fill what I considered a much-needed gap in the literature on flexible working and the future of work, by investigating theoretically and empirically the potential risks and benefits flexible working carries, especially in light of the current socio-economic and cultural contexts. In this book, I sum up a range of studies I have published over the years using the most recent data from across Europe, with some focus on the UK and Germany. However, I reference work by others using both qualitative and quantitative empirical data, from the US, Australia, India, Korea, China and other parts of the world.

Outline of the book

The book is divided into three sections and 11 chapters. The first section sets out the issue, by providing definitions of flexible working and how it came about. It also examines the extent to which flexible working is used/provided and summarises the outcomes of flexible working identified in the literature. The second section presents the core of this book, namely the concept of the flexibility paradox with a sociological framework of why it happens, how its manifestation may be different for men and women, and the role flexibility stigma plays in all of this. It also provides some empirical evidence to prove that the flexibility paradox does happen. The third section examines the roles of contexts, focusing on work cultures, gender norms, insecurity/precarity and negotiation powers of workers, and institutional factors. It also examines the role of context by exploring how COVID-19 has shifted the way we work, the way we think about flexible working, and potentially the mechanisms of the flexibility paradox.

The first section starts off with Chapter 2 that investigates the extent to which flexible working is on the rise. I first examine the demand for greater flexibility in work, to show that it is no longer a perk but a must-have that many workers find essential for their future prospective jobs. I then examine the extent to which flexible working is done and how this has changed over the years. This chapter further outlines some of the key legislative developments across the world in terms of the right to flexible working to provide an indication of the different approaches made by governments in enabling a true 'right to flexible working'.

Chapter 3 explores the opposing nature of flexible working – namely as a performance-enhancing tool against the work-life balance, or diversity enhancing tool. It reviews the existing theories that explain flexible working in a sociological and management, organisational studies perspective. The chapter provides empirical evidence of the provision of and access to flexible working using company- and individual-level data from across Europe. The results show that despite popular belief, rather than family and care demands, performance demands are more useful in understanding who has access to flexible working arrangements. Furthermore, disadvantaged workers and those with possibly the most need for flexible working arrangements are sometimes the least likely to have access to such arrangements.

Chapter 4 explores the outcomes of flexible working, such as productivity and performance, work-family and well-being outcomes. The chapter summarises the results from a number of studies across the world, including meta-analysis/systematic reviews. The chapter will also provide results from European data to explore whether flexible working results in better work-life balance satisfaction and lower work-family conflict, and how this association varies across gender lines. The key message of this chapter is that flexible working, unlike the assumptions made by many policy makers, may not necessarily be effective in relieving workers from the conflict felt due to the demands arising from work and family life. This may also be a result of the conflicting nature of flexible working mentioned in the previous chapter. However, it can increase the work-life balance satisfaction of workers, especially women, by enabling women and others with care demands to maintain their labour market positions during times of high family demands.

The second section of the book starts off with Chapter 5, which provides the theoretical underpinning of the flexibility paradox and the resulting self-exploitation. This chapter first summarises the ideas of previous scholars – for example the theories of social exchange, enforced intensification and enabled intensification (Kelliher and Anderson, 2010; Lott and Chung, 2016), 'Arbeitskraftunternehmer' (entreployee) (Pongratz and Voß, 2003), and the theory of autonomy-control paradox observed in the high-power professional environments (Mazmanian et al, 2013; Putnam et al, 2014). These theories provide an understanding of the organisational structures and other control mechanisms that can lead to the flexibility paradox phenomenon, yet do not provide a more structural sociological framework to understand why it happens. This chapter contextualises these theories by proposing a new way of understanding flexible working using social theories of autonomy and control in modern-day societies. Foucault's theories of homo-economicus and the subjectification of self (Foucault, 2010) provide a broader framework of understanding power in contemporary society. Namely, we now live in a society where all interactions take the form of economic exchanges, where workers internalise these ideas of capitalism, forcing workers to manage their own risks and be responsible for their own failures. In this context, 'freedom' over one's work is more likely to lead to an easier way to exploit worker's labour, because the failure to do so will only result in the worker themselves bearing the associated risk of income insecurity, unemployment or loss of position within the organisation/labour market. This becomes especially true given that such move to an individualised risk management is also evident in our social security systems (Abrahamson, 2004). This approach is similar to that of the concept or theories of the 'entrepreneurial self' (Bröckling, 2015), which argues that increasingly, workers are made to organise their own work processes in a self-determining, self-control, 'entrepreneurial' manner to transfer their own labour potential into concrete performance. This chapter also examines whether this phenomenon is on the rise especially with the millennial (and xennial) generation, who have been born into the world of gig-economy and the demise of the collective (Harris, 2017). Finally, the chapter explores some of the key indicators of such societal change by exploring the idea and data around passion at work.

Chapter 6 provides the empirical evidence of the flexibility paradox. I present my own research, carried out with colleagues, that uses data from the UK and Germany to show how workers who gained more control over their work were those who ended up working longer (unpaid) overtime. These results are supplemented with empirical studies from other countries, such as India, China and the US, arriving at the same conclusions. I also present analysis using data from across 30 European countries to show how flexible working leads to mental encroachment of work on other spheres of life, that is, flexible workers also worry and think about work when not at work more often than those without such control. In sum, these studies point to the fact when workers get more freedom over work, they actually increase their workload, letting work encroach on family and private leisure time, resulting in workers working all the time and everywhere. The chapter also looks at whether there may be variations across occupational lines, and gender and parental status which opens up to the question posed in the following chapter on the gendered paradox.

The next chapter, Chapter 7, examines the gendered nature of the flexibility paradox. Because men and women face different levels of household demands, women are unable to 'self-exploit' themselves in the formal labour market and adhere to the 'ideal worker' norm as much as men when working flexibly. Furthermore, drawing again from Foucault's idea of subjectification, the education of children and the so-called, 'intensive parenting' (Hays, 1998), calls for mothers to invest in their children's brain and their enrichment as if investing in a company that will yield future profits to ensure the future financial stability of the family. Again, I present my own research and that of others to provide empirical evidence of this from across the world, for example the UK, Germany, Sweden, Germany, Poland and the US. The results show that men have higher tendencies to work longer when given more control over their work, and they are thus compensated better for this increase in work intensity. Contrarily, flexible working allows women to expand their parenting time and housework activities – self-exploitation in the household context. I also present the ideas of 'the exploitation model' (Sullivan and Lewis, 2001; Hilbrecht et al,

2008) – namely that through flexible working women are able to maintain their role as the main person responsible for childcare and housework, while also being able to take part in the labour market – exploiting their labour in both home and labour market spheres to the max. Through this I argue that flexible working enables maximum engagement of labour of households without disrupting neither the norm around gender roles nor the ideal worker norm, originally based in the male-breadwinner female-caregiver model. I also present how such exploitation of women's labour results in low levels of mental health and high levels of stress among women and to stigmatised views of flexible working, ultimately resulting in negative career penalties for women.

Chapter 8 explores the ideas of flexibility stigma, namely the idea that workers who use flexible working arrangements to address work-family demands are somehow less productive and less committed to the organisation. These stigmatised views against flexible workers exist because of the prevalence of the ideal worker norm (Acker, 1990) and work devotion schema especially among professionals (Blair-Loy, 2009). Our work cultures still equate long hours worked in the office/workplace as sign of commitment and productivity, and that the 'ideal worker' is a worker who prioritises work above all else and has no other responsibilities outside of work. These views of the ideal worker makes the flexible worker, who may be utilising flexible working to meet the demands of housework and childcare, deviate away from the image of a 'good, productive worker'. Some scholars argue that men may experience a double stigma – namely, that flexible working for care purposes makes men deviate away from both the masculine breadwinner image and the ideal worker image. However, I argue that women, especially mothers, experience the double-whammy stigma – existing biases against mothers' capacity to work (Budig and England, 2001) is compounded by the stigma against flexible workers. I use my own study and those of others, including experimental studies (for example, Brescoll et al, 2013; Munsch, 2016), as evidence of the gendered stigma negatively impacting women and mothers more. Actually, men are more likely to hold stigmatised views against flexible workers.

The next section of the book examines the role of contexts. This section potentially tries to overcome the bleak pictures drawn in the previous section to paint a possible brighter scenario to argue that the flexibility paradox need not happen if we change the context in which it is used. Chapter 9 examines contexts such as cultural norms around work, work-life balance and gender roles, national level policies, workers' bargaining or insecurity positions and the prevalence of flexible working. I do this by summarising studies, including my own, that explore how contexts shape flexible working practices in terms of how widespread flexible working arrangements are in a country (for example, Lyness et al 2012; den Dulk et al, 2013), who gets access to it (for example, Chung, 2019a) and how it is used, stigmatised views on flexible working, and the extent to which the flexibility paradox occurs (for example, Mills and Täht, 2010; Drobnič and Guillén Rodríguez, 2011; Lott, 2015; Kurowska, 2020). This enables us to see what steps must be taken to ensure that flexible working can result in positive outcomes both for workers and companies. The studies show contexts matter – normative views around work, work-life balance and gender roles – which is shaped by national level family policies and workers' bargaining powers – can shift workers' access to flexible working arrangements and the prevalence of stigmatised views against flexible workers. This then helps shape the outcome of flexible working to one that is more positive, potentially eliminating the flexibility paradox.

Given the timing of this book we need to look into one major change that occurred that could potentially change the context of flexible working forever. That is, the COVID-19 pandemic. In 2020, as many countries across the world were experiencing high rises of COVID-19 cases, countries went into different levels of lockdown with workers being required to either work from home or not work at all. This provided us with a unique natural experimental setting of what happens when half of the workforce is required by the state and employers to work flexibly. This is the topic of Chapter 10, where I examine the impact of COVID-19 on the provision of flexible working, on flexibility stigma, on the patterns of the flexibility paradox and its gendered outcomes. Again I draw on a number of studies, including our own, using unique data collected during the first lockdown in the UK (Chung et al, 2020b). In sum, I argue that although we do see some patterns of change especially in terms of the perceptions of flexible working among both workers and managers, the patterns of the flexibility paradox still remains, with many workers working longer hours, working harder, with blurring boundaries leading to work encroaching on family life. What is more, although we do find evidence of men using flexible working for care purposes during the first lockdown periods, the gendered patterns of the flexibility paradox still exist – in that women seem to utilise it more to meet family demands. This provides us with the evidence that the expansion of flexible working alone is insufficient in solving the problems of the flexibility paradox. In other words, without disrupting norms around work, work-life balance and gender roles we are unlikely to completely eliminate the flexibility paradox and its gendered outcomes.

The final chapter, Chapter 11, brings together the contents of this book to summarise what it means for workers to be more flexible and have more autonomy over when and where they work. The chapter first explores some remaining questions, such as, will we see an expansion of flexible working post-pandemic, how flexible working will impact workers' well-being outcomes, and gendered division of labour in the future. The chapter then goes on to provide some recommendations to avoid flexible working leading to self-exploitation and further traditionalisation of gender roles.

The recommendations are outlined for policy makers at the national and international level, companies and managers, and workers. These include issues around shifting work and work–life balance cultures and gender norms, providing better rights to flexible working and protection of workers when working flexibly, as well as the possible move to shorter working hours. I end with some reflections especially for workers themselves to think about in light of the findings I present here in the book about self-exploitation.

How to read this book

This book is long, and possibly longer than I expected it to be. So here is a quick tip on how to read it, depending on why you decided to pick it up.[8] This is not a novel, you don't have to read the whole book. Those of you who are only interested in the summary of the book and its key messages, this chapter pretty much sums it up so read this and the final chapter – Chapter 11 – which talks about what we should do about it. For those of you who are only interested in the theory of the flexibility paradox and the key contributions of this book, jump straight into Chapter 5. Also read Chapter 7 which talks about the gendered patterns of the paradox, and Chapter 8 on flexibility stigma as they form the main crux of my argument. For those of you who don't trust me and need further evidence of the paradox occurring, you can read Chapter 6 which mainly summarises key evidence to prove to you that the paradox actually happens and Chapter 9 provides evidence of why changing contexts matters. For those of you interested in the historical trends of flexible working, and the origins of how such arrangements started to be used/provided, Chapters 2 and 3 are where you can find these. For those who are interested in future scenarios, you should definitely read the chapter on COVID-19, Chapter 10 and Chapter 11, where I outline what I expect to happen in the future in regards to flexible working patterns. Those of you interested in looking for policy solutions and recommendations in light of introducing flexible working, Chapter 2 outlines some of the key policy developments in the areas of flexible working, and Chapter 4 provides a summary of the meta-analysis of the outcomes of flexible working and can be useful to provide support as to why flexible working should be introduced. Finally, I use a gender lens throughout the book, but Chapters 7 and 8 are especially dedicated to the feminist reader. I hope you like it.

Quick word on methodologies

This book brings together a large body of work that I have carried out over the years, many of which have been published in different journals or books (for a full list see http://heejungchung.com). I will not provide detailed information of these studies, for example data, methods and the regression tables, given that they are already available online, all of them open access, as the project was funded by a UK Research Council. I also ran additional analyses to supplement some of the analysis carried out in the articles to update or add to the findings. The majority of the additional analyses done in the book is based on the European Working Conditions Survey of 2015, which was at the point of publication the most recent data available. More information about the data and the variables used, their operationalisation can be found in the Appendix. Full tables are provided in the Appendix, and coefficient graphs and figures of outcomes are in the main body of the book in the hope that it may be easier to visually understand the results. This is how you read coefficient graphs – dots represent the effect (+ positive association, - negative association). The further the dot is away from zero, the stronger the effect/association. The lines around it are coefficient lines (95 per cent) – namely representing how much of this effect is down to randomness. The shorter lines indicate that we can be more confident that this happens around that point. The lines should not overlap with zero – if it does it means that the association found may be by chance. But don't worry too much, I tried to explain it more fully in the text. I also draw on a lot of work by others, again all references are provided in the chapters and in the reference list at the end of the book for the reader to explore further. If readers would like more details on specific analyses of my own, they can contact me for more information.

The take-home message

I want to make something very clear before we move on to the main book which essentially examines flexible working in a critical way. My goal is not to argue that we should stop the expansion of flexible working, or that we should stop giving workers more control over their work. I am a great supporter of flexible working, and providing workers with control over their work is a very welcome step towards making work better. Rather, the book's main argument is that the blind introduction of flexible working as a way to promote workers' well-being and facilitate gender equality in the workplace isn't really going to work unless broader changes within our labour markets and work, gender cultures are made. Flexible working is an amplifier, only providing as good outcomes as our current working and gender cultures allow. In this sense, this book is also written to show that in many ways flexible working is a good case study to take a critical look at some of the issues around the current state of work, how we balance work with other aspects of our lives, and how we divide work both paid and unpaid work between men and women. By examining how 'freedom' and 'control over one's work' is enacted and the patterns of outcomes it results in, it provides us a better understanding of the way we are constrained by the larger structural factors that guide our behaviours. In other words, autonomy over work and flexible working can be an incredibly useful tool for both managers and workers, but only if we start changing the context in which it is used. Otherwise, it will lead to exploitation patterns which unfortunately will not benefit the worker, the company, the family or society.

Notes

[1]   Based on a survey of academics from the Times Higher Education (Bothwell, 2018) in 2018, about two thirds of all academics surveyed worked more than nine hours a day, and 70 per cent also worked during the weekend, clocking in an additional half-day to a day's work.

[2]   Based on the Conversation tracker alone, it has been read by more than 85,000 people, shared by more than 800 people on social media, and has been translated into a dozen languages and covered by media around the world. Read it for yourself at: https://theconversation.com/flexible-working-is-making-us-work-longer-64045

[3]   From the podcast The Solo Collective (1 April 2021, Episode 5)

[4]   www.gov.ie/en/press-release/6b64a-tanaiste-signs-code-of-practice-on-right-to-disconnect/

[5]   www.theguardian.com/technology/2018/aug/23/elon-musk-120-hour-working-week-tesla

[6]   https://edition.cnn.com/2019/04/15/business/jack-ma-996-china/index.html

[7]   www.theguardian.com/business/2021/mar/22/goldman-sachs-boss-responds-to-leaked-report-into-inhumane-working-hours

[8]   BTW thank you so much for picking this book up and purchasing it! Otherwise, you might be one of those lucky ones who I force-fed this book to.

2

The demand for and trends in flexible working

Introduction

This chapter examines the definition of and the growing demand for flexible working. Flexible working is no longer a nice perk ring-fenced for higher-status workers, but a must-have many workers find essential. This is especially the case after the COVID-19 pandemic, which I will look into in greater detail in Chapter 10. In this chapter, I will focus mostly on the pre-pandemic developments of flexible working. The chapter also explores the extent to which governments have responded to the demand for more flexible working by examining some of the most recent legislative changes increasing workers' right to work flexibly implemented across the world. Following this, some empirical data showing the trends in the provision and access to flexible working is provided using cross-national European data sets, accompanied by some data from other countries like the US. Based on this, what we see is that flexible working is growing when we look at developments in national legislation and company-level data. However, there is no clear evidence showing growth in workers' access to flexible working when we examine data from the past couple of decades before the COVID-19 pandemic.

What is flexible working?

Definitions

But before we go on, what exactly is flexible working? Flexible working can entail employees' control over when, where and how much they work (Kelly et al, 2014; Chung and van der Lippe, 2020). There are different arrangements relating to employees' control over when they work. Flexitime enables workers to alternate the starting and ending times of work. Working time autonomy is when workers have greater freedom to control their work schedule and their working hours. The biggest difference between flexitime and working time autonomy is that some constraints still remain in flexitime; for example, adhering to core hours (for example 10am to 2pm) or a defined number of hours workers can work in a week (for example 37 hours per week). Condensed or compressed hours is where workers work a full-time load (for example 40 hours) but condensed into, for example, four days (that is, ten hours a day). Annualised hours is an arrangement where employees work a certain number of hours over the course of a year, but they have some flexibility about when those hours are done – for example, with some busy months where workers work longer hours (but without overtime compensation), followed by quieter months where they work shorter hours. There are variations to this annualised hours system, where hours can be calculated over a shorter period of time than a full year – for example, over six months, as is the case in Korea. Teleworking, or homeworking, allows workers to work outside of their normal work premises, for example working from home or in other public spaces such as cafes or co-working spaces. Flexible working can also entail workers having control over the number of hours they work, mainly referring to the reduction of hours of work (temporarily) to meet personal demands. Common patterns of such reduction of hours include part-time working – namely working less than 30 hours a week; term-time-only working – this is when workers work only during school term times (for example 38 weeks of the year); job sharing – namely when two or more workers share one full-time job; phased retirement, where workers reduce their working hours and work part-time before they retire so that their retirement is phased out across a longer span of time; and temporary reduction of hours – which is when workers are allowed to reduce hours temporarily for a specific period of time.

Box 2.1: Types of flexible working mentioned on the UK government website

Job sharing: Two people do one job and split the hours.

Working from home: It might be possible to do some or all of the work from home or anywhere else other than the normal place of work.

Part-time: Working less than full-time hours (usually by working fewer days).

Compressed hours: Working full-time hours but over fewer days.

Flexitime: The employee chooses when to start and end work (within agreed limits) but works certain 'core hours', for example 10am to 4pm every day.

Annualised hours: The employee has to work a certain number of hours over the year but they have some flexibility about when they work. There are sometimes 'core hours' which the employee regularly works each week, and they work the rest of their hours flexibly or when there is extra demand at work.

Staggered hours: The employee has different start, finish and break times from other workers.

Phased retirement: Default retirement age has been phased out and older workers can choose when they want to retire. This means they can reduce their hours and work part-time.

Source: www.gov.uk/flexible-working/types-of-flexible-working

Flexibility as an arrangement or an approach?

This book focuses mostly on workers' control over when and where they work. However, I argue here that flexible working, especially in relation to the increased demands for flexibility we observe among workers, isn't really confined to a certain type of arrangement such as working from home or flexitime. In fact, the focus should be more about control, autonomy or freedom to choose a working pattern that fits with one's preferences and other demands in life while meeting one's employer's staffing and business needs. In this sense, flexible working can be understood as a part of a 'flexicurity' strategy (Wilthagen and Tros, 2004). The flexicurity approach argues that a successful labour market strategy needs to meet employers' need for flexibility while protecting employees' need for employment or income security. However, in this case, it is more about meeting employees' need for flexibility at work to meet personal demands, while protecting employers' security of having enough staff at the right time to carry out the work that needs to be done, or the security that their business will not be harmed by such demands.

This is especially important to consider when we think about jobs in manufacturing, such as factory workers, or in the services sector, such as health and social care workers or retail workers. For these workers, flexitime in the more traditional sense can be difficult and working from home almost impossible because of the nature of their job which confines them to space (for example, facing clients or using machinery) and time (for example, machine operating times and shop opening times). However, it is not the case that flexibility cannot be sought out in these jobs. Self-rostering (Thornthwaite and Sheldon, 2004) or 'work schedule patching' (Kossek et al, 2019) are common practices used in such sectors where workers work as a team to fill in the staffing demands of managers, while meeting their own work-life demand.

There is another example that I regularly use to respond to employers that ask how they can introduce flexible working practices when the nature of the work doesn't allow for such flexibility. This example comes from a company with about 50 personnel; about 20 were doing some sort of research and development work (software programming and hardware development), about 10–15 doing some sort of administrative work, and 10–15 manufacturing the product they were selling. The company allowed the R&D team to work flexibly, that is, have flexitime, and in some cases, with the approval of the manager, work from home on occasion. The management team, however, felt it was unfair to the rest of the staff whose work did not allow for such flexibility. However, the manufacturing section of the company had another solution. They had collectively decided to operate a 'team flexitime'. They came in to work much earlier than the rest of the company, around 7–8am, and finished work at around 3–4pm, leaving them the rest of the day for other things. Given that their production team worked as a group, a collective decision was made as to when the group should start work. However, there was flexibility in that it did not need to follow the standard 'nine-to-five' schedule in addition to some individual flexibility within that flexible working pattern in agreement within the team. Again, I consider this also to be a part of flexible working in the broader sense. Finally, it is worth noting that increasingly many jobs, once thought not possible to do flexibly such as health care work, are now becoming more flexible. A good example of this is health care consultations being carried out on the telephone or online during the COVID-19 pandemic. We can expect this to happen more often in the future enabling many more occupations more freedom over where they carry out their jobs.

The demand for and provisions of flexible working

The demand for flexible working

How popular is flexible working and to what extent are workers able to work flexibly? A 2018 UK study showed how three quarters of workers wanted more flexibility in their work.[1] This demand was especially strong among women and millennials – defined as those born around the early 1980s to the mid-1990s. A similar result was found in the 2018 Deloitte Millennial Survey across 34 different countries. Although financial income was still the top workplace characteristic young people chose when looking for a job, next were positive work culture and flexibility, with more than half of those surveyed saying this was 'very important' (Deloitte, 2018). Those who had flexibility in their work were more likely to say that they expected to stay at their current company for at least five years. The lack of flexibility, on the other hand, was a key factor driving workers to find new positions. A 2018 study of UK workers found that a quarter of all workers, and 40 per cent of millennial workers, have refused a job due to a lack of flexibility (Franklin, 2018). Finally, there are also reports on how workers believe flexible working to be the most important motivator in increasing their productivity at work. One report shows how nine out of ten workers say flexible working motivates them to be more productive at work.[2] This demand for flexible working has exploded during and after the COVID-19 pandemic (Chung et al, 2020b; CIPD, 2021; Jung, 2021), where the majority of workers whose work could be carried out at home had the opportunity to do so across the world. As examined in Chapter 10, the majority of workers reported wanting to work from home at least two to three days a week post-pandemic.

Government response to the demand for flexible working to date

How have governments responded to these demands? Here, I focus on the UK, the Netherlands, Italy, Finland, Australia and Korea. These countries represent some of the countries where an active debate on the right to flexible working has occurred, and represent different regimes of welfare states (Esping-Andersen, 1990), modes of capitalism (Hall and Soskice, 2001), care/family policy/gender regimes (Bettio and Plantenga, 2004; Korpi et al, 2013) and working time regimes (Chung and Tijdens, 2013). It is interesting to note that the majority of these policies have only been implemented recently. I expect that there will be more national legal reforms to give workers more rights to flexible working in the future. This is in light of the new European Commission directive on work-life balance which entered into force in the summer of 2019, the COVID-19 pandemic which drastically shifted preferences and attitudes towards flexible working, and the development of software/digital technologies we have seen in the past years.

European Commission directive on work-life balance

After the introduction of the European pillar of social rights, and a series of consultations with European policy stakeholders, the European Commission passed a bill on a new Work-Life Balance directive (see this link: https:// eur-lex.europa.eu/legal-content/EN/TXT/?uri=CELEX%3A52017PC0 253). The new legislation replaces the Maternity Leave directive, by expanding a number of policies relating to working families after childbirth. The directive includes the introduction of paternity (second parent) leave of ten working days compensated at least at the level of sick pay; making parental leave as paid leave, and making two of the four months of parental leave as non-transferable, earmarked for each parent; the introduction of a five-days-per-year carers' leave. Most importantly, the directive includes the right to request flexible working arrangements available to all working parents of children under eight years old, and all carers. Previously, parents had the right to request reduced working hours after the birth of a child. The new directive allows workers to request flexible working hours/ flexitime and flexibility in place of work – that is, the ability to work from home. The directive also includes a number of non-legislative measures to ensure a better use of the aforementioned policies. This includes ensuring protection against discrimination and dismissal for parents and carers when taking up the policies, and encouraging a gender-balanced use of family-related leave and flexible working arrangements. The directive entered into force in 2019 and its full implementation by the Member States is expected to be completed by 2024.

UK

The British right to request flexible working was introduced in 2003 'under the banner of enhancing parenting choice' (Lewis et al, 2008) in the context of a lack of other means for parents to address work–life balance issues, for example, through well-paid leave and public childcare (Chung and van der Horst, 2018). This was a policy through which the then Labour-majority government aimed to address women's employment agenda without incurring significant costs for the government. The scope of the law includes a range of arrangements as noted in Box 2.1. Initially, the right was only available for parents of children under the age of six and children with a disability up to the age of 18. In 2007, this was extended to carers of adults, and parents with children below the age of 17, and finally extended to cover all workers as of June 2014. The right, however, is currently restricted to those who have been in continuous employment with their current employer for the past 26 weeks, and only one application can be made in a 12-month period. Employers can reject this request on various business grounds (ACAS, 2016). A recent survey of working mothers in the UK showed that a quarter of mothers had their flexible working requests turned down, and this number increased to 35 per cent for those who were on maternity leave at the time of the request (Workingmums, 2016). A more recent survey of over 12,000 mothers by the UK Trades Union Congress showed that half of all surveyed had their request turned down or not fully accepted (TUC, 2021b).

In 2019, the Conservative government held a consultation to make changes to the current paternity leave, parental leave and flexible working rights.[3] Two suggestions were made on the right to request flexible working. First, to require employers of large companies (of 250 employees or more) to publish their family-related leave and pay and flexible working policies so it is widely accessible to everyone (possibly in a government portal). Second, to require employers to consider advertising jobs as flexible – stating the possibilities for it to be flexible and/or the organisation's policies on flexible working. The more recent consultation on the right to flexible working in 2021 also includes the expansion of the right to include all workers from the first day of their job, enabling more than one request per year (possibly two or three), putting the onus on managers to explain why the request was rejected, and finally requiring managers to respond quicker to the request (three months maximum).[4]

The Netherlands

The Netherlands is famous for its flexibility in the labour market, especially in relation to the high proportion of part-time workers. For example, in 2015, 84 per cent of all women between the ages of 25 and 49 years old with children were in part-time jobs. However, more than half of women without children were also in part-time work (52 per cent). One key reason for this is the Dutch Working Hours Adjustment Act (Wet Aanpassing

Arbeidsduur) introduced in 2000 as a part of the Dutch Flexicurity social exchange (Wilthagen and Tros, 2004). The law allows workers employed in organisations of ten or more employees to ask for an adjustment of their working hours – that is, reduction to part-time, but also allowing for the increase of hours back to full-time. In 2016, this law was changed into the Flexible Working Law (Wet Flexibel Werken)[5] to extend the existing right for workers to request changes to their work schedules and place of work. However, similar to the UK, one request can be made in a 12-month period, and workers must have been employed by the organisation for the previous 26 weeks before making a request.

Italy

Italy is a unique case in that in 2015 it introduced flexible working for a specific segment of the labour force, namely the public administration sector workers, as part of a law on the reorganisation of public administration. One of the innovative aspects of this approach was that the introduction of flexible working was not solely focused on its ability to meet workers' work-life balance, but very much embedded in the narrative of enhancing performance outcomes – in this case public services. Rather than using the term 'flexible working', they used the terms 'agile work' and 'smart working' to give workers more control over their work schedules (start/end times of work) and to work from home. Smart working was included in the law as an objective to be achieved, measured in quantitative terms – more specifically it was noted that within three years at least 10 per cent of employees of each administration must be able to make use of teleworking and smart working (ELENA, 2018). Furthermore, the directive recommends a number of fundamental pillars for such experiments/implementation including strengthening the work organisation according to result-oriented models; including how teleworking and agile work are going to be applied in the Performance Plan and in the Performance Measurement and Evaluation System; evaluating the innovative organisational ability of managers; enhancing the skills of individuals and groups; empowering workers and fostering relationships based on trust; guaranteeing and verifying the fulfilment of the work performance (Viale, 2018). Another innovative aspect of this policy reform was that the Italian government did not only introduce the right to request flexible working as a stand-alone initiative; they also promoted the idea of shifting the work organisation and performance plans/goals and included specific goals on empowering workers and enhancing trust between managers and workers, and ensuring goals are met through shifting the evaluation systems of managers and organisations.

Some of the early trial results of the implementation have shown that workers with the ability to work flexibly show improved levels of productivity, work–life balance satisfaction, and decreased levels in sickness and absences (ELENA, 2018). The 2017 decree also includes granting contribution relief to companies in the private sector that provide innovative work–life balance measures in their collective bargaining agreements/company policies. However, it is unclear whether further developments will be made to provide a legal right for smart working for the entire workforce.

Finland

One of the most recent and most radical additions to the policies on the right to flexible working comes from Finland. In March 2019, Finland passed a new Working Hours Act which came into force in January 2020, with the aim of updating rules governing working hours to meet the changes in the economic structure and in the ways people work. This included stronger rights for workers to work flexibly.[6] The key innovation here was that the new law changed the concepts of 'workplace' and 'working time'. 'Workplace' has now been changed to 'working place' which means that work is no longer tied to a specific location, and can be done anywhere. Working time, similarly, has been changed to a more simplified definition of 'time spent working', again not tied to work done within the office. Furthermore, the law specifically states that workers are able to freely decide when and where they work for *at least half* of their working time, with the employer deciding on the rest (up to 49 per cent). This effectively gives workers the right to decide when and where they work, as long as the worker works the agreed (weekly) working hours. The law also provides more flexibility in the calculations of hours – allowing for working hours to be banked/accumulated – up to 60 hours at the end of a four-month period, to be used as days off. Furthermore, additional overtime premiums or holiday pay can also be transferred into time off.[7] It has been noted that such legislation and rights are only possible due to the high levels of trust and high demands for better work–life balance found in Finland, as well as the relatively short average working hours and low tendency for long-hours work in the country.[8] The family-friendly nature and the strong union power of the country may have contributed to this reform (more in Chapter 9).

Australia

On 1 December of 2018, Australia introduced a new legislation that grants workers the right to request flexible working, based on the ruling by the Australian Fair Work Commission.[9] The right is, however, restricted to those who have been working with the same employer for the past 12 months, and are expected to work with the employer on a continuous and regular basis in the future. It is also further restricted to those with care responsibilities (parents of school-age children or younger, caring for friend/family member) or those with a disability, those aged 55 or over, or those experiencing or helping someone who is experiencing domestic violence. Flexible working is defined here as flexible schedules (flexitime), flexible place of work (working from home) and the reduction of hours (part-time, job share and so on). Employers are obliged to take into consideration the consequences for the employee when the request is rejected, providing a written response specifying the reason for the refusal, and possibly suggesting a solution. Employers can only refuse a request on reasonable business grounds, including the following listed on the government website: the requested arrangements are too costly; other employees' working arrangements cannot be changed to accommodate the request; it is impractical to change other employees' working arrangements or hire new employees to accommodate the request; the request would result in a significant loss of productivity or have a significant negative impact on customer service.

Korea

Flexible working arrangements were introduced in Korea in 2014 alongside policy packages aimed at addressing the work–life balance of workers. Flexible working in the Korean context can be defined as follows (Korean Ministry of Employment and Labor 2018). Flexible working hours (탄력적 근로시간제) entails the ability to work different hours as long as a certain number of hours of work is met across a specified time period. This is normally a week (40 hours across one week but different number of hours per day), but can be expanded to six months. Selective working hours (선택적 근로시간제) is also a type of flexitime but where workers need to work a given number of hours per day (for example eight hours), however, they can choose their start and end times of work. This can be distinguished into complete selective working hours and partial selective working hours, where in the latter, workers are bounded by certain core hours they need to work (for example 10am to 3pm). Discretionary working time (재량 근로시간제) is similar to working time autonomy, where workers are not bound by working hours, and workers decide their own working hours. Here work is more based on the projects workers need to complete, rather than the working hours they need to fulfil. It should be noted that this arrangement can only be applied to the occupations that are defined in the Korean Labour Law Article 13.[10] Finally, flexible working can also entail the capacity to work from home (재택 원격근무제) where workers can carry out work from home (재택) or from another location (원격) and their working hours are assumed based on the work done (사업장 밖 간주근로시간제). In 2018, the Korean government restricted the maximum weekly working hours to 52 hours from the previous 68 hours a week for all large companies with 300 or more employees (Chan, 2018). The regulation was expanded to cover medium-sized companies (50–299 employees) in January 2021, and small companies (5–49 employees) in July 2021. Korean companies have been introducing flexible working arrangements to overcome some of the restrictions in this legislation by calculating weekly hours over a longer period of time through flexible working hours (six months). Some companies have circumvented the introduction of the maximum working hours regulation altogether by allowing workers discretionary working time, where weekly working hours restrictions become rather meaningless. In 2019, the Korean socio-economic council/tripartite organisation agreed on the extension of the flexible working hours regulation (탄력적 근로시간제), for working hours to be calculated across a six-month rather than the previous three-month period (Hangyoreh, 2019). There has been a lot of criticism against this move, with the Korean Federation of Trade Unions arguing that the extension of the calculation period will leave the 52 hours regulation useless (YTN, 2019). Such use of flexible working leading to, or in the Korean case maintaining, overwork is a theme we will touch upon in Chapters 5 and 6.

Empirical data on the use and provision of flexible working

Provision of flexitime across Europe[11]

So how is flexible working provided and taken up by workers? Has there been a rise? In the European Company Survey, human resource managers were asked: 'Does your establishment offer employees the possibility to adapt – within certain limits – the time when they begin or finish their daily work according to their personal needs or wishes?', which we consider flexitime. Unfortunately, the data set does not ask managers about teleworking practices. Figure 2.1 provides the average proportion of companies that said they provide flexitime to at least one of their employees in 2009 and 2013. On average, 65 per cent of all companies across Europe provided flexitime to their employees in 2013. This is an increase from 57 per cent in 2009, and 48 per cent in 2004/05 (Chung, 2020a). When we change the definition of companies providing flexitime to those providing it to at least 20 per cent of its workers, the proportion drops to 54 per cent of all companies in 2013, but still again up from 45 per cent in 2009. We find a large cross-national variance across Europe – the Northern European countries such as Finland, Denmark and Sweden alongside Austria are the champions of flexible working with more than 80 per cent of all companies providing flexitime to their workers in 2013. Companies based in Southern Europe do not provide flexitime widely. In Bulgaria, Cyprus and Greece, less than half of the companies surveyed provided flexitime in 2013.

Figure 2.1: Proportion of companies providing flexitime across the European Union in 2009 and 2013

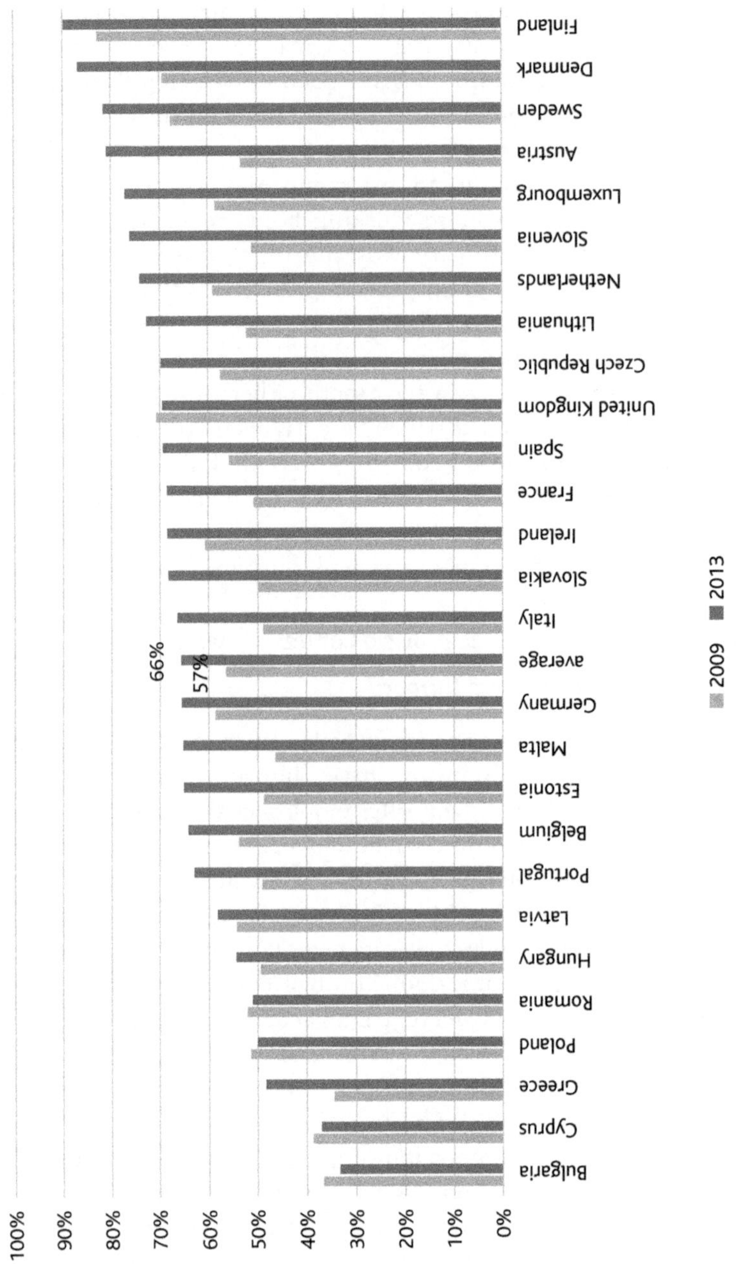
100%
90%
80%
70%
60%
50%
40%
30%
20%
10%
0%
Bulgaria
Cyprus
Greece
Poland
Romania
Hungary
Latvia
Portugal
Belgium
Estonia
Malta
Germany
average
Italy
Slovakia
Ireland
France
Spain
United Kingdom
Czech Republic
Lithuania
Netherlands
Slovenia
Luxembourg
Austria
Sweden
Denmark
Finland
66%
57%
2009
2013

Source: European Company Survey (ECS), 2009; 2013 (establishment weighted). N= 24,475 (2009), 24,316 (2013)

Access to flexible working

The provision of flexible working arrangements as described by HR managers may not necessarily reflect workers' access. Workers' positions within the company and various workplace cultures – including stigmatised ideas towards those who take up flexible working – influence the real access workers have towards flexible working (Eaton, 2003; Kossek et al, 2006; Cooper and Baird, 2015). Despite having formal policies stated either or both at the national and/or company-levels, this does not guarantee that flexible working arrangements are accessible to workers, and can be unevenly implemented across work places depending on mid-level and line managers. It is thus important to examine data gathered at the individual level. I examined the most recent round of the European Working Conditions Survey of 2015. More information about the data and variables are available in the Appendix.

As Figure 2.2 shows, more than a quarter of all dependent employed workers across the 30 Europe Union member states had flexible schedules in 2015; approximately 20 per cent had access to flexitime and another 6 per cent to full working time autonomy. Despite the fact that regulations on flexible working have thus far mostly been regulated only at company level in most countries, there is a wide cross-national variation in workers' access to flexible working with a clear pattern. Similar to what was found in the company-level data, Northern European countries – such as Sweden, Denmark, Norway, the Netherlands and Finland – are the ones where more workers respond that they have access to flexible working arrangements. In

Figure 2.2: Proportion of employees with flexible schedules across 30 European countries in 2015

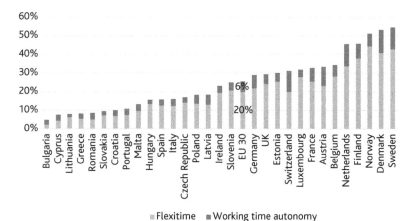

Source: European Working Conditions Survey (EWCS), 2015

Note: weighted averages/sorted by the proportion of workers with flexitime + working time autonomy

Figure 2.3: Proportion of dependent employed who teleworked/worked from home at least several times a month in the past 12 months across 30 European countries in 2015

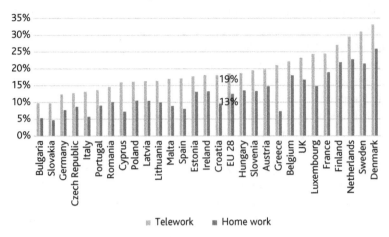

Source: European Working Conditions Survey (EWCS), 2015

Note: weighted averages/sorted by the proportion of teleworkers

the first three countries listed, more than half of employees have access to either flexitime or working time autonomy. On the other hand, in Eastern and Southern European countries, access is limited. In Bulgaria, less than 5 per cent of workers responded that they have access to flexible schedules (flexitime and working time autonomy). Similarly, in countries such as Cyprus, Lithuania, Romania, Greece, Slovakia and Croatia, this number does not reach 10 per cent.

Similar patterns emerge when examining the patterns of teleworking across Europe (see Figure 2.3). More than a quarter of workers in Northern European countries worked at home or in other public spaces (such as cafes) regularly (several times a month or more often) in the past 12 months in 2015. In Denmark, the number goes up to one in three (33%) employees. Again, Eastern and some Southern European countries, now alongside Germany, are those where this is more limited. It is no coincidence that the countries where workers have better access to flexible working are also those well known for being family-friendly with some of the most generous family policies at the national level (Korpi et al, 2013; Ferragina and Seeleib-Kaiser, 2015), or where workers' bargaining powers are stronger (den Dulk et al, 2013; Chung, 2018; Chung, 2019a). We will discuss this in greater detail in Chapter 9.

Has there been a growth in flexible working?

Has there been a growth in the number of workers working flexibly over the years? We could expect an increase in the proportion of workers with access to and use of flexible working arrangements over the past couple of decades. This is due to the increase in the demand for flexible working as mentioned earlier in this chapter, the expansions in the legislations enabling better access to such arrangements, and technological developments/changes in the nature of jobs in the past years.

However, when examining the data on the access to and use of flexible working arrangements, we cannot observe a clear pattern of growth. When examining the proportion of companies that say they provide flexible working arrangements, there seems to have been some progress with more companies saying they are providing flexitime to their employees. As mentioned earlier, in 2004/05 less than half of all companies surveyed said that they provided flexitime arrangements to their workers, while this number grew to two thirds in 2013. However, this growth has not been translated into growth in workers' access to flexible working arrangements. Examining workers' access to flexitime and working time autonomy through the European Working Conditions Survey data from 2005 to 2015 in Figure 2.4, it seems like access to these arrangements has remained relatively stagnant over the ten years, although there are differences across countries (available upon request). Even in 2005, approximately a quarter of workers had access to some sort of arrangement that gave them flexibility in their schedule, which is similar to the rates for 2015. Looking at our top country Sweden, surprisingly the proportion of workers with access to flexible schedules was at 58 per cent in 2005, higher than the rate of 54 per cent in 2015.

A similar pattern emerges when we look at country-specific data sets. Looking at the four waves of the UK BIS Employee Survey of Work-Life

Figure 2.4: Trends in flexitime and working time autonomy across 29 European countries (EU28+ Norway)

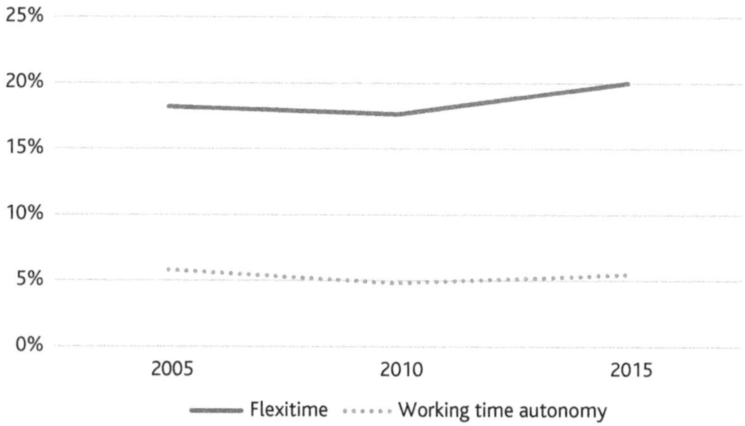

Source: European Working Conditions Survey (EWCS)

Balance between 2000 and 2011, the take-up of flexitime and teleworking has not changed much (Tipping et al, 2012) (Table 3.1 of the report). For example, in the first wave of the Work-Life Balance survey in 2000 approximately 24 per cent of all workers surveyed took up flexitime, and this number remained stagnant at 23 per cent in 2011. Actually, the rate went up between waves two and three (years 2003 and 2006), when the rate was slightly higher at 26 per cent, and then we saw a fall back in 2011. Similarly, in the European Working Conditions Survey, there seemed to have been a slight decrease in workers saying they had access to flexible schedules in 2010. This may be due to the 2008/09 financial crisis. As we will see later (Chapter 9), high levels of unemployment and the general insecurity of workers may result in workers not being able to access flexible working arrangements (Chung, 2018; Chung, 2021c). There has been a slight increase in workers who note that they regularly work from home from 11 per cent in 2006, to 13 per cent in 2011, according to the UK Work-Life Balance Survey.[12]

Looking now beyond Europe, I examined data from the US to see the trends in the access/use of flexible working arrangements. Figure 2.5 examines the trends in flexible working based on the US General Social Survey. As we can see, the proportion of workers who have access to schedule flexibility (often or sometimes can change start and end times on a daily basis) has not changed much over the past 14 years, with approximately 55 per cent having the ability to do so. The proportion of workers with the ability to work from home (at least once a week as part of their job) has had a modest increase from about 24 per cent in 2002 to 27 per cent in 2018. However, we should also be wary of considering this as an increase

Figure 2.5: Trends in flexible schedules and working from home in the US from 2002 to 2018

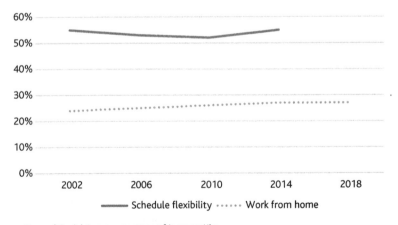

Source: General Social Survey; courtesy of Jaesung Kim

Note: there was no data available for schedule flexibility for the year 2018

Figure 2.6: Trends in the reason why workers work from home in the US from 2002 to 2018

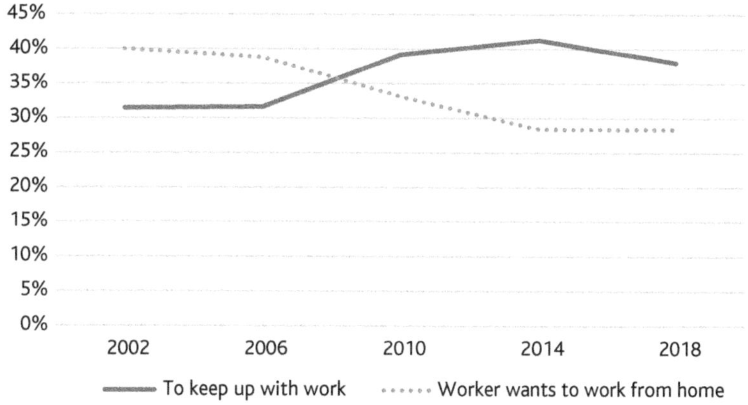

Source: General Social Survey, https://gssdataexplorer.norc.org/trends/Quality%20of%20 Working%20Life?measure=whywkhme_r

in workers' control over their place of work. As Figure 2.6 shows, the proportion of workers that say they work from home in order to catch up on their increasing workload has increased significantly, from 31 per cent in 2004 to 41 per cent in 2014, although it decreased slightly in 2018 to 38 per cent. Accordingly, the proportion of workers who work from home because they like to has decreased from 40 per cent to 28 per cent between 2002 and 2014.

In other words, despite the increased demand for flexible working, there hasn't been an obvious increase in the number of workers with access to flexible working across the past decade or two if we look at the more general working population. Furthermore, it is questionable whether the increase we see, especially in workers' ability to work from home, can be considered a development in the increase in workers' control over where they carry out their work. From what we gathered from the data, it looks more like there has been an increase in workers' ability to work from home in addition to the normal working hours in the office, possibly due to the advancements in technologies that allow us to do so. In other words, we already see a pattern of flexible working relating to the encroachment on family/leisure time.

Conclusion

This chapter outlined the growth and demand for flexible working. As some of the evidence explored in the beginning of the chapter has shown, there has been a growing demand for flexible working, where for many workers it has become an important working condition that can determine whether or not workers will take or keep their jobs. This chapter has also explored how governments across the world are responding to such demands by introducing the right to (request) flexible working arrangements. We expect more changes in legislations to occur in the coming years due to the COVID-19 pandemic and the experiences workers and managers have had over this period. We expect changes to occur in Europe in light of the new European directive on work-life balance that came into force in 2019.

However, it is clear that the trends in workers' perceived access to flexible working has not increased as much as one would expect. Despite the growing number of companies that say they have introduced flexible working arrangements, workers' access to flexible working arrangements have remained relatively stagnant. This is not the case during the COVID-19 pandemic, which, as we will explore later, resulted in an explosion of flexible working across the world. What is more, it seems like what has increased in terms of flexible working may not necessarily be the type of flexible working that is aimed at helping workers balance work with family life, but rather to enable workers to catch up on work, to make workers work better, or possibly more. The concept of the dual nature of flexible working is a point that we will be investigating in the next chapter.

Notes

[1] *The Independent* www.independent.co.uk/news/business/news/flexible-work-life-balance-remote-employment-a8223791.html

[2] www.cbronline.com/opinion/race-productivity-flexible-working-beats-pay

[3] UK government Open Consultation on the 'Good Work Plan: Proposals to support families' www.gov.uk/government/consultations/good-work-plan-proposals-to-support-families

[4] www.gov.uk/government/consultations/making-flexible-working-the-default

[5] For more information: https://wetten.overheid.nl/BWBR0011173/2016-01-01

[6] See https://nordiclaw.fi/new-working-hours-act-of-finland-enters-into-force-1-january-2020/

[7] For more, see www.borenius.com/2019/04/02/new-working-hours-act-approved-by-the-parliament/

[8] www.bbc.com/worklife/article/20190807-why-finland-leads-the-world-in-flexible-work

[9] For more, see www.fairwork.gov.au/employee-entitlements/flexibility-in-the-workplace/flexible-working-arrangements

[10] This includes workers doing research- and development-related work; work-related design or analysis of information processing system; journalism; fashion, interior, industrial design; advertising and broadcasting; film industry production; accounting, legal affairs; patent office; any work that is done on commission, for example consulting, advise, counselling and so on.

[11] For more information about the data and variables, see Appendix, and Chung (2014).

[12] The European Working Conditions Survey data on teleworking is not comparable across time so no time comparisons could be made.

3

The dual nature of flexibility: family-friendly or performance-oriented logic?

Introduction

In the previous chapter, we examined the extent to which flexible working is widespread across the world. This chapter continues on from the previous chapter by examining why companies provide flexible working arrangements and who – which individuals – gets access to and uses flexible working. Through these analyses, this chapter aims to show that despite popular belief, provision of/access to flexible working may be still driven by performance-enhancing goals, rather than work-life balance or well-being goals. When examining who has access to flexible working arrangements, family and care demands of workers have limited explanatory power. Rather, it is better explained by the type of work carried out, the relative value the worker has – that is, their skill level, and position of seniority/power they carry, and in general how much performance outcomes employers can expect from these workers. This explains why disadvantaged workers, possibly with the most demand for such flexibility, are the least likely to gain access to such arrangements. This results in a rather polarised access to flexible working arrangements across the labour market. This chapter will look into these issues further. First, I explore the dual nature of flexible working – namely the different purposes it meets. I will then examine the theories explaining why employers provide flexible working arrangements. Finally, the chapter presents empirical evidence testing these theories, and reviews other already published work. This is done to argue that performance outcome goals may trump work-family goals when examining workers' access to flexible working policies – depending on the flexible working arrangement in question.

The dual nature of flexible working

Flexible working as a family-friendly arrangement

Karasek (1979) in his study on the determinants of job strain explains how job decision latitude or job control helps workers reduce the negative impact high-job demands brings. Here job demands relate to one's workload or responsibility, while control is autonomy over various aspect of one's work including decisions about the way in which it is done and, more important for this book, when

37

and where it is done. Demerouti, Bakker and colleagues (Demerouti et al, 2001; Bakker et al, 2003; Bakker and Demerouti, 2007) refines this model to a job demands and resources model. In this model, job demands refer to 'those physical, psychological, social, or organizational aspects of the job that require sustained physical and/or psychological (cognitive and emotional) effort or skills and are therefore associated with certain physiological and/or psychological costs', while job resources entail 'those physical, psychological, social, or organizational aspects of the job that are either/or functional in achieving work goals, reduce job demands and the associated physiological and psychological costs, or stimulate personal growth, learning, and development' (Bakker and Demerouti, 2007: 312). Flexible working is a major part of job resources, as a broader aspect of autonomy over one's work. In general, autonomy over one's work or general job resources improves workers' well-being through two ways. One through enabling workers to manage job demands, such as heavy workload, to fit around family/private life demands. Another is the motivational process, namely by fostering work engagement and providing an intrinsic motivational role. In this model, flexible working and generally more autonomy over one's work has been seen as a job resource that can alleviate or moderate some of the negative influences high levels of job demands can have over one's job stress and work-family conflict (Voydanoff, 2005). This is why in most studies flexible working is considered a family-friendly arrangement that is offered by employers, on the one hand, to meet workers' work-family demand, and on the other, to meet employers' HR need – namely, staff recruitment and maintenance.

In the 2013 UK Work-Life Balance survey of employers conducted by the UK Business, Energy & Industrial Strategies (BEIS),[1] employers were asked about the effects of introducing flexible working and leave policies in their companies (Figure 3.1). Almost two thirds of those surveyed agreed that it increased employee motivation and commitment, and more than half agreed that it helped with employee relations, absenteeism, labour turnover. Fewer said it had a positive effect on productivity and ease of recruitment, although we can see an increase in those who responded positively to this item since the last wave in 2007.

Flexible working as a high-performance management system

Flexible working arrangements are also used to enhance performance outcomes of the company (Osterman, 1995; Ortega, 2009; Brescoll et al, 2013; den Dulk et al, 2013). High-performance or high-involvement strategy scholars argue that when workers have more control or discretion over their work, this will increase their performance outcomes (Appelbaum et al, 2000; Davis and Kalleberg, 2006). Appelbaum and colleagues (2000) observe that compared to previous times where workers carried out tasks set by managers, managers in manufacturing sectors in the 1980s and 1990s started to view workers and

Figure 3.1: Proportion of employers who answered that the introduction of flexible working and leave policies had the following positive effect within companies

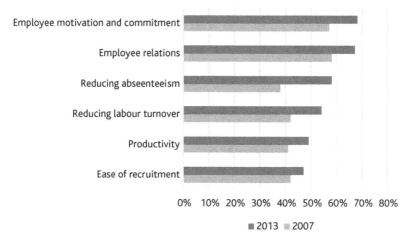

Source: UK Work-Life Balance Survey waves 4 & 3, BEIS, N=2,011 (weighted averages)

their participation as an important source of competitive advantage in the global market place. This gave birth to the high-performance work system (HPWS). HPWS is where work is organised to enable more involvement of front-line workers into the decision-making processes. This could take form in many ways, including shop-floor production teams, self-managed work teams, employee participation in problem-solving or quality improvement teams, giving workers higher levels of communications on work matters with themselves, managers, as well as customers and so on (Appelbaum et al, 2000: 7). A part of HPWS is giving workers more autonomy over job tasks and method of work. In this sense, giving workers control over where and when they work can be seen as an essential part of this system, rather than solely an employee-friendly benefit (Chung and Tijdens, 2013). Thus, employers provide workers with more control over their hours, expecting increased efficiency – for example workers increasing their work intensity or working their most productive hours (Kelliher and Anderson, 2010) – see Chapter 5 for more. In fact, many scholars have noted that organisations created flexible working policies not necessarily to meet workers' demands but to serve their own business interests (Hall and Richter, 1988; Regan, 1994; Clark, 2000).

Examining the European Survey of Working Time 2004/05 (Riedmann et al, 2006) – which surveyed a representative sample of companies of ten or more employees across 21 European countries, 68 per cent of managers noted that flexitime was introduced to enable better combination of work and family/personal life for employees. However, almost half (47 per cent) of employers also noted that they introduced flexitime to make working hours more adaptable to variations in the workload, 22 per cent mentioned commuting problems as a reason for its introduction, and 14 per cent said it was used to reduce paid overtime hours. Furthermore, 54 per cent of managers in the same survey responded that flexible working allowed for better adaptation of workloads, and 22 per cent said they were able to thereby reduce paid overtime. In sum, although enabling workers a better work-life balance is a major reason why employers introduce flexible working arrangements, performance/cost are also frequently mentioned as key reasons for, or at least noted as some of the outcomes of, its introduction.

Theories on the determinants of flexible working provision and access

Many scholars ask the question: what is the driving force behind the introduction of flexible working arrangements? (for example Osterman, 1995; Wood et al, 2003; Swanberg et al, 2005; Davis and Kalleberg, 2006; Ortega, 2009; Chung, 2018; Chung, 2019c). In other words, are flexible working arrangement provisions driven more by performance goals or family-friendly goals? Similarly, others have discussed the three distinctive principles employers use to decide who gets access to flexible working arrangements; namely, principle of need, equity and equality (see also Lambert and Haley-Lock, 2004; Swanberg et al, 2005). The goals or principles employers aim to achieve not only shape whether or not flexible working arrangements are provided, but to whom it is provided within the company/labour market.

Principle of need/family-friendly demands

For many, the general assumption is that flexible working is provided based on the principle of need, that is, those with a greater need are given better access to flexible working arrangements. Many studies have shown that those with the most family demands are most likely to request flexible working arrangements (Golden, 2009; Skinner and Pocock, 2011). Similarly, companies employing more workers with greater family/care responsibilities are expected to face increased internal pressure to be responsive to work-family issues and make flexible working arrangements more readily available (Goodstein, 1994). Because women are expected to carry out the bulk of the housework, childcare and other types of care (Bianchi et al, 2012; Dotti Sani and Treas, 2016; Taylor and Scott, 2018), many expect that women with care responsibilities are those with the greatest access to flexible working arrangements. It is also assumed that jobs/occupations where women are over-represented are those where flexible working and other family-friendly arrangements are more readily available (Goodstein, 1994). In fact, some studies, especially those using company-level data and managers' perceived provision of flexible working, have shown that companies with more female workers are more likely to provide flexible working arrangements (for example Bardoel et al, 1999; Dex and Smith, 2002; Wood et al, 2003; Kerkhofs et al, 2008). The idea that female-dominated workplaces are the better providers of flexible working and other family-friendly arrangements can be linked to the theory of compensating differentials (Filer, 1985). This theory argues that the lower pay found in female-dominated jobs/ occupations can be justified because these workplaces have better working conditions and better access to family-friendly benefits. Accordingly, the persisting gender wage gap is expected to be explained by the fact that women trade off access to flexible working for higher-paying jobs (Goldin, 2014). However, many recent studies, especially those looking at individual-level data and workers' perceived access to flexible working, have shown that female-dominated workplaces are where access to flexible working arrangements are most limited (Glass, 1990; Adler, 1993; Glass and Finley, 2002; Glauber, 2011; 2012; Chung, 2019c; Magnusson, 2019). This may be because rather than responding to the demands for flexible working, employers are more interested in the enhanced performance/outcomes gained from introducing the arrangements.

Principle of equity/expected performance outcome

Principle of equity is similar to the idea that flexible working is primarily used to meet performance-oriented goals – that is, employers will provide flexible working arrangements to those from whom they can reap the most benefit out of. When performance goals are important, employers may be more reluctant to provide women, especially mothers, flexible working arrangements. This is because due to social norms about whose responsibility it is to care, and whose responsibility it is to be the breadwinner (Scott and Clery, 2013), employers expect women to prioritise care and housework above paid work (Budig and England, 2001). Thus, employers may not expect to be able to gain any performance outcomes from providing mothers/ women with flexible working arrangements (Brescoll et al, 2013; Chung and van der Lippe, 2020). This is explored further when we examine the gendered flexibility paradox in Chapter 7, and in Chapter 8 where we discuss the stigma around flexible working.

Again, if principle of equity takes precedence, the provision of flexible working is expected to be driven mostly by the idea that the company will benefit from workers having more control over when and where they work because workers can do their jobs better in this way. Although companies can also increase productivity/performance outcomes by enabling better work–life balance or well-being of workers, this indirect increase of profits may not be as important or as evident for many managers. Based on the principle of equity, we can expect flexible working to be used more in knowledge-intensive fields (Brescoll et al, 2013) and in more 'innovative companies' aiming to enhance their competitive edge (Nagar, 2002). Furthermore, workers in higher-status/skill level jobs will have more access in the expectation that it will enhance their productivity. There is plenty of evidence to show that high-skilled workers and workers in higher-paid occupations are much more likely to gain access to flexible working arrangements that give workers more control over when and where they work compared to low-skilled workers or workers in lower-paid occupations[2] (for example, Glass, 1990; Golden, 2001; Nagar, 2002; Kelly and Kalev, 2006; Golden, 2009; Ortega, 2009; Clawson and Gerstel, 2014; Glass et al, 2016; Wiß, 2017; Chung, 2019a; Magnusson, 2019). Similarly, when performance goals are important, flexible working will be used as part of the wider high-performance work systems package. This means that flexible working arrangements are provided to workers alongside control over other aspects of the job – namely, tasks, order, speed and so on – and other arrangements such as self- managed teams, job rotations and performance-related pay (Ortega, 2009).

Higher status

Some scholars (Adler, 1993; Schieman et al, 2009) argue that flexible working is a part of a higher-status position. The reason for this is that with higher status, workers are given more responsibility/workload at work and are expected to increase their commitment to work (Blair-Loy, 2009). Control and discretion over one's work can then be considered to be a resource given to workers to allow them to deal with such increased demands from work, and the two go hand in hand as an integral part of higher-status positions (Schieman et al, 2009).

In the same vein, workers in disadvantaged positions – for example, low-wage, low-skilled, lower-educated workers – will be the least likely to have access to flexible working arrangements. This is due to the fact that employers do not invest in the lower-paid segments of the labour market because they do not expect large profit gains from this segment of the workforce. Again there is ample evidence of this in practice across countries (for example, Swanberg et al, 2005; Golden, 2009; Wiß, 2017; Chung, 2019a), where those possibly with the most need for flexible working are the least likely to gain access to it (see also, Stewart and Bivand, 2016; TUC, 2017).

Bargaining power

Examining access to flexible working arrangements across Europe (Chung, 2018), I also found that insecure workers, even having taken into account the different skill levels and occupational levels of workers, were significantly less likely to have access to flexible working arrangements. This is because in addition to skill levels, workers' relative bargaining power may be relevant in explaining their access to flexible working arrangements. This is especially the case when we consider the stigma people hold towards flexible workers (for more see Chapter 8), which may prevent those without much negotiation power from taking up flexible working arrangements, due to the potential consequences for their job and income security.

Power resource theory argues that welfare states are shaped by the power that is mobilised by wage earners, whether through political parties or through interest organisations such as trade unions (Korpi, 1989). In addition to the direct impact trade unions have on shaping national policies, when there are strong unions within the company or even at the national level, this can lead to a 'contagion from the Left' (Korpi, 1989: 316) influencing the way employers act in providing family-friendly benefits at company level. What is more, organised labour within the establishment might allow for the introduction of family policies that managers would not have adopted (Seeleib-Kaiser and Fleckenstein, 2009). In this case, unionised workplaces with employee representatives should be the ones where family-friendly, flexible working arrangements will be most prevalent. Empirically, the results are rather mixed – some saying that unions are important when it comes to enhancing provision and access to flexible working arrangements (Seeleib-Kaiser and Fleckenstein, 2009; Berg et al, 2014), others noting that there is no significant effect (Chung, 2018; Chung, 2019a), and some noting that this depends on the country (Wiß, 2017). Some studies argue that rather than unions, managers are important in the introduction of family policies at company level. For example, companies with supportive managers will be more likely to provide workers with family-friendly, flexible working arrangements (Hammer et al, 2009; Minnotte et al, 2010; Kossek et al, 2014) or are places where workers feel like they are more able to take up the arrangements (Cooper and Baird, 2015).

Structural factors

The factors we observed in the previous sections can be considered agency factors – that is, factors that relate more to the willingness of managers and/or the push they get from workers and unions to provide flexible working policies. We can also consider structural factors – that is, factors that relate to structure of the company that enables or prohibits the company from being able to provide flexible working arrangements (Dex and Smith, 2002; Seeleib-Kaiser and Fleckenstein, 2009; Wiß, 2017). Due to the administrative costs involved in providing these arrangements, larger companies may find it easier to administer the use of flexible working arrangements and may have more resources to provide it. Having said that, small and medium-sized companies may be able to provide more informal or ad hoc arrangements (Dex and Scheibl, 2001). The type of work that is being done has always been noted as one of the biggest constraints to the introduction of flexible working arrangements by managers (Wanrooy et al, 2013). There are jobs where it is harder to apply flexible working arrangements than others due to, for example, production structure (machinery, clients' demands and so on) or sensitivities towards certain business cycles. This would mean that certain jobs in sectors such as manufacturing, construction, education, retail, and health and social services may be restricted in their application of flexible working arrangements – especially teleworking/working from home. However, as we will see in Chapter 10, COVID-19 has changed these dynamics. Public sector employers, have been perceived to be better at providing various types of family-friendly arrangements because they are not as sensitive to business cycles (Evans, 2001; Chung, 2008).

Empirical data analysis results

In this section, I will examine the determinants of the provision of flexible working using cross-European company data – namely the European Company Survey (ECS) of 2013, and the access to and use of flexible working arrangements using individual-level data – namely the European Working Conditions Survey (EWCS) of 2015. More about the survey can be found in the Appendix

Provision of flexitime – company-level analysis

Examining the ECS of 2013 (Figure 3.2 – for detail see Table A3.1), we can see evidence for both family-friendly and high-performance reasons why companies provide flexitime. The proportion of women in the company, the existence of an employee representative, and a good working climate are all factors that contribute to determining whether or not a company provides flexitime to its workers, and how widely it is available within the firm. Having said that, they are not as powerful as high-performance explanations; for example, the proportion of skilled workers in the company and whether or not the company uses other types of high-performance work systems such as performance-related pay and self-managed teamwork. However, performance-related pay is negatively associated with the likelihood that flexitime covers a wider group of workers. We can also see that although having an employee representative is positively associated with the likelihood of a company providing flexitime to its workers, it has a negative association with the proportion of workers accessing flexitime. Structural factors, such

Figure 3.2: Explaining company-level provision of flexitime across Europe (28 countries) in 2013

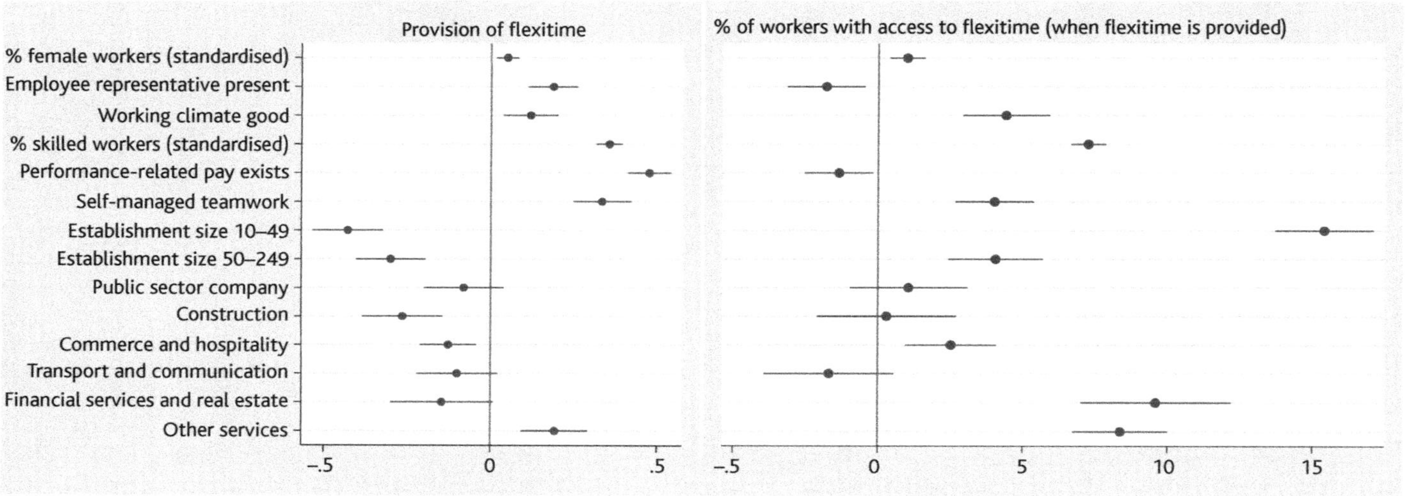

Source: ECS, 2013, author's calculation. Coefficient plot of two regression tables, detailed table in Table A3.1
Note: percentage of female workers and skilled workers has been standardised. All other variables are dichotomous variables

as the size of the company and which line of business they are in also matter. Bigger companies are more likely to provide flexitime; however, smaller companies are more likely to provide it to a broader group of workers if they do use it. Construction, commerce and hospitality sectors are less likely to provide flexible working arrangements, as are, to a certain extent, financial services and the real estate sector. However, both financial services and the real estate sector, and other services sectors provide flexitime to a larger group of workers when they do provide it.

Access to flexitime/working time autonomy – individual-level analysis

Figure 3.3 shows the results of the individual-level analysis examining the factors that relate to workers' access to flexitime and working time autonomy. Here working time autonomy means having full control over when and to a certain degree how much you work (as long as you get the work done), while flexitime entails a more limited discretion over one's work – for example controlling the start and end times of work. Detailed regression tables are available in Table A3.2.

Similar to what is found in the company-level analysis, we do see a mix of evidence in terms of family-friendly and performance-oriented goal outcomes. First, there is some evidence that flexitime is provided to those in greater need of work-family policies – namely, those with preschool children, with care responsibilities, or have a disability are more likely to have access to it. Furthermore, those who have supportive managers are more likely to say they have access to flexitime. However, we can see that none of the aforementioned variables are significant in explaining workers' access to working time autonomy. High-performance or higher-status logic can explain access to flexitime and working time autonomy and has more explanatory power compared to variables that relate to the family-friendly logic (see also, Ortega, 2009). Occupational status and educational levels are two of the most important factors in determining who has control over their schedules – be it with flexitime or working time autonomy, with managers and (associate) professionals, and higher-educated workers having greater access. In addition, those who have higher levels of income security – that is, higher household income/pay, in supervisory roles are the ones with better access. This supports the idea that flexible working is a type of control one gains over one's work as one gains higher-status jobs/ positions. On the other hand, those who feel that their jobs are insecure were less likely to have access to flexible schedules (flexitime/working time autonomy), again supporting the worker bargaining position thesis. However, contrary to expectations, those with open-ended contracts were less likely to have access to working time autonomy. This may be because of

Figure 3.3: Explaining individual-level access to flexible schedules (flexitime + working time autonomy) across Europe (28 countries) in 2015

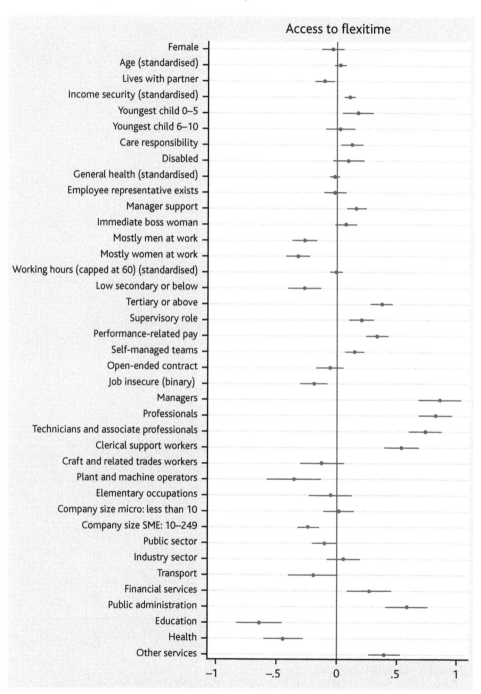

(continued)

Figure 3.3: Explaining individual-level access to flexible schedules (flexitime + working time autonomy) across Europe (28 countries) in 2015 (continued)

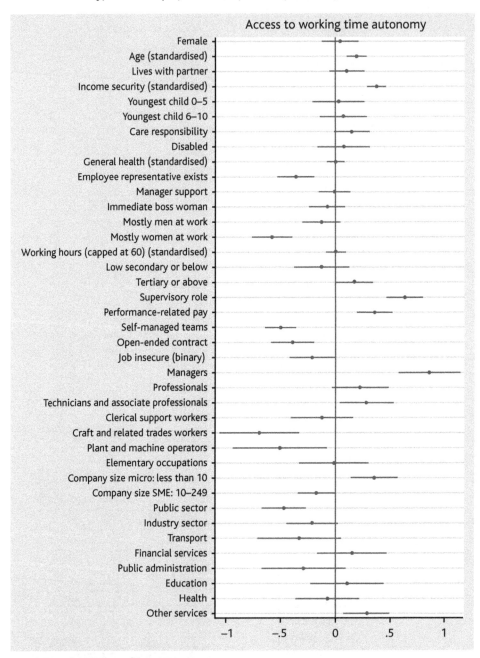

Source: EWCS, 2015, author's calculation.
Note: Age, income security, general health, and working hours have been standardised. All other variables are dichotomous variables. Coefficient plot of two regression tables, detailed table in Table A3.2. N level 1=23408, N level 2=28 countries.

Figure 3.4: Explaining which workers teleworked regularly across Europe (28 countries) in 2015

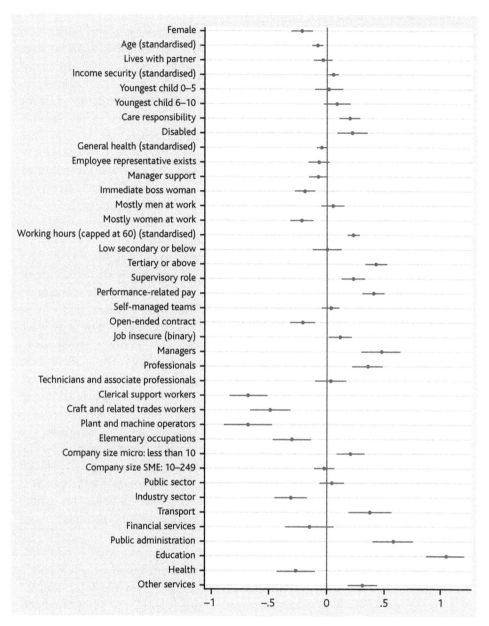

Source: EWCS, 2015, author's calculation.
Note: Age, income security, general health and working hours have been standardised. All other variables are dichotomous variables. Coefficient plot of two regression tables, detailed table in Table A3.2. N level 1=23197, N level 2=28 countries.

the inclusion of people who are on so-called 'gig' type freelance contracts who are more flexible in terms of the hours they work, yet whose contracts are not permanent.

Looking more at company-level characteristics, workers working in companies that provide performance-related pay are more likely to have access to both flexitime and working time autonomy, yet their use is not associated with self-managed teams. Public companies are less likely to provide working time autonomy arrangements to their workers, while for flexitime there are no clear differences between public and private sectors. Workplaces where men and women were equally represented were the ones where access was highest for both flexitime and working time autonomy. Female-dominated workplaces are those where access was most limited especially for working time autonomy (see also, Chung, 2019c; Magnusson, 2019). Company size mattered. Medium-sized companies with 50–249 employees were the ones where access to both flexitime and working time autonomy was most limited. Workers in small companies with less than 50 employees were most likely to have access to working time autonomy. This may be because larger companies are more likely to provide formal access to flexible working due to the resources they have, while smaller companies may be able to provide more informal ad hoc arrangements, and can be more flexible with its provision (Dex and Scheibl, 2001). This may leave medium-sized companies caught between the two where it is difficult to implement formal policies due to lack of resources or staff to implement these arrangements, while not being able to rely solely on informal arrangements due to its implication on the fairness across the company. Finally, looking at differences across sectors/line of business, we see that financial services and real estate sectors, as well as the public administration sectors are the ones where access to flexitime is greater, while education, health and social care services access is worse. For working time autonomy there is not much sector variation, other than the fact that workers in the other service sectors have better access to working time autonomy. Workers in this sector, which includes research, arts, and also technical-related sectors, also have better access to flexitime.

Figure 3.4 examines the characteristics of workers who telework regularly – here defined as those who work from home or other public spaces (such as cafes) several times a month or more often (see Table A3.2 for detailed results). The results are similar to that found for flexible schedules. Family-demands logic somewhat explains which workers telework. For example, having care responsibilities and being disabled increases your likelihood of teleworking. Having a young child in the household increases your likelihood of working from home yet not for teleworking (see Table A3.2). However, the higher-status/performance logic factors are far more powerful in explaining workers' likelihood to telework. Workers in higher occupational groups – managers and professionals, higher-educated, with higher incomes, in supervisory roles, working in a company that applies performance-related pay are those who are most likely to have regularly teleworked. On the other hand, in a similar vein, women, workers in female-dominated workplaces, with a female boss, and those in lower-paid jobs are less likely to have teleworked. Contrary to this, those with open-ended contracts are less likely to have teleworked, and those who feel that their jobs are insecure are more likely to have teleworked. This may be due to the fact that the teleworking measured here may also be capturing more the need to work from home or other public spaces to catch up on/ do more work possibly to overcome their insecure positions. This also explains why teleworking is associated with long working hours (see also Chapters 5 and 6).

Looking at company-level characteristics, unlike flexitime, management support is not associated with teleworking, and workers in small companies were most likely to have teleworked. Sectoral variations exist. Industry sectors or health and social care sectors are those where workers are less likely to have teleworked. Public administration and other service sectors are those where teleworking is more common. Financial services and real estate sector workers are more likely to have worked from home regularly compared to other workers (Table A3.2). Interestingly, education sector workers have also noted that they have teleworked (from home and in public spaces) frequently. However, this may be due to teachers needing to work from home to catch up on work, especially during term time. Teachers are well known to work long (unpaid) overtime especially in countries such as the UK (Henshaw, 2019), clocking on average 12 hours of overtime per week in 2020 (TUC, 2021a). Thus, what we may be seeing here is workers working at home on top of their regular working hours rather than working their regular contracted hours from home (see also Figure 2.6 in Chapter 2).

Outside Europe

The results of this chapter have been replicated by many others using data from across the world. For example, many studies confirm that the access to flexible working arrangements in the US is better explained by performance logic rather than family-friendly logic (Lambert and Haley-Lock, 2004; Swanberg et al, 2005; Kossek and Lautsch, 2018). Similar conclusions are made by those using cross-national comparative data sets covering countries in Asia and the Americas (Lyness et al, 2012). All point to the fact that although workers in lower-paid jobs are more likely to benefit from flexible working arrangements, they are the least likely to have access to it.

Conclusion

For many, flexible working is generally considered part of family-friendly arrangements that is mostly used to allow workers a better balance between work and family life. However, as this chapter has examined, this is a rather simplistic view. In reality, flexible working is used not only for family-friendly purposes but also for performance-enhancing goals as a part of the larger high-performance systems strategies or given as a part of a package of working conditions for higher-status workers to enhance their performance. This is evidenced by the analysis of the most recent cross-European data sets, but also through a number of different studies that cover different countries.

In fact, examining both company-level provision data, as well as the individual's perceived access to flexitime, working time autonomy, teleworking/homeworking, we find that high-performance/higher-status variables had much stronger explanatory power in explaining who provides and who has access to these arrangements. One key result found in this chapter – which will become important to remember when we explore the gendered flexibility paradox in Chapter 8 – is that, women and workers in female-dominated workplaces have the worst access to flexible working arrangements. This contradicts the ideas of family-friendly logic in the provision of flexible working and many of the assumptions behind the logic of compensating differentials (Filer, 1985). In other words, the idea that women choose flexibility over pay or that the low pay found in female-dominated workplaces/occupations can be explained by the better working conditions that allow workers to fit work around family demands better, can be put to rest. Based on the evidence we see, it seems like women and workers working in female-dominated workplaces are not only paid less (Macpherson and Hirsch, 1995), but they also lack control over their work (Chung, 2019c). This may in a way explain why we can see an over-representation of women in part-time work and a larger prevalence of part-time work in female-dominated workplaces (Nicolaisen et al, 2019). Namely, due to lack of flexibility at their jobs, women have no choice but to reduce their working hours to better adapt work around family demands (Chung and van der Horst, 2018). The reason why women and those with care responsibilities have limited access to flexible working arrangements can also be linked to the stigmatised views around their flexible working, which we will explore further in Chapter 8. In general, however, it is important to note that it may be largely due to the already existing biases against disadvantaged workers' capacity to work and be productive that can explain the limited access to flexible working arrangements for these groups of workers.

In sum, despite popular belief, flexible working is not necessarily used solely for family-friendly purposes and its provision/access can be better explained by what employers perceive as the pay-offs will be through its implementation. Obviously there may be cross-national variations in the extent to which performance logic versus family-friendly logic is being used (see, for example, den Dulk et al, 2013; Riva et al, 2018; Chung, 2019a). This is something we will be looking at in Chapter 9, when we examine the role of contexts in the provision and outcomes of flexible working. However, in general, the work–life balance of workers may not be the first thing on the manager's mind when it comes to the provision of flexible working. This obviously has implications for the outcomes of flexible working. If flexible working is provided more with a performance logic in mind, we could expect that while it may increase performance outcomes for companies, it may not necessarily lead to better work–life balance for workers. This is what we will be examining in the next chapter.

Notes

[1] For more information about this survey please see: www.gov.uk/government/publications/fourth-work-life-balance-employer-survey-2013

[2] In this book, I try not to use the term low-skilled jobs. In David Graeber's (2018) book, *Bullshit Jobs*, he argues that many of the professional and especially managerial jobs are bullshit jobs, that provide no true value to society. Contrarily, the more societally meaningful jobs that are crucial to the day-to-day running of societies are the ones in the so-called lower occupational ranks, such as waste collectors and fruit pickers. Also the skill levels needed to carry out a task may not necessarily be low-skilled just because it does not require formal education. Rather what really distinguishes these jobs are the fact that they are paid less. Thus I will use the term low(er)-paid, sometimes alongside lower-skilled.

4

The outcomes of flexible working

Introduction

In the previous chapter, we explored the question whether or not flexible working is more of an arrangement used by employers to enhance performance outcomes mainly given to higher-status workers, or is more of a family-friendly arrangement as many assume (Osterman, 1995; Ortega, 2009). We concluded that although there is evidence that both family-friendly and performance/higher-status logics partially explain the provision and access to flexible working arrangements, the explanatory power of the latter was much stronger. Thus, flexible working is not actually necessarily provided to workers who need it most, but to workers in higher-skilled/paid occupations and taken up by those in stronger bargaining positions within the company. This chapter explores the question of the nature of flexible working, but this time, by looking at the outcomes of flexible working. More specifically, I will empirically examine whether flexible working helps workers relieve the conflict felt between work and family life (work-family conflict). If flexible working were to be provided for workers to better meet private life demands, it would help workers reduce the conflict felt between the demands coming from the two spheres, and increase workers' satisfaction towards work-life balance. If flexible working does not result in enhancing workers' work-life balance, this makes us re-evaluate the nature of flexible working and how it is implemented. Obviously, the goals of better work-life integration and increased work performance are not necessarily at odds with one another. Performance-enhancing flexible working may also help workers to shape work around private life demands, and family-friendly flexible working can benefit companies due to the improvement in workers' well-being (Rapoport et al, 2002). This chapter provides us with some evidence of this being the case.

Before we move onto the empirical evidence, this chapter summarises existing literature on the outcomes of flexible working, focusing mostly on meta-analysis or systematic reviews – that is, studies that combine the results of a number of studies (statistically) together. Some key themes that will be touched upon are performance and productivity outcomes, well-being, and work-life balance. Through this, the chapter provides evidence that despite the assumptions made by many who promote flexible working as a major tool to address the work-life balance needs of workers, flexible working may increase the conflict felt between work and family if not implemented properly. One reason for this is partially explained through the fact that flexible working increases boundary blurring, which leads to work encroaching on family life. Through this, the chapter opens up for the next section of the book which goes into greater detail about this encroachment processes, namely, the flexibility paradox.

Summaries of existing studies

Performance outcomes

One of the key concerns employers raise when discussing the introduction of flexible working in their organisation is the worry that workers will abuse the control or freedom they are given, which will lead to negative performance outcomes for the company.[1] However, on the contrary, there is a wealth of research on the so-called 'business case' for flexible working, that evidence positive performance outcomes of flexible working (for an overview and meta-analysis and systematic review, see Beauregard and Henry, 2009; de Menezes and Kelliher, 2011; Allen et al, 2015; Kelliher and de Menezes, 2019).[2] Kelliher and de Menezes (2019) discuss the two ways in which flexible working can help increase performance outcomes for companies. First, flexible working can have a direct link with performance outcomes. Studies have linked flexible working directly with worker productivity and organisational performance, for example, profit and return on investment, labour productivity and so on, showing both positive and negative, but also insignificant outcomes (for example, Chung, 2009; de Menezes and Kelliher, 2011; Bloom et al, 2015; Kelliher and de Menezes, 2019; Boltz et al, 2020). What is more consistent from previous studies is the positive association between the use of flexible working arrangements with reduction in turn over intention, and increased levels of job satisfaction, organisational commitment and loyalty among the workforce (see also, Masuda et al, 2012; Moen et al, 2017; Ruppanner et al, 2018a). This in turn increases worker retention, and reduces worker recruitment problems (Aryee et al, 1998; Kerkhofs et al, 2008; Kossek and Ollier-Malaterre, 2019) which can result in major cost-savings for companies. Another way flexible working can improve performance outcomes for companies is by reducing sickness and absenteeism, and improving health and other well-being outcomes of workers (Gajendran and Harrison, 2007) which helps improve performance indirectly.

Workers' well-being

There is a lot of evidence around flexible working improving well-being outcomes for workers (Gajendran and Harrison, 2007; Moen et al, 2016; Avendano and Panico, 2018). This can be for several reasons. Flexible schedules may allow workers with certain needs better able to work by enabling work schedules to fit to the biological rhythms or other care demands of the workers. Workers who may have a hard time coming into work when feeling ill may still be able to carry out parts of their work if they do not have to commute and are able to work from home. Having said that, this may also increase the likelihood of the worker not having sufficient recovery periods which can deteriorate their well-being. Not having to commute in itself can also improve well-being due to the reduced risk of catching germs and viruses, and experiencing other potential health hazards. This can explain why flexible working can reduce sickness, absenteeism and improve well-being outcomes for workers on the one hand, and on the other, enable those with a disability or other care demands to take better part in the labour market (Jones, 2008; Chung and van der Horst, 2018). In addition, providing workers more control over their work involves a level of trust and freedom. This sense of autonomy may also drive workers to have higher levels of job satisfaction and organisational commitment (Gajendran and Harrison, 2007). As we have shown in Chapter 2, given that the demand for flexible working is quite high among workers in general, it is not hard to understand why providing workers with flexible working arrangements will increase workers' loyalty, organisational commitment and job satisfaction, while reducing their intention to leave their job. Especially in countries where flexible working arrangements are not as common, we would expect this to be even stronger. Another major reason why flexible working is associated with positive well-being outcomes is due to the reduction in stress due to a better work–life balance, which we will examine next.

Work-life balance

Job demands and resources theory (Bakker and Geurts, 2004; Voydanoff, 2005; Schaufeli et al, 2009) suggests that having control over one's work can act as a resource to help facilitate workers meet demands coming from both their work and other spheres of life, as well as enabling a better balance between the two (see Chapter 3). Here control and flexibility over one's work is a resource one can use to tackle demands of work (long-hours work), family (childcare demands) or other private life demands (Kelliher et al, 2019). For example, even if you need to work long hours, it is much better to choose when to work rather than having to, for example, work in the office from 8am to 8pm. Border control theory (Clark, 2000) or boundary management theory (Kossek et al, 2006) similarly argue how the flexibility and control workers have over the time and space boundaries between work and other spheres of life, and the possibility to blend the activities together, can enable workers a better balance between the two. Especially given that normal fixed working hours (for example 9am to 5pm) and family/private life schedules/demands (for example school pick-up times at 3pm) are not necessarily compatible, the control over the borders may help workers resolve some of the conflicts arising from this incompatibility. Teleworking allows workers to address family demands by providing a possibility to blend/integrate the work and family domains, for example, taking care of a sick child or putting a load of washing on while working from home. In addition, workers with long commutes will have more time and energy for childcare and/ or work when they no longer need to travel into work by working from home (Peters et al, 2004; Chung et al, 2020b).

However, the evidence is mixed. Some studies show that job autonomy and flexible working relieve work-to-family conflict (for example Chung, 2011; Michel et al, 2011; Allen et al, 2013; Kelly et al, 2014) especially during the transition into parenthood (Erickson et al, 2010). Some studies using meta-analysis approaches that combine and consolidate a number of studies together show that the association is rather weak (Michel et al, 2011; Allen et al, 2013). Others show that flexible working, especially teleworking or working from home arrangements, can significantly increase work-family conflict (Duxbury et al, 1994; Golden et al, 2006; Chung, 2017; Yucel and Chung, 2021). Many scholars argue that rather than being one singular relationship, the relationship between flexible working and work-family conflict may depend on one's gender (Yucel and Chung, 2021), the organisational contexts (van der Lippe and Lippényi, 2020) and national contexts (Lott, 2015; Chung, 2021c). Namely, contexts such as the family-friendly nature of the context, workers' bargaining power, work and gender culture contexts and the prevalence of flexible working all matter in explaining the association. This is something we will look into in greater detail in Chapter 9.

Many studies have shown that flexible working may be bad for work-family conflict due to its boundary blurring effect (for example Golden et al, 2006; Kossek et al, 2006; Lott, 2020). Role-blurring hypothesis (Ashforth et al, 2000; Schieman and Glavin, 2008) argues that greater flexibility and control over one's work can increase the blurring of the work-family spheres. While in previous times there was high segmentation between work and family with a clearer distinction between the two spheres. As work boundaries become more flexible, the boundaries between the work and family spheres become more permeable – as in one domain can leak into or encroach the other (Clark, 2000). The border crossing or integration of the two roles may help workers address the demands coming from both spheres especially for those who prefer such integration (Kossek et al, 2006). However, it can also increase the likelihood of work spilling over to family spheres, increasing potential work-family conflict more often than when stronger boundaries are in place. What is more, as mentioned in the previous chapter, providing workers with more control over their work is not only done to meet employees' demands but also to enhance performance (Rapoport et al, 2002; Ortega, 2009; Lyness et al, 2012). Due to this, workers have been shown to work harder and longer when working flexibly (Kelliher and Anderson, 2010; Noonan and Glass, 2012; Lott and Chung, 2016; Chung and van der Horst, 2020). Even when flexible working is specifically used for family-friendly purposes, when workers fear the stigma or negative career consequences attached to it (Williams et al, 2013; Chung, 2020b) (more in Chapter 8), they may try to overcompensate for this by working harder and longer. A summary of different studies that show how flexible working leads to workers working harder and longer, and the underlying mechanism behind this phenomenon is the focus of Chapters 5 and 6, so we will not go into too much detail here. However, what is important for this chapter is that if flexible working increases work intensity and working hours of workers, it is likely to increase their work-family conflict, since work intensity and long working hours are some of the main causes of work-family conflict (see Byron, 2005; Michel et al, 2011). We explore this relationship further in the empirical analysis section of this chapter.

Enhancing employment of mothers and carers

Another reason why flexible working can also increase work-family conflict is by enabling workers to work longer than they would have otherwise. Many women end up dropping out of the labour market or move into part-time jobs after the birth of their child(ren) (Gornick et al, 1997; Stier et al, 2001; Miani and Hoorens, 2014). For example, in the UK, looking at the working population aged between 25 to 49 in 2015, the employment rate of men and women without children was on a par at approximately 85 per cent. On the other hand, when comparing mothers and fathers of the same age group, the gap was evident, with fathers' employment rate at 92 per cent and mothers' at 71 per cent. What is more, more than half of mothers employed were in part-time employment, or to put it another way, mothers were seven times more likely to be in part-time employment than fathers, and three times more likely to be in part-time employment compared to women without children. Part-time jobs in most cases entail occupational downgrading (Connolly and Gregory, 2008, 2009; Gascoigne and Kelliher, 2018), resulting in career penalties/income loss across the life course and is considered one of the key causes of the persistent gender pay gap (Costa Dias et al, 2018b) or the so-called motherhood penalty (Budig and England, 2001). One of the main reasons why women work part-time and drop out of the labour market is due to the fact that women carry out, and people expect them to carry out, the majority of housework and childcare duties (Craig and Mullan, 2011; Bianchi et al, 2012; Scott and Clery, 2013; Dotti Sani and Treas, 2016).

Figure 4.1: Comparing women's likelihood of reducing their working hours on flexitime

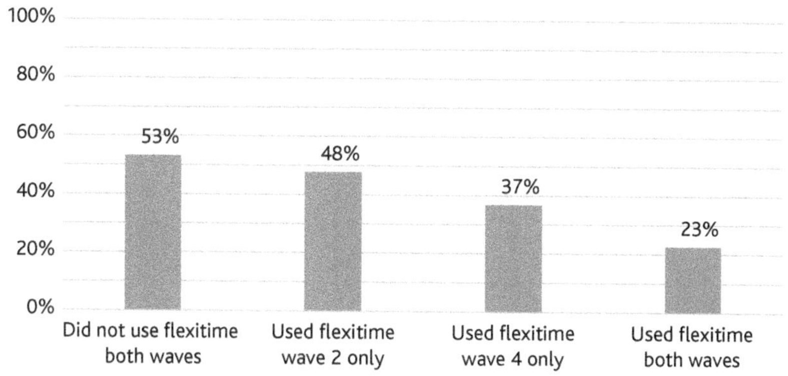

Source: Chung and van der Horst (2018: 61)

When women have more control over when and where they work, they may be better able to maintain their labour market position post-childbirth. This was the main question asked in the paper Chung and van der Horst (2018). We used the UK Household Panel, Understanding Society data set (University of Essex, 2015) waves 2 (2010/11) and 4 (2012/13) to run a quasi-experiment to see whether access to/use of flexible working arrangements would reduce the likelihood of women dropping out of the labour market or reducing their working hours. To do this, we tracked the employment patterns of women who gave birth between waves 2010 and 2013 to see how many dropped out of the labour market, and how many reduced their working hours significantly – here measured as half a day (four hours) or more a week.[3] Here we wanted to compare those with versus those without access to/or using flexitime/teleworking, to see if there were any significant differences in these labour market outcomes. The outcome was remarkable. We found that more than half of women who were not using flexitime/teleworking in waves 2 and 4 reduced their working hours by at least half a day after the birth of their child. This was not the case for mothers who were using flexitime especially in both waves – only 23 per cent reduced their working hours (see Figure 4.1). In other words, being able to use flexitime reduced the likelihood of mothers moving into part-time jobs/working shorter hours after childbirth by half. Similar results were found for women with and without access to teleworking (see Figure 4.2). What is more, we also found evidence that for first-time mothers, the access to and use of flexible working arrangements such as flexitime/teleworking, can help them stay in the labour market. Namely, they were less likely to drop out of the labour market once their child was born.

This is not an isolated finding. Fuller and Hirsh (2018) examined Canadian-linked workplace-employee data set (WES) from 1999 to 2005 to see how

Figure 4.2: Comparing women's likelihood of reducing their working hours on teleworking

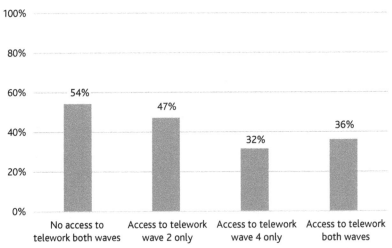

Source: Chung and van der Horst (2018: 60)

workers' control when and where they work – or in this paper termed as the use of temporal and spatial flexibility – helped moderate motherhood penalties. They found that flexitime helped mothers by reducing the barriers to better paying establishments, while teleworking or the ability to work from home allowed mothers to compete better within establishments. In sum, they argued that flexible working allows mothers to stay and compete in higher-waged establishments or higher-waged jobs. Although both studies only looked at mothers and their employment patterns, this could hold for other workers with similar care and other family/social responsibilities. For example, studies have provided some evidence that flexible working may help workers with informal care responsibilities to maintain their labour market positions (Henz, 2006).

If flexible working allows workers to work longer and in higher-waged, yet perhaps more stressful, work environments than they would have otherwise been able to, this can lead to an increase in the conflict workers feel between work and family. This type of conflict can also lead to higher levels of stress. Chandola, Booker and colleagues (2019) use the Understanding Society data to compare workers' stress levels to see how different flexible working arrangements can help reduce it. They find that women with children, especially two or more children, had higher levels of allostatic load indicating high levels of chronic stress. Reducing working hours helped reduce stress, yet flexible working arrangements did not make any significant difference. One key reason behind this outcome may be because flexitime and teleworking allows mothers to maintain work while also meeting the childcare/household demands they are expected to carry out[4] which can overstretch them and increase stress (see also Chapter 7 and Ruppanner et al, 2018b).

Work-life balance satisfaction

The increase in work–family conflict that may come with increased flexibility and control over one's work may not necessarily go hand in hand with one's work–life balance satisfaction. Studies have shown that women in countries with generous family policies that help mothers stay in employment, such as generous public childcare provision, may have higher work–family conflict. However, they also show higher levels of life satisfaction (Yamauchi, 2010; Schober and Schmitt, 2013). This can be explained through role-expansion (Grönlund and Öun, 2010). Role-expansion theory argues that having too many roles can lead to role-overload where one may feel stress due to competing demands. However, having multiple roles can also be beneficial because they offer different meaning and guidance for one's life (Nordenmark, 2004). In other words, role-expansion can help buffer against stress because 'problems and failures in one sphere can be compensated for by success and satisfaction in the other' (Grönlund and Öun, 2010: 180). For example, as a working mother, I sometimes feel like I am not doing very well on both the mother or the worker front – let alone the spouse or friend front. However, because I have both roles (and many others such as a bassist in a punk band or a football coach and player), work failures do not feel like a big deal if I have successes and joys I experience at home with my family, or possibly with friends and through hobbies, and vice versa. Similarly, flexible working can potentially enhance workers' lives and work-life balance satisfaction because it enables workers to carry out multiple roles without having to sacrifice one or the other. Again, we know that flexible working is useful in allowing mothers to maintain their employment positions (Chung and van der Horst, 2018), and enter into high-paying yet stressful jobs (Fuller and Hirsh, 2018). Even if this can lead to increased work–family conflict, it may also result in a higher level of work–life balance satisfaction. In the next section, I test these associations out using empirical data drawn from across European countries.

Empirical analysis results

Data and variables

Using the EWCS of 2015 (see Appendix for more detail). I look at five variables representing work–family conflict and work–life balance satisfaction (detailed results are in Table A4.1). Details on how the variables are derived are also available in the Appendix. First, I examined the association between flexible working and the work-to-family conflict outcomes (Figure 4.3). Despite the assumption towards flexible working and its role in relieving work-family conflict of workers, we can see that workers with certain flexible working arrangements felt higher levels of conflict, but this varied depending on gender (see also, Yucel and Chung, 2021). Both men and women who teleworked regularly were approximately 1.2 times more likely to feel that they always or most of the time felt too tired after work to do any household jobs. Similarly, men and women who teleworked regularly were about 1.4 times more likely to feel that their job prevented them from spending time with their family. Working time autonomy also increased the feeling that work conflicted with one's capacity to carry out household jobs, yet this association was only found for men (1.3 times more likely) and not for women. Flexitime, on the other hand, significantly reduced the feeling that one's job prevented them from spending time with their family, but only for women. Although not the focus of this book, I also examined how employer-led shift work and the capacity to take a couple of hours off from work influenced one's work-family conflict levels. Women who were working in employer-led shift work were less likely to feel conflicted between the time spent with family and time spent at work, but this was not the case for men. Workers with the ability to take a couple of hours off work to tend to personal issues were less likely to feel both types of work-to-family conflict to the point it can reduce the feelings of conflict to about half. This held for both men and women.

Next, I examined how flexible working related to the feeling that family demands conflict with work demands (Figure 4.4). It is first worth noting that women were much more likely to experience family-to-work conflict (FWC) compared to men (see Table A4.1). Examining how flexible working relates to this feeling, we see that teleworking increases the likelihood of not being able to concentrate on work due to family demands for both men and women. For men, teleworking also increases the likelihood of feeling that family demands prohibit them from spending the time they need on work. Women with more control over their working hours – working time autonomy – were also more likely to feel that they always or most of the time felt that they could not concentrate on work because of family issues, whereas for men, it led to the feeling that they were unable to spend as much time as they wanted to on the job. These results show that flexible working can lead to not only feeling that work spills over to one's family life, but also the feeling that family demands prohibit work roles. However, as we will show later, teleworking and working time autonomy is more likely to lead to longer working hours, and long overtime especially for men. This may entail that what we're capturing here, especially for men, is impacted by a different expectation towards work or work-life balance – namely in feeling the need to work longer/harder.

Figure 4.3: Association between flexible working and work-to-family conflict

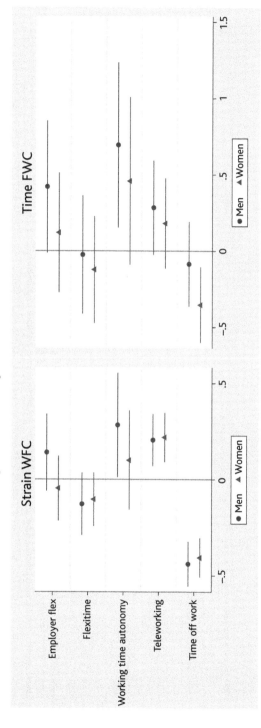

Source: EWCS, 2015, author's calculation

Note: In the X axis, higher numbers indicate higher likelihood of feeling conflict, and lower numbers indicate lower likelihood of feeling conflict
Strain-based work-family conflict – always or most of the time feel that they are too tired after work to do some of the household jobs which need to be done;
Time-based work-family conflict – always or most of the time found that your job prevented you from giving the time you want to your family.
Coefficient plot of two multi-level logistic regression analysis with a number of control variables including household, individual and company-level
characteristics. Detailed table in Table A4.1. N level 1=23818 (strain wfc) and 23717 (time wfc), N level 2=30 countries. All variables are dichotomous variables.

Figure 4.4: Association between flexible working and family-to-work conflict

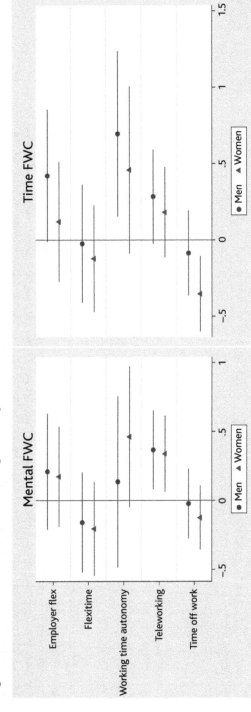

Source: EWCS, 2015, author's calculation

Note: In the X axis, higher numbers indicate higher likelihood of feeling conflict, and lower numbers indicate lower likelihood of feeling conflict. Mental FWC – always or most of the time found it difficult to concentrate on your job because of your family responsibilities. Time FWC – always or most of the time found that your family responsibilities prevented you from giving the time you should to your job.
Coefficient plot of two multi-level logistic regression analysis with a number of control variables including household, individual and company-level characteristics. Detailed table in Table A4.1. N level 1=23818 (strain wfc) and 23717 (time wfc), N level 2=30 countries. All variables are dichotomous variables.

If flexible working can increase the conflict felt between work and family, how does flexible working then relate to work–life balance satisfaction? In the previous figures we saw that flexible working is positively associated with the feelings that work demands prohibit family roles, and family demands prohibit work roles. However, as flexible working may enable workers to meet both work and care/private life demands, this can help increase satisfaction between work and family life through role-expansion. This is what seems to be the case when we examine how flexible working relates to the perceived work–life balance satisfaction, or more specifically how workers felt that their working time fit with other commitments outside of work. As expected (Figure 4.5), those with more control over their working hours – namely working time autonomy – were those who felt that their working hours fit better with other aspects of their lives, such as family or other social commitments. However, this association was found only for women. It may be that having more control over your work provided some benefits in allowing one to fit work around other responsibilities and

Figure 4.5: Association between flexible working and satisfaction with working hours fit

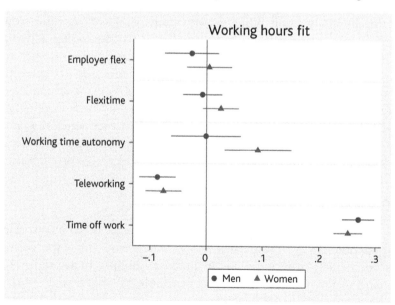

Source: EWCS, 2015, author's calculation

Note: Higher numbers indicate a better fit between work and family life. Working hours fit measured through how well your working hours fit in with your family or social commitments outside work (ranging from 'Not at all well'=1 to 'Very well'=4).
Coefficient plot of two multi-level logistic regression analysis with a number of control variables including household, individual and company-level characteristics. Detailed table in Table A4.1. N level 1=23888, N level 2=30 countries. All independent variables are dichotomous variables.

possibly the sense of control that increased their feeling of satisfaction. It may also be that those with working time autonomy were more likely to have been able to combine work with family life better without sacrificing one or the other – for women, mostly their work/working hours. It is not too surprising that we do not find this positive association for men. Especially given that we found that working time autonomy increased the feeling that work conflicted with family life/household responsibilities. What is more, working time autonomy is more likely to lead to longer working hours for men. We will explore such gendered outcomes of flexible working and the flexibility paradox in greater detail in Chapters 6 and 7.

Unsurprisingly, those who have worked at home or in other public spaces regularly, that is, teleworked, were those who felt that their working hours did not fit with other aspects of their lives. This can be explained by the results shown in Figure 4.3 in terms of work-to-family conflict, combined with the patterns observed for tele/homeworking on work encroaching/ spilling over onto family life which we will see in Chapter 6. However, this may also be due to the way in which the data was collected. We are unable to capture or differentiate between the workers who have the ability and the control/freedom to work from home as a part of their normal working hours versus workers who do a full day's work in the office and work additionally at home or in other spaces to catch up on work. In other words, if teleworking measured here largely indicates workers doing additional overtime at home – it is naturally going to be associated with workers feeling like working hours do not fit well with private life demands. Yet, given that we already control the total number of hours workers work we can expect that there is an association that indicates some element of teleworking, and not only overwork, leading to a worse balance between work and family life/other aspects of life. Again, the ability to take a couple of hours off work is important in ensuring that workers feel a better work-life balance.

Conclusion

The goal of this chapter was to examine the outcomes of flexible working. This was done firstly by summarising key studies that examine the 'business case' for flexible working. This included examining meta-studies that combine a large number of findings to examine whether flexible working can help company performance and increase productivity either directly or indirectly. The latter included examining the role of flexible working in removing a number of HR problems such as sickness/absenteeism, turnover, or improving a number of factors that are crucial in enhancing productivity – such as increasing workers' well-being, morale, loyalty, commitment, and job satisfaction. Although the evidence was mixed for the direct association between flexible working and performance outcomes, there was more evidence to support the idea that flexible working helped improve a range of different outcomes that can indirectly help improve a firm's productivity and performance.

The evidence on flexible working improving workers' work–life balance, or reducing the perceived conflict between work and family life was not as clear-cut, with many studies showing that flexible working can increase work–family conflict. This was mirrored in the analysis of the European Working Conditions Survey (EWCS), which showed that flexible working arrangements, especially those that allow for more boundary blurring and blending such as working time autonomy and teleworking/homeworking, can increase work–family conflict. This poses a paradoxical question. If flexible working is a very popular and commonly adopted policy tool by companies and countries to specifically address the work–life balance needs of workers, why does it not relieve work–family conflict? One key factor examined in this chapter was a more positive one and also one that meets a key policy goal that flexible working was intended to meet; namely, that flexible working arrangements allowed workers who were unable to carry out (long hours of) work due to care or other responsibilities to maintain their labour market positions. By enabling workers to stay in employment and maintain their working hours, flexible working can increase the feeling that you are conflicted with work and family demands due to your increased capacity to meet both. This explains why although flexible working was associated with higher levels of conflict, it was also associated with higher work–life balance satisfaction. The finding that the latter association was especially true for women evidences how flexible working may be especially beneficial for those whose labour market capacities are limited due to private life demands. Another major reason why flexible working may not necessarily reduce feelings of work–family conflict comes from the fact that flexible working tends to increase spill-over of work into family life/other aspects of one's life. This explains why the arrangements with more boundary blurring/blending and possibly more 'flexibility' – namely working time autonomy and teleworking – were more problematic. Why is it that when workers are given more freedom and control over their work, they end up expanding work rather than their private life or leisure, as many would believe? This is the paradoxical question which we will be exploring in greater detail in the next chapter.

Notes

1 In fact, Boris Johnson the PM of the UK at the time of writing equated working from home to 'time off' www.theguardian.com/world/2021/mar/27/boris-johnson-branded-irresponsible-over-back-to-the-office-call

2 Systematic reviews are a type of literature review that uses systematic methods to collect a body of literature that examines specific topics/similar questions and aims to synthesise findings. Meta-analysis is a form of systematic review that uses statistical analysis method to

combine the results of multiple studies addressing similar questions, using similar variables. In this sense, meta-analysis allows us to combine the results of a number of studies in a more simplistic way.

3   We played around with different measures to indicate 'reduction of hours', from one hour or more, to a full day or more and found similar outcomes.

4   More on how flexible working 'allows' women to meet their care/household demands without making reductions in their work demands will be examined in Chapter 7.

5

The flexibility paradox: why more freedom at work leads to more work

Introduction

In the previous chapter, we ended with a puzzle of if flexible working was commonly adopted by many companies and countries as a way to address the work-life balance demands of workers, why is it not helpful in reducing their work-family conflict? One major reason for this is because flexible working can lead to the spill-over of work-to-family and other spheres of life, resulting in workers working longer and harder. Several theories help us understand this phenomenon better, for example, the 'autonomy-control paradox' (Mazmanian et al, 2013; Putnam et al, 2014), the social exchange, enforced, and enabled intensification theory (Kelliher and Anderson, 2010), and the 'entreployee' theory (Pongratz and Voß, 2003) which we will examine in this chapter. Much of the exploration in understanding why the flexibility paradox happens has focused on the employer-employee relationship (Kelliher and Anderson, 2010), or the organisational/professional context (Pongratz and Voß, 2003; Mazmanian et al, 2013; Putnam et al, 2014). This chapter, and ultimately this book, contributes to the ongoing debate by exploring the larger societal context that drives the flexibility paradox – and later on, the gendered flexibility paradox (Chapter 7) and flexibility stigma (Chapter 8). More specifically, by drawing from Foucault's theory of homo-economicus, subjectification and the subjugation of the individual (Foucault, 2010), I understand flexibility and 'freedom' at work as another example of how power in contemporary society has moved away from the disciplinary society to a society of control (Hardt and Negri, 2001). Similar to what is being argued in the theory of the 'entrepreneurial self' (Bröckling, 2015), I argue that capitalistic ideas of productivity, performance and profit has now been internalised by workers and understood as their own drive and passion. Thus, increasingly workers are made to organise their own life in an 'entrepreneurial' manner where they need to transfer their own labour potential into concrete performance, that is, where workers manage themselves without the need for direct managerial control (Pongratz and Voß, 2003). These theories help us understand why when workers are given more freedom and control over their work, rather than increasing their leisure time, end up being more devoted to work, increasing the hours and efforts they put into work. The chapter also questions whether this phenomenon is on the rise especially with the millennial (and xennial) generation, as a generation who have been born into the world of gig-economy without a collective voice or power (Harris, 2017). Finally, the chapter explores some of the key indicators of such societal change by exploring the idea and data around work centrality and passion at work.

Theories behind the flexibility paradox

Gift exchange, enabled and imposed intensification

One of the first theories that was developed in order to understand why flexible working can lead to the intensification of work was put forward by Kelliher and Andersen (2010). In their study of UK-based organisations and workers' use of remote working and part-time/reduced-hours work, Kelliher and Andersen argue that intensification of work through flexible working can take place in three ways, namely imposed intensification, enabled intensification, and finally social exchange theory.

Imposed intensification is where employers increase the worker's workload while introducing flexible working. Here, they use the case of a worker whose hours have been reduced to part-time while their workload has not reduced accordingly, a common phenomenon also observed in other studies (Tomlinson, 2006; Durbin and Tomlinson, 2010; Young, 2018). This would result in the worker needing to work when they are not scheduled to work or working harder during the hours they are working. Kelliher and Anderson only observe this type of imposed intensification for the reduced-hours workers in their study. Despite having moved to a part-time job, many respondents were doing the same amount of work as full-time workers. Enabled intensification is where flexible working enables workers to work harder or longer. For part-time working or reduction of hours, workers may be more productive because they work fewer hours and thus may be more able to expend greater effort, are less likely to feel fatigue, and may not feel the need to take as many breaks. As we examined in Chapter 4, studies evidence how flexible working decreases performance reducing issues such as sickness and absenteeism (see also, de Menezes and Kelliher, 2011), which can increase performance outcomes as a whole (Beauregard and Henry, 2009). What is more, despite the popular belief that those working from home would have more distractions coming from the home sphere (Felstead et al, 2003; Harris, 2003), Kelliher and Andersen found that the majority of their teleworking interviewees experienced fewer distractions working from home (see also, Bloom et al, 2015). This, however, may be different for men and women due to their expected responsibilities at home as we will examine further in Chapter 7. The authors also note that the intensification of work of those working from home took the shape of not being able to 'switch off from work' as they were held on an 'electronic leash' (Kelliher and Anderson, 2010: 94).

Finally, there is the social exchange theory of work intensification through flexible working. Because flexible working policies are designed to encourage employee commitment and motivation, flexible workers show increased efforts at work due to enhanced motivation. However, based on the social exchange theory, Kelliher and Andersen also argue that the provision of flexible working can be considered a part of a transaction between workers and employers; employers when giving workers the ability to work flexibly puts some sort of obligation onto the worker to reciprocate the gift. This exchange happens between the worker and the employer, and among co-workers in that: 'Flexible workers, aware of a negative effect on co-workers, may feel the need to increase their effort in an attempt to ameliorate such (negative) reactions (towards those working remotely)' (Kelliher and Anderson, 2010: 87). The topic of negative effect of flexible working, and stigma around flexible workers is examined in greater detail in Chapter 8. In their study, most workers working remotely or reduced hours felt an increased sense of loyalty and commitment towards the company due to their ability to work flexibly, and they did not feel exploited despite having intensified their work. Rather, the feeling of gratitude was found to be the dominant discourse among the workers they interviewed, and the reason why workers ended up working harder or longer (see also Chapter 7 and Sullivan and Lewis, 2001; Hilbrecht et al, 2008). In this study, this exchange was not explicitly done or negotiated in advance, but evolved over time, where workers were generally prepared to exert additional effort in exchange for more flexibility (Kelliher and Anderson, 2010). Other studies have also found such behaviours. Bathini and Kandathil (2019), examining an Indian IT company, found what they coined, an 'orchestrated negotiation exchange', where employees agreed to the intensification of work with managers only in exchange for being able to do the work at home. Unlike the social exchange theory, the exchange is done in a much more explicit manner and in advance, where the ability to work flexibly is only given under the condition that workers intensify their work. In this sense, this is similar to the enforced intensification process identified by Kelliher and Andersen (2010).

Self-exploitation

One additional mechanism, identified by others (for example, Mazmanian et al, 2013), that can be added to this list is the phenomenon of 'self-exploitation' (Pongratz and Voß, 2003) that happens when workers gain flexibility or more autonomy over their work. This is where workers use their freedom and autonomy to increase their work intensity as a way to increase their own competitiveness to progress further in their careers (Lott and Chung, 2016; Chung and van der Horst, 2020). This then creates a spiral of increased competitiveness among workers, shifting the work culture to become more competitive (see also, Mazmanian et al, 2013). The theory of self-exploitation is unlike enabled intensification in how the intensification or increase in outputs are realised. In enabled intensification, the intensification is largely gained through the processes of making work efficient or effective, for example, through enhancing the well-being or the per-hour productivity of the worker, or removing any other barriers that prohibit this. In comparison, the concept of self-exploitation entails the workers ending up working harder and longer to maintain their position, status, their job or their competitive edge. It borrows Marx's concept of exploitation of labour, which is defined as the phenomenon where workers sell their labour power to capitalists for less than their full value they produce through their labour, due to the lack of power (or in this case, lack of capital) they have (Cohen, 1979; Zwolinski and Wertheimer, 2017). Pongratz and Voß (2003) argue that in previous times this exploitation has mostly taken place through the management's tight control over workers' production processes. For example, in previous times, managers used a Taylorism approach, where they enforce a highly rigid and detailed control over how and when workers work. However, in the new form of management, with the introduction of the high-involvement systems (Wood and De Menezes, 2010) or high-performance systems (Appelbaum et al, 2000), as we explored in Chapter 3, managers attempt 'to free up the usual boundaries of the traditional employee in the workplace in nearly all dimensions – time, space, content, qualifications, cooperation etc. – and enhance their (employee's) own responsibility through strategies of increased flexibility and "self-organization" in the workplace' (Pongratz and Voß, 2003: 3). In other words, there has been a shift in managers' belief that in order to extract profit or value out of workers, it is actually more beneficial to provide workers with autonomy and freedom over their work rather than micro-manage workers' work processes. However, this freedom over one's work is not true freedom. Rather, it was provided in combination with emerging forms of systematic control that workers need to meet, for example individualised performance-related pay, target settings or with the dawn of long-hours work culture and presenteeism (Williams et al, 2013). This enforces the process of self-exploitation, a newer and more efficient way of extracting profit from labour. The next section examines how such processes have occurred through changes in the organisational/ professional contexts.

Organisational culture and self-exploitation

Mazmanian, Orlikowski and Yates (2013) explored the question why professionals would willingly use devices, that is, Blackberries or 'crack-berries' as they were called in those days, that would restrict them to the demands of the job/employer/client by needing to be available all the time – by being 'technologically connected to work at all hours of day and night' (Mazmanian et al, 2013: 1337). Their conclusion was that the workers knew that these devices and method of working resulted in being more controlled by their employers/work. However, workers enjoyed the flexibility and capacity to do their work when and where they wanted because these devices enhanced the temporal and physical flexibility of their work. Mazmanian and colleagues coined this 'the autonomy paradox' – that when workers gain greater control over when and where they can work, it led to a 'collective spiral of escalating engagement, where they end up working everywhere/all the time' (Mazmanian et al, 2013: 1338). Building from this, Putnam et al (2014: 427) talk of 'the autonomy-control paradox' – namely, the more autonomy workers have over their work, the harder and longer they tend to work, and the more they let organisations control their lives which in turn leads to workers feeling constrained and controlled by their work. A key element of this paradox, or why it is considered a paradox, is how other elements of control are introduced when providing workers with the autonomy over when and where they carry out their work. As they argue in their paper: 'Autonomy refers to the freedom, independence and discretion an individual has in scheduling work and task activities (Hackman and Oldham, 1975), whereas control stems from direct and indirect ways that professional socialization, cultural norms and supervision constrain behaviors (Kunda, 1992)' (Putnam et al, 2014: 427). Putnam et al (2014) argue that some of this control can be more direct or visible such as fixed deadlines, work quotas or rigid task expectations. However, the more important is the 'unobtrusive control' set through professional workplace norms. Similarly, Mazmanian et al (2013) argue that normative, bureaucratic and identity control is used as a mechanism to increase workers' commitment and limit real autonomy, especially in light of the demands of the market and uncertainty about the future. Alongside the autonomy given to workers was an introduction of a new form of work culture, namely, one in which workers are expected to prioritise work above all else, work perpetually and without any other obligations outside of work, that is, the ideal worker culture (Acker, 1990; Williams, 1999) and the work devotion schema (Blair-Loy, 2009). This can be considered the typical hegemonic masculine work culture (Berdahl et al, 2018), which is based on a male-breadwinner model, where men (can) fully engage in work, and focus only on work, due to the support of the female member(s) in the household who carry out the unpaid domestic work (housework and childcare) and other reproductive work. In this work culture, to exert yourself as someone important in the organisation, you need to 'perform' long-hours work (Reid, 2011), that is, present yourself as someone who is working long hours whether or not you actually do it. The key notion here is that long-hours work (in the office) is still considered the most reliable measure to monitor one's performance and commitment towards the organisation. Due to this, to survive in the workplace especially in the context of intense competition or insecurity, workers tend to act like they work long hours. In fact, a study based on the US Time Use Survey (Yanofsky, 2012) has shown that those who estimate that they work more than 75 hours a week tend to over-estimate their working hours by around 25 hours. Similarly, those who believe they work between 65 and 74 hours a week over-estimate on average around 18 hours, and so on, until you get to those who say that they work around 40 hours a week, only over-estimating about a couple of hours. This data essentially shows that very few people actually work more than 50 hours a week. Actually, those who reported that they were working shorter hours, for example, less than 24 hours a week, tended to under-estimate their working hours. In other words, long-hours work is more of a normative performative measure workers need to adhere to, as a measure to show others their level of commitment, their status and importance within the organisation or overall society (Gershuny, 2005; Blair-Loy, 2009). Putnam and colleagues (2014) further argue that the manifestation of this work culture can also be in the shape of workers working harder and longer trying not to inconvenience other workers, or to maintain a certain level of professional reputation. This sentiment of using the newly given autonomy to perform the ideal worker image is best illustrated in a quote in Mazmanian et al's (2013) paper by a junior associate of an investment bank who talks about how mobile devices allow him to carry out a performance of engagement – of being able to perform the ideal worker role, by being connected to work during his vacation: 'I think you keep in the flow more if you're able to keep in touch. If I'm on vacation and I see what's happening with a project, I can write back and question their thoughts. I think it makes the junior people more engaged' (Mazmanian et al, 2013: 1342). Or Hillary, a law partner, talking about how her Blackberry allowed her to present herself as a responsive and competent knowledge professional – again used to signal her motivation as a commitment (see also Cristea and Leonardi, 2019):

> It allows me to just get A+++ on the response schedule, without actually having to do more work. It's just a click, click, click. Because if I can leave the office at 5 and a client on the West Coast sends me an email at 8 p.m., I can just put a two-second, two-line, 'Yep, got it, I'll look at it tomorrow.' And they're like, 'Oh my God, how great; she checks her email at 8 p.m.' And I'm like, home, eating dinner. (Mazmanian et al, 2013: 1344)

Putnam et al (2014: 428) argue that workers are not aware of the norms of unobtrusive control, that is, of flexible workers being controlled by their socialisation practices, changes in workplace norms or the ideal worker image. They argue that workers' autonomy over their work disguises the sources of where the control comes from – rather than an external control, it is understood as an internal personal process – a personal choice. This is echoed in Mazmanian et al's (2013) piece, where they argued that workers were fully aware that there had been a shift in the culture of what it means to be performing efficiently and competently as a professional with everyone feeling the need to be connected all the time. However, workers did not see this as restricting their autonomy and participants were quick to downplay the negative implications of this new culture on stress, limited downtime and blurring of boundaries by reframing it as an individual choice through using terms such as 'type A personalities' and 'workaholic'. What is more, they saw the restrictions on their own autonomy as a testament to their performance and competence as responsible professionals. Mazmanian and colleagues argue that this is due to the process in which collectively these workers fully internalise the new standard of what it means to be competent and motivated, shifting the collective norms around what it means to be an ideal worker: 'It's just freedom. Freedom to connect. You can connect whenever you want and not be prevented by where you are or what you're doing. It just feels liberating' (Janice, an associate at a law firm, in Mazmanian et al, 2013: 1344).

Entreprenurialisation of self and careers

The aforementioned studies understand the autonomy-control-paradox as a phenomenon largely relating to workers in high-powered, professional settings, rather than linking it to larger societal structures which can impact workers across the board. Interestingly, this development of understanding the autonomy-control-paradox as a social phenomenon has been done by German sociologists. This includes Hans Pongratz and Günter Voß in their theory of *Arbeitskraftunternehmer 'entreployee'* or self-entrepreneurial worker (Voß and Pongratz, 1998; Pongratz and Voß, 2003) and by Ulrich Bröckling (2015) in his theory of *Das unternehmerische Selbst*, the entrepreneurial self. Pongratz and Voß, exploring the processes of change in labour control, detail how the previous Taylorism approach of rigid and detailed surveillance of work activities encountered limitations on costs and was seen to discourage innovation and flexibility among workers. In fact, economics studies have detailed how it is specifically when you start micro-managing and controlling workers that you see workers limit their productivity and performance, rather than when you give workers more freedom and autonomy (Falk and Kosfeld, 2006). Thus, Pongratz and Voß argue that there has been a change in management approach to reduce direct labour control practices to encourage 'employee responsibility'. This is done through 'outsourcing' the previous management functions of work, that is, the realisation of labour potential into concrete performance, to workers themselves. They argue that this gave rise to the '*entreployee*', a worker who needs to develop their own labour power in an entrepreneurial manner in a way an entrepreneur will do with any product of a business. An entreployee is someone who is 'continuously redefining their own capacities and potentials within the company (and in the larger labour market), by organizing the work process in a self-determining, "entrepreneurial" manner' (Pongratz and Voß, 2003: 6). The key characteristics of an entreployee are as follows: 1) the control of work rests in the hands of the worker ('*self-control*'), with the new organisation of targets and goals to be met such as deadlines and output targets; 2) they regard their own labour power as a commodity that needs active development and exploiting as the only 'capital' available for workers to secure a living, and they accept this as an integral part of their life ('*self-rationalisation*'); 3) this results in a higher level of '*self-commercialisation*' where workers constantly generate capacities and performance. Workers need to able to continuously promote or 'market' their capacities within the company as well as outside the company to the broader labour market, and become the salesmen of their own work capacity (Pongratz and Voß, 2003). In this sense, Pongratz and Voß (2003) see a new rise of the commercialisation of life, and the need to systematically reorganise all individual resources into a kind of business. Drawing from Sennett's (1998) study of flexibilisation of work and self, and Hochschild's (2001) work on blurring boundaries of work and home, they argue how increasingly we see a growth in the commercialisation of self, where the production and commercialisation, that is, marketing, of one's individual work capacities and expertise becomes a part of one's daily life. They further argue that the advent of the entreployee was made possible due to the societal changes that occurred, namely globalisation, neo-liberalism and the individualisation of life styles and life courses (Beck, 1992). Their work ends with the engagement of *subjectification of work* (Hardt and Negri, 2001; Foucault, 2010) to understand 'the new ambivalence and contradictions experienced increasingly by those involved in market-based labor structures' (Pongratz and Voß, 2003: 18). They argue that workers are not helpless victims of this process of increased commercialisation of self, but rather a co-participant. This closely echoes the observations made by Mazmanian et al (2013) that workers, despite being subjected to the increased level of control with more restrictions of their lives through the introduction of the new working regime, did not consider the changes as restrictions but rather new ways or opportunities in which they can perform their competencies and standing as a professional.

Subjectification of self

The subjectification of self and the links to larger societal structure is developed by Bröckling in his book *The Entrepreneurial Self* (Bröckling,

2015). Bröckling picks up where Pongratz and Voß left off by applying the argument of the entreployee to go beyond the workplace, that the notion of the entrepreneurship is now applied to everyday life not only of oneself but of the family. The book aims to understand the knowledge and practices that have caused individuals to see and govern themselves as individuals, which goes beyond just the pure notion of individualisation. Here, individuality is understood as a paradoxical coercion, a form of duty to become an individual, done within the socio-political conditional framework which force people to act autonomous yet in doing so, they also have only themselves to blame for their failings, that is, the 'paradox of freedom' (Bröckling, 2015: 3–6). Bröckling's work draws heavily from Foucault's understanding of subjectification and governmentality.

To understand subjectification of self, we need to start off with Foucault's notion of *homo-economicus* and the application of the economic market exchange values to all aspects of one's life domains and to the social fields (Foucault, 2010). Foucault defines homo–economicus as 'an entrepreneur, an entrepreneur of himself … being himself his own capital, being for himself his own producer, being for himself the source of [his] earning' (Foucault, 2010: 226). This mirrors the entreployee concept of Pongratz and Voß, explored earlier, where the autonomous worker who only has his labour power, or as Foucault borrows from Becker's work (1964) '*human capital*', to exchange within the market becomes an entrepreneur who engages in the commercialisation of this product (self-commercialisation). However, Foucault goes further to say, it is about generalising the 'enterprise' form within the social body or social fabric, where an individual needs to make the individual life itself, as well as his relationship with his family, household, property and society into permanent and multiple enterprises (Foucault, 2010: 241). Here, even a household unit can be considered a firm where the investment in human capital and future profit generation becomes one of its main goals. This will be explored further in Chapter 7 when we discuss the gendered nature of self-exploitation. In short, for women, self-exploitation takes the form of investing more time and energy in childcare when gaining autonomy over their work, done to ensure that the future profit generation of the household is maintained. In this process of subjectification, the enterprise becomes the universally generalised social model of functions which is then applied to all aspects of life including those that are of non-economic domains. Thus social relationships between individuals also take the form of business exchanges between companies, and possibly more importantly the relationship between the individual and the state also takes the framework of market exchange.[1]

Coming back to Bröckling's work, his goal was to investigate how this subjectification manifests in today's society. He aims to uncover how strategies and managerial concepts (such as creativity, empowerment, quality management and concepts of project) operate in society to force people into this new form of 'self'. The key message is that people are not asked if not forced into the new 'freedom' to optimise themselves into a society where all interactions mirror that of market transactions and economic exchange. It is no longer an issue of management of one's career, but rather of life, asking for behaviour modifications for continuous self-optimisation to be able to compete in all aspects of life. Drawing from Rose's (1999) work, he argues that the entrepreneurial society asks that 'people ought not only to maximise their self-control, self-esteem, self-awareness and health, but also their work performance and their wealth. They will be better equipped to do this in proportion as they more actively assume responsibility for their own lives' (Bröckling, 2015: 28). In this way, even the examination of self, and self-help becomes a part of optimising the 'product' of self for future market gains. Another key element here is the 'outsourcing' of risks and failures not only in the labour market but also in life to the individuals themselves, many of which were once the remits of the welfare state (see also Abrahamson, 2004; Bauman, 2013). In many countries, the safety net and social security once provided by the welfare state no longer become necessary in a society of entrepreneurial individuals when individuals themselves are the ones responsible for the successes and failures of their livelihood. This clears the way for neo-liberal governments, and the destruction of the welfare state and social security systems to take place. As Bröckling notes, 'If the thrust of neo-liberal government is towards generalizing competition, modelling society as a whole on the market, then it will ineluctably come to mould subjectivity on the figure of the entrepreneur' (Bröckling, 2015: 60).

In sum, the autonomy over work given to workers, in terms of the locational and temporal flexibility, can only be fully understood when we consider the context in which it was provided. As elaborated in this section, it was provided with additional organisational level control (Mazmanian et al, 2013), leading to the development of a new work culture or the norm of working all the time and everywhere (Putnam et al, 2014). In this new norm, managers and companies were able to offload the risks and responsibilities of performance (or the responsibility of realising labour power potential into performance outputs) onto the workers themselves (Pongratz and Voß, 2003). This again was framed within a broader context of a neo-liberal society where individuals were made responsible for their own (and their families') risks and failures in life (Bröckling, 2015). The retrenchment of the welfare state, and the individualisation of social risks exacerbated this trend. More importantly, individuals themselves consider this as the norm, where it is not an enforced social structure but a natural matter of fact to maintain themselves and their families as one would do a business or company, that is, the internalisation of capitalist ideals (Foucault, 2010). Essentially, put in simpler terms, our whole society has now geared individuals from an early age to be the master of their own destiny to ensure that they succeed in life. This is reinforced by removing the previous protective mechanisms in place (such as job guarantees or income protection) as well as moving away from the collective identity of society to that of a society of individuals, highlighting the competitive nature of the relationships between the individuals (and their families).

Understanding this broader context of society, it is no wonder why more freedom at work leads to more work and self-exploitation, removing the need for the harsher and more explicit disciplinary measures to make people adhere to capitalist regimes (Hardt and Negri, 2001). However, as a keen reader may have noticed, the question arises whether these contexts in which flexible working and autonomy over one's work have been introduced are inevitable, if they are found across all organisations and countries, or if there are variations. We know that the neo-liberal trends were not necessarily equally strong across all countries. This brings us to the importance of contexts which we will go into greater detail in Chapter 9. The short answer is yes, there are variations in which these contextual factors play out, with varying outcomes for flexible working. These variations are crucial for us to explore as it provides us with potential solutions to the problems raised, with potential actors across different levels (family, organisation, country) who can help alleviate the flexibility paradox phenomenon. But for now, I will explore two examples of the manifestation of the subjectification of workers – in other words, some empirical evidence that shows the prevalence of cultural norms and practices that enable the subjectification of the workforce in our societies.

Manifestations of the paradox: passion at work as the basis for self-exploitation

In this section, I want to provide examples of manifestations of the subjectification or internalised capitalism of workers, the new cultural norms that developed in this new world of the entrepreneurial self that are tangible and visible in everyday life. There are several we can explore, but here I focus on the always-on culture and the need to be constantly busy and productive and the importance of passion at work in the new work-centred society. Another manifestation of this can be considered the prevalence of flexibility stigma where we as a society stigmatise workers who signal that they want a better work-life balance. These types of stigmatisation of flexible workers have also been identified in previous studies (Kelliher and Andersen, 2010; Mazmanian et al, 2013). We examine this in Chapter 8.

Passion

One of the manifestations of this rise of the 'entrepreneurial self' or 'entreployee' is the rise in notion of having to fulfil your passion through your work. As we have seen in Chapter 1, our society has become more work-centred over the past decade, with work taking a more important role in people's lives compared to previously. What is more, the pursuit of passion through one's work has become deeply romanticised in contemporary discourse (Kim et al, 2020). In previous times, it was much more acceptable for someone to say you work to earn a living for yourself and your family, with clearer boundaries between the two (see also Schor, 2008). For example, in the 1989 International Social Survey Programme (ISSP) data, 36 per cent of those in Germany and 30 per cent of those in the UK agreed or strongly agreed that a job is a way of earning money but no more than that. By 2015 this had shrunk to 31 per cent and 27 per cent respectively. Possibly a more significant change can be seen when we learn what people think a job means for them. We see an increase in the number of people who agree that they would enjoy work even if they didn't need the money in the past decades. For example, again in the ISSP data, in the UK, only 49 per cent agreed that they would enjoy work even if they didn't need the money in 1997, while by 2015 this number had risen to 61 per cent. Similarly, in 1989, only 52 per cent of those in Germany agreed that they would still enjoy work even if they didn't need the money, while by 2015 this number had risen to 70 per cent.

Work now has to be interesting and has to allow individuals to follow their passion. According to the ISSP 2015, when asked how important it is in life to have an interesting job, we can see that almost half of those surveyed across the world said that it is 'very important', with up to 87 per cent of those in Venezuela saying this was the case, 51 per cent in the US, 53 per cent in Denmark and 44 per cent in the UK (see also Figure 5.1). When we consider those who consider an interesting job important as well as very important, the numbers are around the 90 per cent mark for most countries. It was only in some of the East Asian countries where this sentiment was not as prevalent, with only 17 per cent of those surveyed in China, and 21 per cent of those in Japan saying it was very important. However, even in these countries when we consider those who find it important as well as very important the numbers rise to more than a third of the surveyed population.

This need to have an interesting job and the need to pursue your passion through your job isn't necessarily something unique to those in professional careers. As shown in Figure 5.1, although those in higher-skilled occupational groups such as managers, professionals and associate professionals are more likely to say having an interesting job is very important (50 per cent or more), we see that even those in the somewhat medium/lower-paid jobs – such as elementary occupation (36 per cent) – also believe that having an interesting job is important in life. Passion in one's job is something that is now asked of almost everyone regardless of their role or position.

Figure 5.1: The proportion of those surveyed responding that it is 'very important' to have an interesting job across occupations (average across countries)

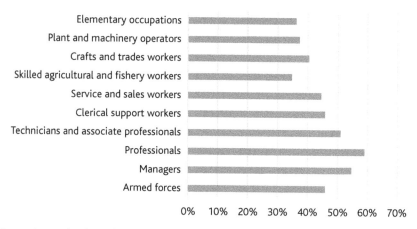

Source: International Social Survey Programme (ISSP), 2015

Busyness as a badge of honour

The current work culture does not stop at the need to have passion in your work. With passion comes the idea that you should be devoting your time to it with a constant need to be productive (Bröckling, 2015). This is why we are also experiencing a norm where busyness at work, and in life, becomes a badge of honour (Gershuny, 2005; Blair-Loy, 2009; Schulte, 2015). Gershuny (2005) argues that work, not leisure, is now the signifier of dominant social status, and the assertion of busyness reflects one's position in or an aspiration to high social status. In other words, busyness reflects one's importance and value not only in organisations (Reid, 2011) but also in society, where it shows that you are of great worth that is highly demanded and thus do not have time for leisure pursuits. It shows others that you are also passionate about the work you do, and that you are willing to spend the limited resource all of us have – time – on work. Studies have shown that people like to present themselves as busy as a source of conspicuous consumption – to show others of one's higher-status position, that is, to indicate your importance, and your important contribution to society. However, it goes beyond this and can provide individuals with confirmation of self, and of self-worth (Bellezza et al, 2017). In other words, we live in a society where you need to be busy at work to feel you are worthwhile not only through the eyes of others, but even through your own eyes.

Having passion in your work can be great and believing your work is meaningful is important for one's well-being and mental health (Ryan and Deci, 2000; Kim et al, 2020). However, too much passion, especially in a society where work is the centre of life, can be highly problematic.

Passion paradox

The problem with passion at work is that when you are passionate about work, it is more likely that you yourself and others around you feel it is okay for you to be exploited. A clear evidence of this comes from the study by Kim and colleagues (2020a). They found that the more you are passionate about your job, the more people considered it legitimate to exploit your labour. Here exploitation of one's labour included asking the worker to leave their family to work on a weekend, work unpaid overtime hours, and handle tasks that were not in the job description. The way in which this exploitative behaviour was rationalised was because participants believed that the passion or being able to do what you love in itself is the reward that does not need additional remuneration. This is the same type of thinking that comes to people's mind when discussing whether musicians or artists should be paid to do their job. Many people may think that since you want to do it, and it is something you love, you should not expect financial renumeration. The problem is that one, these people also need to earn a living, and two, we are increasingly seeing this rise in passion or love for one's job as a way to justify exploitation and low wages in jobs across the sector. What is more, Kim and colleagues found this relationship held in a reverse direction, in that those who are or whom people felt were exploited, were more likely to be considered to be passionate about their work, in a way justifying the extent to which they are asked to do more. Similarly, studies have shown that those who show passion in their work are more likely to feel conflict between work and other aspects of their life, most likely due to this increased level of overwork, and thus are more likely to experience symptoms of burnout (for example Vallerand et al, 2010). This type of pattern is also found in purposeful work, or work that has more societal value. For example, doctors, nurses, care workers, as well as those who work in NGOs who may be more passionate about their work due to the (perceived) societal value it holds, are more likely to overwork or be overworked (both in terms of time but also of emotional labour). In many cases this is done with little or insufficient pay, and results in high levels of burnout (Shanafelt et al, 2012; Timm, 2016; Moss, 2019).

Millennial burnout

This type of passion–exploitation association may be even more prevalent in the younger generation. In recent years, an article written by Anne Helen Petersen talking about the millennial generation as the 'burnout generation' (Petersen, 2019) has caused a sensation across the world. Despite some rather dominant perceptions of young people or 'millennials'[2] as being lazy, entitled and spoiled, she argues that they are the ones who have internalised the idea of busyness as a status symbol, that one should be working all the time, and that they need to performance manage every aspect of their life.

In fact, the idea of having to have passion at work, and needing to succeed is quite prevalent in the mindset of the younger generation. The 2018 survey carried out by the Pew Research Center of American teenagers between the ages of 13 and 17 found that 93 per cent of boys and 97 per cent of girls responded that having a job or career they enjoy would be extremely or very important to them as an adult (Horowitz and Graf, 2019). Having a job one enjoys was so popular that about three times as many teenagers found it very/extremely important compared to those who believed having a family was very important (39 per cent). At the same time, the need to attain academic achievements can lead to high levels of anxiety and stress among teenagers. Ninety-six per cent of teenagers saw anxiety and depression as a major issue among people their age in their community, and 88 per cent of those surveyed said they personally felt pressured to get good grades. In comparison, the more common aspects of drugs, sex and rock and roll ranked very low in the list – with only 15 per cent feeling pressured to do drugs.

Harris (2017), in his book *Kids These Days*, maintains how this is due to the younger generation having been socialised from birth to believe that everything they do is a part of an 'investment' and everything they do should contribute to their success as an adult competing in the labour market. In other words, this is a generation where the socialisation of the homo-economicus or internalisation of capitalism starts from birth. He argues that risk management used to be a business practice, but is now dominant in child-rearing. Similarly, the idea of optimising – a key concept identified in Bröckling's work – is now standard in parenting starting from extra curriculum activities to play dates. This is linked to the themes of the gendered nature of the subjectification process which we will explore in Chapter 7, where I argue that the subjectification of individuals to this newly entrepreneurial state results in parents, especially women, (having to) invest significantly in enrichment activities for children – that is, intensive parenting. This idea of performance management needing to be applied to every aspect of one's life and the increasing need for optimisation has to be understood within the labour market context most young people are in. Workers today, especially younger workers are much more exposed to employment and income insecurity compared to previous generations (Chung et al, 2012) (see Chapter 1). This has been exacerbated further due to the recent COVID-19 pandemic (Dias et al, 2020). However, Harris argues that it is unlikely for the millennial generation to engage in collective action given that they 'have been structurally, legally, emotionally, culturally, and intellectually dissuaded from organizing in their own collective interest as workers' (Harris, 2017).[3] This again encapsulates the ideas of the individualised self as separate competing entities, as denoted in the entreployee/entrepreneurial self (Bröckling, 2015), leaving us to believe that possibly the phenomenon may more evident among the younger generations. This means that the tendencies for the flexibility paradox may increase in the future.

Conclusion

This chapter examined the theories that can help us understand the flexibility paradox. Combining existing theories (Kelliher and Anderson, 2010; Mazmanian et al, 2013; Putnam et al, 2014), we were able to understand why the flexibility paradox happens within an interpersonal/employment relations framework or within the organisational or professional context. To better understand the larger societal contexts/structures that drive the flexibility paradox and the gendered paradox, I drew from German sociological theories on the entrepreneurial self and entreployee (Pongratz and Voß, 2003; Bröckling, 2015), and Foucault's (2010) notion of homo-economicus and the subjectification of the self in capitalist societies. These theories combined enables us to understand how capitalistic notions of value and competition are now internalised by the individual. Individuals and their families act as individual enterprises who are responsible for investing in themselves and their families to ensure they are profitable now and into the future, and individualises any potential risks they encounter as their own failures. Within this context, it is not surprising to see that when given more freedom and control over work, or when boundaries between work and private lives are blurred as is the case with flexible working, workers expand work and let work encroach on their private lives. The next chapter provides empirical evidence of the flexibility paradox that is drawn from a wide number of countries and data sets to better provide support for such patterns occurring.

Notes

[1] Foucault's theory then leads on to issues around governmentality and the applications of this into the wider systems within society such as the welfare state, the legal and the justice systems. This is the entire life work of some scholars in politics and sociology which I do not even attempt to go into.

[2] I put this term in quotation marks because despite, technically, some millennials being in their 40s with children, a mortgage, and so on, the media and certain groups of people use the term to indicate 'young people'.

[3] Having said that, there has been some exciting work by 'younger' generations around unionising gig economy workers such as the IWGB https://iwgb.org.uk/. So I do not fully agree with Harris on this point.

6

The empirical evidence of the flexibility paradox

Introduction

In the previous chapter, I examined a wide range of theoretical underpinnings of the flexibility paradox – namely when workers have more control over when and where they work, they may end up working harder and longer, and with work encroaching on other spheres of life. This chapter will provide a summary of evidence of this flexibility paradox from across the world. This includes my own original research with colleagues exploring the association between flexible working and overtime using longitudinal data from the UK and Germany. I also present findings looking at the association between flexible working and work spill-over examined using data across 30 European countries. Others' work showing evidence of the flexibility paradox from across Europe, the US, India, China and other countries using both qualitative and quantitative methods are also presented. The results show that flexible working leads to work encroaching on other spheres of life not only in terms of the time spent actually working, but also thinking about work. However, as the latter part of this chapter shows, there are different variations across the population. Here I show that the flexibility paradox may depend on the workers' gender, parental and occupational status. What is more, the way in which flexible working is introduced may also matter. The final points open up for Chapter 7 where I elaborate further how the self-exploitation patterns of the flexibility paradox may look very different for men and women. It further opens up questions for Chapter 9 which explores the importance of contexts.

Evidence of flexible working and longer working hours
Association between flexible working and long hours of work

There was evidence of flexible working being associated with longer working hours, where those who work flexibly, compared to those who do not, work longer hours or longer overtime hours. Many cross-European and national studies look at the association between working hours and access to/use of flexitime, and other types of arrangements that gave workers more control over when they work. Results show a U-shaped curve, where short working hours (for example less than 35 hours) and long working hours (50/60+ hours) were both associated with better access to flexitime – with long hours showing stronger associations (Drago et al, 2005; Golden, 2009; Lyness et al, 2012; Chung, 2019b).

Similarly, various studies have provided evidence that teleworking/working from home is linked to longer working hours (for example Walrave and De Bie, 2005; Ojala, 2011; Tipping et al, 2012; Beauregard et al, 2013), although some studies refute this (Wheatley, 2012). For example, Noonan and Glass (2012) examined data from the US National Longitudinal Survey of Youth, along with the US Census Current Population Survey to show that those who telework are more likely to report longer overtime hours compared to those who do not. A report by the European Foundation and the ILO (Eurofound and the International Labour Office, 2017) examined the working hours of telework/ICT-mobile (T/ICTM) workers using the EWCS of 2015. Here T/ICTM workers are defined as those who work from home or locations other than their employers' premises frequently (at least several times a month or more), and use ICT (new information and communication technologies) always or almost all the time. They found that T/ICTM workers, especially home-based teleworkers, and high-mobile T/ICTM workers were much more likely to work longer hours compared to those who always work at their employers' premises or those who only occasionally work remotely.

As these studies only examine *the association* between working hours and flexible working, it is unclear whether flexible working is the *cause* of the longer working hours and overtime work. It could also be the case that those who were already working very long hours, possibly those who were already devoted to their work, were using flexible working to better adapt to their workload to private demands (see also, Karasek, 1979; Schieman and Young, 2010). Also, those who were working long hours may have been the ones given the opportunity to work flexibly due to their managers trusting them with such arrangements. In other words, looking at cross-sectional data that is gathered at one point in time does not provide us sufficient evidence that flexible working, and not other factors, *leads to* longer working. Thus to explore this further, we need to draw evidence from longitudinal studies that track individuals over time.

Flexible working leading to long hours of work

Yvonne Lott and I (Lott and Chung, 2016) examined the German Socio-Economic Panel (SOEP) to see how workers end up working longer overtime hours when they start to work flexibly – namely, using flexitime and working time autonomy. The SOEP is a representative panel study of German households with over 12,000 households and 32,000 persons interviewed every year, and thus provides us with data on year-on-year changes of individuals in their working status, household status as well as flexible working status (Haisken-DeNew and Frick, 2005). We only examined those who were employed, excluding self-employed or under

65, and only including those with contracted working hours. We used the question: 'Nowadays, there are a number of different types of working hours available. Which of the following possibilities is most applicable to your work?'. Responses could include: 1) 'fixed daily working hours' (fixed schedules); 2) 'Working hours fixed by employer, which may vary from day to day' (employer-oriented flexibility); 3) 'flexitime within a working hours account and a certain degree of self-determination of daily working hours within this account' (flexitime); and 4) 'no formally fixed working hours, decide my own working hours' (working time autonomy). The reference category is fixed schedules. The goal of the study was to follow individuals across time (here, between 2003 and 2011) to see how *changes* in workers' working time arrangements, that is, if you move from a fixed schedule to a flexible one, leads to longer overtime hours. Overtime hours is measured as the difference between the actual hours worked by workers compared to their contractual hours. Here, the key benefit of longitudinal studies is that you can examine changes in the pattern of behaviours of an individual across time, taking into account anything else that may influence these changes, such as work devotion tendencies across individuals, changes in jobs/positions/authority, other working conditions such as job insecurity and household changes (number of children, breadwinner status). This way, we can be more assured that it is the changes in flexible working patterns that leads to longer working hours and overtime, and not other factors, although direct causality is always very difficult to guarantee.

The results of our analyses showed that first, comparing *across* groups of workers, those working flexibly (flexitime and working time autonomy) worked longer overtime hours compared to those with fixed schedules. For example, those who had working time autonomy worked almost four hours more overtime compared to individuals with fixed schedules. Next, examining changes occurring *within* an individual across time, we found that when workers switched from fixed schedules to flexitime they clocked in more than half an hour more overtime per week. This change was larger for those who moved from fixed schedules to working time autonomy, of almost one and a half hours more overtime (see Figure 6.1). In other words, through following the behavioural changes within an individual using longitudinal data, we found more conclusive evidence that flexible working *leads to* longer overtime working. Although half an hour, and one and a half hour per week doesn't seem like a lot, we need to understand this is in addition to the overtime hours people were doing already. What is more, as these numbers indicate the mean, we expect some workers to have increased their overtime hours much more.

Similar results have been found in a study I conducted with Mariska van der Horst using data in the UK (Figure 6.2) using the UK Household Longitudinal Study (UKHLS) (Chung and van der Horst, 2020). The UKHLS

Figure 6.1: Predicted overtime (in hours) of workers with fixed schedules, employer flexibility, flexitime and working time autonomy for men and women

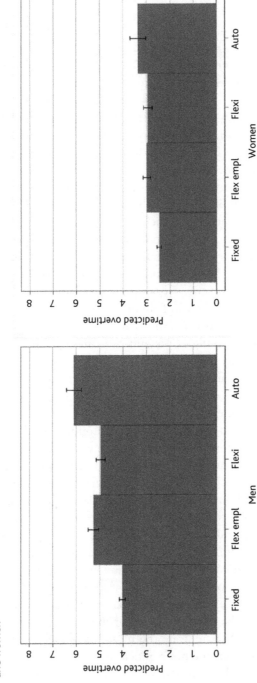

Source: Lott and Chung, 2016

Note: The lines on top of the boxes indicate 95% confidence intervals. Predicted overtime (in hours) based on predictive margins; within-estimates separately for men and women (full estimation results in Table 2); SOEP 2003, 2005, 2007, 2009 and 2011.

Figure 6.2: Increase in unpaid overtime hours due to increased schedule control for men and women

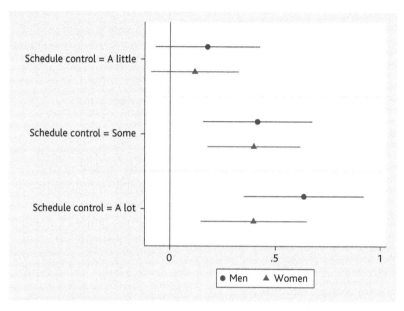

Source: UK Household Longitudinal Study (UKHLS), Chung and van der Horst (2020)

Note: reference group: no control.

is similar to the German data set in that it follows individuals across time to see changes in their working patterns, alongside other individual, work, and household characteristics that may influence these patterns. The design of the analysis was similar to that used for the German data study, where we followed the changes occurring within an individual's behaviour over time. We looked at how changes in one's flexible working patterns result in changes in unpaid overtime hours. Here, we focused specifically on unpaid overtime to better capture the flexibility paradox – not overtime done to gain additional money for financial reasons, but the hours workers put in additionally to gain a competitive edge or to reciprocate back to their employers. Here schedule control was measured by asking workers how much control they had over the starting and ending times of work, as a part of a series of questions asking about workers' control over other aspects of their work – for example task, order and so on. We found that when workers gained access to 'some' or 'a lot' of schedule control, this led to longer unpaid overtime hours compared to when workers had 'no' control. The increase in the unpaid overtime hours was about half an hour a week on average, although there were differences across groups as we will explore in the next section.

Glass and Noonan (2016) looked at salaried workers (not hourly paid workers) in the National Longitudinal Study of Youth data set from 1989 to 2008 and examined how teleworking was linked to increased overtime hours of workers. They found that when there was an increase in teleworking hours, it was mostly on top of the hours worked in the office, rather than replacing the hours done in the office. In other words, teleworking was more of a way to increase the overtime hours of workers, again leading to an encroachment on family life.

Flexible working, mental spill-over and additional work effort

Flexible working not only leads to work encroaching on one's private life through hours spent doing paid work, but it also leads to work encroaching on one's mental space. I examined the relationship between flexible working and two types of work-to-home spill-over using the 2015 EWCS (Figure 6.3). Here, work-to-home spill-over is measured as workers' likelihood of thinking about work when not at work, and their likelihood of regularly working during their free time to catch up on work.

As we can see, those with flexitime and working time autonomy are more likely to think about work when not at work, or regularly work during their free time compared to those with fixed schedules. For example, those with working time autonomy were about 1.7 times more likely to think about work when not at work, and almost twice as likely to work during their free time compared to those with fixed schedules, even taking into account a number of job-related factors such as occupational level, managerial roles, working hours, the type of work done and so on. Those using flexitime were about 1.3 times more likely to think about work when not at work, and 1.5 times more likely to work during their free time to catch up on work compared to those with fixed schedules. Similarly, those who telework – or work at home or in other public spaces regularly –were almost twice (1.9 times) as likely to think about work when not at work and almost 3.5 times more likely to work during their free time compared to those who do not telework. However, it should be noted that this may be due to the way teleworking was measured – which doesn't distinguish between work done outside of the office as part of regular working hours or work done to catch up on work due to workload (as found in the study by Glass and Noonan (2016)). In other words, those who need to work outside their normal working hours (during their free time) may be doing those hours in public spaces or at home.

The results mirror what was found by Felstead and Henseke (2017) using the Skills and Employment Survey. They examine how teleworking is associated with work intensity and spill-over of work to private lives. Work intensity in the paper includes the degree to which workers feel that they work hard, work longer than formally required, and how much discretionary effort workers feel like they put in. Work-to-home spill-over include workers'

Figure 6.3: Association between flexible working and work-to-home spill-over by gender

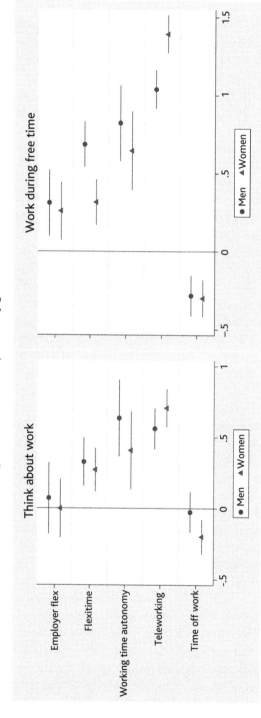

Source: EWCS, 2015, author's calculation

Note: Reference category: fixed schedules, X axis – higher numbers indicate a higher likelihood of spill-over of work-to-family life, lower numbers indicate lower likelihood of spill-over occurring.

Think about work – always or most of the time think about work when not at work, working during free time – workers who work during free time to meet work demands at least several times a month.

Coefficient plot of two multi-level logistic regression analysis with a number of control variables including household, individual and company-level characteristics. Detailed table in Appendix 6.1. All variables are dichotomous variables.

inability to switch off at the end of the working day, and the difficulty of unwinding and relaxing after work. Their results show evidence that working from home was associated with workers working harder, longer, putting more discretionary efforts. Working from home was also linked to workers' reduced capacity to detach themselves from work and relax. Lott (2020) similarly examined how flexible schedules can lead to increased levels of cognitive work-to-home spill-over, using German longitudinal panel data (GSEOP) of 2011 and 2012. Cognitive work-to-home spill-over is measured by the degree to which respondents agree to the following questions. 'I am often already thinking about work-related problems when I wake up', 'Work seldom lets go of me; it stays in my head all evening', 'If I put off something at work that needs to be done that day, I can't sleep at night'; and disagrees to 'When I come home, it is very easy to switch off from thinking about work'. She found that although flexitime was not associated with cognitive work-to-home spill-over, working time autonomy was positively associated with it. This brings into question whether there are variations across different types of flexible working arrangements – which we will explore in the next section. She also found that overtime hours, feeling of time pressure due to high work volumes, and interruptions at work fully mediate the relationship between flexible working and cognitive work-to-home spill-over. In other words, having more autonomy over one's work leads to workers not being able to switch off from work when at home because autonomy and control over work increases working hours or pressures of work. This pressure and overwork then leads to cognitive or mental work-to-home spill-over, and workers not being able to switch off from work, rather than something innately wrong with the flexibility and permeability of boundaries themselves. In other words, the main culprit of the problem of work-to-home spill-overs may be the expansion of work, or, as Felstead and Henseke note, needing to or feeling a need to work harder and work longer than required, due to flexible working.

Schieman and Glavin (2008) using the 2002 National Study of the Changing Workforce found that schedule control and job autonomy resulted in higher levels of work-life blurring. More specifically, in their study work-family blurring was measured as how often workers were contacted outside of normal hours, and how often they brought (paid and unpaid) work home. Again they evidence that those with more control over their work schedules and jobs were more likely to experience work-life blurring, and thus, unsurprisingly, increased feelings of work-family conflict. However, the associations were stronger for men. Although for women, control over one's work was insignificant or less relevant in work-family role-blurring and for work-family conflict, for men, control and autonomy over work was much more likely to lead to work blurring into other aspect of one's life and increased feelings of conflict between the two. This raises the question whether the tendencies for overwork and increased work pressure resulting from the flexibility and autonomy over one's work will be the same for all workers or whether there are variations across individuals.

Differences across groups of individuals

Gender and parental status

Various studies suggest that flexible working may entail and is expected to entail different things for different groups of workers (Brescoll et al, 2013; Clawson and Gerstel, 2014). Clark (2000) argues that the outcomes of flexibility and permeability between the borders of work and home domains will depend on the strength of the border, the domain the individual identifies with most, and the priority each domain takes in one's life. In other words, the flexibility of the border between the work and home domains is most likely to lead to the expansion of work and the encroachment on the private lives of workers who (need to) identify closely to the work domain and for whom the work domain takes priority. Sometimes this is not a voluntary choice individuals can make due to the breadwinning role they have. On the other hand, those workers who (are pressured or expected to) prioritise and identify with home domains may be restricted in their ability to expand their paid work. The strength of the work and home domains will differ across workers of different gender, parental status and occupational level largely due to societal norms of what people should and can prioritise.

For many women, family remains a strong domain because women still do, and are expected to do, the majority of housework and care work, including childcare, caring for elderly family members and so on (Bianchi et al, 2012; Park et al, 2013). For this reason, women are more likely than men to use flexible working to facilitate family demands (Singley and Hynes, 2005; see also, Kim, 2020; Kurowska, 2020), especially when family demands/domains are not flexible – for example, school opening times, and when family demands are unpredictable – for example, a child becoming ill. On the other hand, men are more likely to and are expected to prioritise and identify with their work domains as they are considered the breadwinner of the family in many societies. Men in heterosexual relationships may be better able to prioritise work above family or other responsibilities because of the support they receive from their female partners in regards to care and domestic work (Moen and Yu, 2000; Williams et al, 2013). Thus, the permeability and flexibility of the boundaries between work and private life is more likely to result in the expansion of work domains for men compared to women (Sullivan and Lewis, 2001; Hilbrecht et al, 2008; Clawson and Gerstel, 2014; Lott, 2020).

We expect this difference in gender to be especially noticeable during parenthood, as children will expand the demand for parental time in not only childcare but also housework (Craig and Mullan, 2011; Bianchi et al, 2012). This is when most heterosexual couples end up 'specialising' their roles within the household in many countries (Schober, 2013), with mothers moving into part-time work or out of the labour market altogether while fathers end up increasing their working hours (Eurostat, 2016; Nicolaisen et al, 2019). This is also when mothers face a motherhood penalty in their pay and career progression (Budig and England, 2001), partly due to implicit biases against them that they will prioritise family demands above work demands (Williams et al, 2013; Lott and Klenner, 2018). On the other hand, fathers end up gaining a fatherhood bonus (Hodges and Budig, 2010), again due to the implicit assumption that they are responsible for the breadwinning. Having said this, they may face further penalties if they do not live up to this expectation (Rudman and Mescher, 2013) as we will explore in Chapter 8. In sum, if flexible working leads to the expansion of paid working hours/expansion of work, we expect this especially to be the case among men/fathers compared to women/mothers.

This is confirmed in our analysis of the German SOEP data (Lott and Chung, 2016), exploring the association between flexible schedules with overtime hours presented in Figure 6.1. First we can see that men were in general more likely to work longer overtime hours compared to women, that is, men with fixed schedules worked around four hours of overtime work per week, while women with fixed schedules worked around 2.5 hours of overtime. When workers started working flexibly, it was men whose overtime hours increased more. Women, on average, increased their overtime hours by less than half an hour a week when changing from fixed schedules to flexitime, and by less than one hour a week when moving from fixed schedules to working time autonomy. For men, the increase in overtime hours was double of what was found for women. Men moving from fixed schedules to flexitime worked about an hour more overtime per week, and those moving from fixed to working time autonomy worked around two additional hours of overtime.

The same patterns emerged in our analysis using the UKHLS (see Figure 6.2) (Chung and van der Horst, 2020). Men on average worked longer overtime hours compared to women. Men also increased the amount of unpaid overtime hours they carried out when having more control over their schedules, yet the differences was not as clear-cut in the German data. On closer inspection, we found that we need to look at not only gender but also parental statuses as the difference lies between mothers versus other groups of the population (women without children, and men with and without children) (see Figure 6.4). Although for men both with and without young children (here, defined as aged under 12) and women without young children, schedule control, especially a lot of schedule control, led to a significant increase in overtime hours, this was not the case for mothers.

Figure 6.4: Increase in unpaid overtime due to increase in schedule control for parents (living with at least one child under 12) versus non-parents by gender

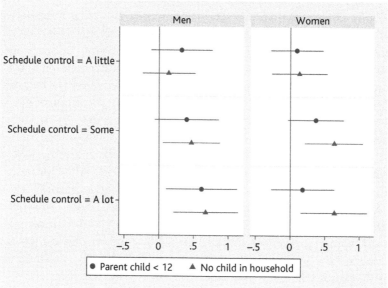

Source: UKHLS, Chung and van der Horst (2020)

The gender differences in the association between flexible working, teleworking and long-hours work/overtime work has also been found in a number of other studies using European data, and various national case studies (Ojala, 2011; Wheatley, 2012; Glass and Noonan, 2016; Eurofound and the International Labour Office, 2017; Lott, 2019). In all of the aforementioned studies, men were shown to work longer (overtime) when working from home compared to women. For example, Glass and Noonan (2016) examining data from the US found that much of the teleworking hours done by mothers were within their normal working hours, whereas much of the teleworking done by fathers were done as part of the hours worked in addition to the normal working hours worked in the office. Lott (2019) compared the overtime hours of mothers and fathers working from home to those who do not, using the German SOEP data. She found that mothers working from home on average did one additional overtime hour compared to those who did not work from home. Fathers worked more overtime compared to mothers in general, but those who worked from home did two additional overtime hours compared to fathers who did not work from home, even having controlled for a wide range of other factors that explain why workers work overtime. In the study by Eurofound and the ILO (2017) one in five men who were categorised as home-based teleworkers worked 48 hours or more per week, while only about one in eight women who worked from home on a regular basis worked 48 hours or more.

Similar patterns emerge when we look at the mental spill-over of work-to-family spheres. As we can see in Figure 6.3, the association between flexible working and work-to-home spill-over was stronger for men. This was especially the case in the association between flexitime and work during their free time. When we restrict the analysis to parents of children under 18, as shown in Figure 6.5, the differences becomes even clearer. The positive association between flexible working, more specifically flexitime or working time autonomy, and work spilling over to private spheres is stronger for fathers compared to mothers – again the biggest gender difference found for flexitime. For mothers, access to flexitime is not significantly associated with a higher likelihood of work spilling over to private life, while for fathers it is. Lott (2020) also finds this in her study examining the association between flexitime and working time autonomy with work-to-home spill-over in Germany, where she finds that this association is only found for men while not for women. Schieman and Glavin (2008) confirm this in their study looking at how schedule control leads to work-to-family spill-over using Canadian data, where the association was only significant for men.

Interestingly, we found an opposite effect for teleworking and increased likelihood for work-to-family spill-over (Figure 6.5), where the effect is slightly stronger for mothers compared to fathers. Mothers who telework were 2.3 times more likely to say that they think about work when not at work, and 4.6 times more likely to say they frequently work during their free time to meet work demands, compared to mothers who did not telework. This was 1.6 times and 3.1 times more likely for homeworking fathers compared to non-homeworking fathers respectively. This leads us to believe that the problems of boundary management between work and family life when working from home may be especially difficult for mothers (see also, Kossek et al, 2006; Kurowska, 2020). This is possibly because mothers who telework may be carrying out their normal hours at home which may make it easier for the mental permeability of work to private spheres (Glass and Noonan, 2016), or because when mothers work from home, they are more likely to be disrupted by family/household responsibilities (Sullivan and Lewis, 2001; Hilbrecht et al, 2008).

Occupational variations

The question arises whether or not the flexibility paradox is limited to professionals and higher-status workers. As we saw in Chapter 5, many of the qualitative observations of the flexibility paradox were drawn from professional workers in the UK or the US. Schieman and colleagues in their higher-status hypothesis (Schieman and Glavin, 2008; Schieman et al, 2009;

Figure 6.5: Association between flexible working and work-to-home spill-over for parents by gender

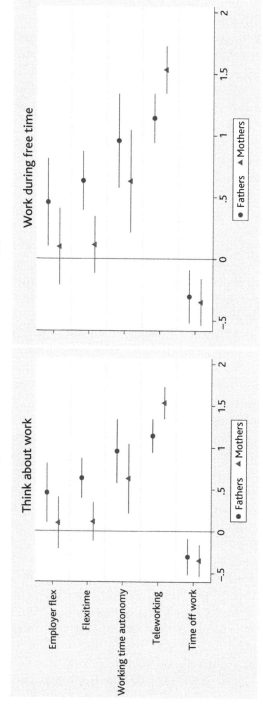

Source: EWCS, 2015, author's calculation

Note: Reference category: fixed schedules, X axis – higher numbers indicate a higher likelihood of spill-over of work-to-family life, lower numbers indicate lower likelihood of spill-over occurring.

Think about work – always or most of the time think about work when not at work; work during free time – workers who work during free time to meet work demands at least several times a month.

Coefficient plot of two multi-level logistic regression analysis with a number of control variables including household, individual and company-level characteristics. All variables are dichotomous variables. Detailed results available upon request.

Schieman and Young, 2010) argue that those in higher-status positions, with stronger work-devotions, may be the ones that are especially likely to experience work to non-work interference when boundaries are blurred. They draw from the work around the notion of the 'greedy institutions' (Coser, 1974), that workplaces – especially American workplaces – are increasingly becoming 'greedy' in that they demand more time commitment and work devotion. Cech and Blair-Loy call this the work devotion schema, namely the 'the moral and institutionalised cultural mandate that work demands and deserves total allegiance' (Cech and Blair-Loy, 2014: 87). Schieman and colleagues argue that it is especially the professionals and workers in high-skill occupations who are more likely to and have been asked to adhere to the work devotion schema. This explains why it is especially among higher-status workers that blurring of boundaries between work and family life increases the likelihood of work encroaching on family rather than the other way around.

Occupational status may also intersect with gender and parental roles. Namely, of higher-status workers, it may be especially the men and fathers in professional and managerial roles who are able to or feel a greater pressure to adhere to the ideal worker culture or work devotion schema through flexible working. Fathers in professional and managerial roles are also more likely to have higher incomes, which reduces the need for their spouses to take on additional breadwinning roles which may subsequently increase the support fathers receive (Clawson and Gerstel, 2014) or reduce the share of housework/childcare they need to provide (Hook, 2006; Bianchi et al, 2012). This enables these fathers to expand their work even further, especially when such conditions are compounded by the breadwinning roles they feel like they need to adhere to. On the other hand, due to the competing demands professional mothers face coming from both work and family domains, mothers' capacity to expand their working hours, especially unpaid overtime hours, may be limited (Blair-Loy, 2009). This discrepancy between professional men and women to exert more time and devotion into their work leads to significant issues of women dropping out of these occupations, or not progressing as much as men, with high gender pay gaps in such occupations (Cha and Weeden, 2014; Goldin, 2014). What is worse, as these occupations become more male-dominated, this may escalate long-hours cultures further because only those who can increase their work devotion remain in jobs (now having eliminated those who cannot) (Berdahl et al, 2018). This creates a playing ground that will further exacerbate the flexibility paradox.

Having said that, workers in lower-paid/skilled jobs may also work harder/ longer when given the opportunity to work flexibly. In Chapter 3 we saw that lower-paid/skilled workers are less likely to have access to flexible working arrangements. This is because managers feel that the job is not suitable for flexible working (Wanrooy et al, 2013). Even if they were, managers do not feel a great need to use such arrangements to recruit or retain workers (Lambert and Haley-Lock, 2004), or it may be because they would not trust workers to use the flexibility to increase productivity (Williams et al, 2013). Thus, when lower-paid/skilled workers get access to flexible working arrangements, they may feel an additional need to reciprocate the gift of flexibility to ensure that they are able to maintain the arrangement. This may especially be the case for women in lower-paid/skilled jobs. They may find it more difficult to gain access to these arrangements in the first place (Brescoll et al, 2013; Munsch, 2016; Chung, 2019), yet rely heavily on flexible working arrangements to balance work with family demands (Chung and van der Horst, 2018; Fuller and Hirsh, 2018; Chung and Booker, forthcoming) especially when they have limited access to other resources (Clawson and Gerstel, 2014; Kim, 2020).

As we can see from Figure 6.6, using the UKHLS (2020) we found that professional men are the ones most likely to increase their unpaid overtime hours with schedule control. For example, professional men with 'a lot' of schedule control, increase their unpaid overtime hours by one hour. On the other hand, men in lower-paid jobs did not significantly increase their unpaid overtime hours when gaining control over their schedules. Although we see that professional women increase their unpaid overtime hours slightly more than women in lower-paid workers when they gain control over their schedules, the differences are small. In Chung and van der Horst (2020) we intersected occupational class with gender and parental status. The results show that for professional workers (men and women) without children and professional fathers, gaining 'some' or 'a lot' of schedule control increased unpaid overtime hours at a similar rate (at around one hour per week for 'a lot' of schedule control). As expected, this was not the case for professional mothers, where gaining 'a lot' or 'some' schedule control did not lead to a significant increase in overtime hours (Chung and van der Horst, 2020).

Thus based on the results, the flexibility paradox seems to be more evident for men and fathers in higher-paid/skilled occupations such as professionals/managerial roles. However, these results may be driven by the fact that we are observing indicators that are biased towards men, and towards the higher occupational group of workers. Boltz and colleagues (2020) examine the question whether flexible working leads to longer hours/increased work intensity focusing on non-professionals doing routine tasks. They use a different approach than subjective measures or by measuring hours worked, by measuring workers' productivity and examining whether an increase in work intensity can explain the increase in productivity gained through flexible working. In an experimental approach, they recruited 535 applicants in Colombia using flexible versus fixed schedule contracts. They found that workers with flexible schedules were 30 per cent more productive compared

Figure 6.6: Increase in unpaid overtime due to increase in schedule control for professionals versus non-professionals by gender

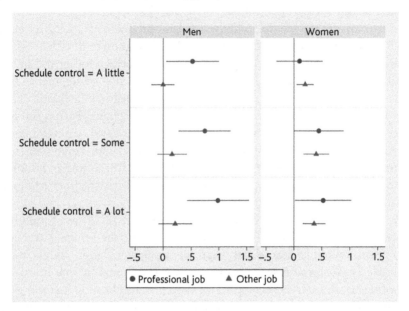

Source: UKHLS, Chung and van der Horst (2020)

to those with fixed schedules. Half of the added productivity was due to the fact that the access to flexible schedules seemed to have attracted more productive workers to the job.[1] They found that there was an added gain in productivity among these workers. It was not due to these workers making fewer mistakes or doing tasks quicker, but more due to the fact that the workers were spending more time doing their job. This was not, however, through increasing the hours worked, but by not taking as many breaks compared to those who had fixed schedules (see also, Kelliher and Anderson, 2010). In other words, there may be an extension of working hours and work intensity due to flexible schedules which may not be observable through our conventional methods of calculating working hours. The added hours or added work intensity of routine workers may be through working more intensively during 'normal' working hours, that is, working without breaks within their contracted hours, rather than working longer overtime hours. A similar result was found by Bloom and colleagues (2015) in an experimental study of Chinese call-centre workers. In this experiment a treatment group was selected to work from home while the control group worked in the office. They found a significant performance increase among those who worked from home. This was partly due to the fact that workers working from home were handling more calls per minute – due to less distraction and noise. However, the largest factor came from workers working from home working more than before, more specifically, working 9.2 per cent more minutes per day. Similar to what was found in the Colombia study, this was not due to workers extending their nominal work day, but by taking less breaks during their shifts. This is why despite not seeing a large significant increase in overtime hours among lower-paid workers in Figure 6.5, this does not mean that the flexibility paradox is not applicable to these workers.

This issue of measurement can also explain why we see a gender discrepancy in the extent to which flexible working leads to work encroaching on private lives. On the one hand, women/mothers cannot increase their overtime hours as much as men/fathers do because it is likely that they have already reached the maximum number of paid working hours they could carry out. Women work fewer hours then men, and are more likely to work part-time due to their housework and childcare responsibilities (Tomlinson, 2006; Costa Dias et al, 2018b). Thus when working flexibly, although women may end up working harder per hour, possibly without breaks as we have seen in the aforementioned study, they are less likely to be able to further extend their working hours (Lott and Chung, 2016). Another important reason why we see a difference between men and women, especially among mothers and fathers, is largely due to the fact that we are only looking at working hours carried out as a part of one's paid employment. When we incorporate the unpaid domestic labour hours and hours spent caring into our definition of 'work' (see also Folbre, 2006) we can see that the increase in the number of 'working' hours is similar for men and women (Lott, 2019). However, it's just that women increase their unpaid hours when working flexibly while men are likely to increase their paid hours. We will explore this issue in greater depth in the next chapter.

Arrangement variations?

The final question raised in this chapter is whether *all types of flexible working* leads to longer working hours and the encroachment on family life. There was already some indication in the variation as we found that flexitime was not as problematic in increasing overtime hours of workers in the German data (Lott and Chung, 2016), and also being least problematic in terms of mental spill-over as found in the previous section (Figure 6.5 and Lott, 2020). In the paper I wrote with Mariska van der Horst (2020) examining the outcomes of flexible working on unpaid overtime working in the UK, we distinguished between flexitime and schedule control. The UK provides a unique opportunity to assess different types of flexible working arrangements because flexible working for family-friendly purposes is installed in the labour law in the Right to Request Flexible Working regulation (see Chapter 2). This right was initially developed specifically to support working parents balance work with care demands. The UKHLS data captures workers' access to and use of arrangements specified in the Right to Request legislation. This is measured by asking workers if they 'personally needed any', whether they have access to and use the following arrangements: flexitime and 'working from home on a regular basis', which can be distinguished from schedule control which we examined in the previous Figures (6.2, 6.4, 6.5 and 6.6). Although flexitime and schedule control both capture workers' control over when they work, we can see they capture different things as demonstrated in Figure A6.1. Although those who have access to or use flexitime are more likely to say they have 'some' or 'a lot' of control over their schedule, many who have 'none' or 'a little' bit of schedule control also have access to and use flexitime. Similarly, more than half of workers with 'some' or 'a lot' of control over their schedules say they do not have access to flexitime.

With this in mind, we examined whether flexitime and working from home also increased the number of overtime hours workers carried out as we found was the case for schedule control. As we can see in Figure 6.7, although when workers get more control over their schedules (schedule control) they are likely to increase their unpaid overtime hours, this is not necessarily the case for flexitime or working from home/teleworking arrangements. Why is this the case? This may be because when survey respondents think about

Figure 6.7: Increase in unpaid overtime due to changes in flexible working for men and women

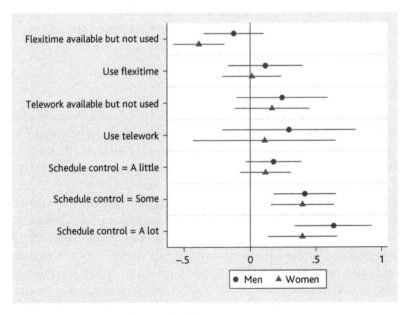

Source: UKHLS, Chung and van der Horst (2020)

Note: reference = no access to flexitime; no access to telework; no schedule control.

flexitime or working from home arrangements in the survey, they may be thinking about working flexibly specifically to meet family or private demands. Respondents may also only consider arrangements they have asked their managers/companies to provide them with specifically to meet family demands, as was defined in the Right to Request. This may be different from the schedule control arrangements that are generally provided to workers to enhance work productivity. However, even if flexible working for family/care purposes does not necessarily result in unpaid overtime hours, or possibly precisely because it does not result in workers extending their work efforts, it can result in negative career outcomes for workers. This is explored in greater detail in Chapter 8.

Another evidence of *how* flexible working arrangements are introduced matters can also be found in the study done by the Work, Family, Health Network in the US (see, Kelly et al, 2014; Kelly and Moen, 2020). This was a multi-site intervention five-year study that implemented a STAR (Support.Transform.Achieve.Results.) workplace culture transformation to see how it impacts workers' productivity, work–life balance, family life and health outcome. Thus, in this case, flexible working was not introduced just as a stand-alone policy, but as part of a wider work culture transformation which redefined issues around productivity, key goals of the team, and work commitment and so on, as well as increased manager and co-worker support towards workers. The results show that in this case, flexible working led to improvements in not only productivity but also helped reduce workers' work–family conflict. This provides us with a new perspective in that the flexibility paradox is not inevitable, that the context in which it is used and introduced matters. This is something we will explore in greater detail in Chapter 9.

Conclusion

By presenting studies using data gathered from across the world, this chapter provided more concrete evidence of the flexibility paradox outlined in Chapter 5. The flexibility paradox was evidenced through studies that show that flexible working was associated with long working hours and mental/physical spill-over of work to non-work spheres. The chapter also provided evidence that followed individuals across time, using longitudinal data, to show how the same individuals when gaining access to flexible schedules and teleworking seem to expand rather than contract their working hours. One interesting finding from these studies was that the patterns of flexible working leading to long-hours work was different across workers in different occupations, gender and parental status. The gender discrepancy can be explained through the fact that men/fathers are more likely to (need to) adhere to the work devotion schema due to their breadwinning roles, and women/mothers are limited in expanding their working hours further due to their care and housework responsibilities. Another reason why we don't see clear-cut evidence of the flexibility paradox through the extension of working hours for women may be related to the fact that we are looking at the wrong hours. In other words, mothers and women in general may expand 'work' hours as much as men do, but for them, this may be more evident only when we also take into account unpaid domestic housework and care hours. This is the topic of Chapter 7. Similarly, the expansion of overtime through flexible working was not as evident for workers in lower-paid occupations. This may be largely due to the measurement of 'overwork' rather than the fact that the flexibility paradox is not applicable to these workers. We also found that there may be some type of flexible working arrangements that may not necessarily result in workers expanding their working hours/efforts. However, as we will explore in Chapter 8, these types of flexible working may result in another negative outcome – namely the stigmatisation of workers who work this way, and career penalties. Finally, the chapter ended with a question about whether the context in which flexible working is introduced may influence its outcomes – which we will explore in Chapter 9.

Note

[1] An experimental study conducted by the Behavioural Insights Team in the UK found that having flexible working options available in job descriptions increased applications to the job by 30 per cent. More information on this study: www.bi.team/blogs/bits-biggest-trial-so-far-encourages-more-flexible-jobs-and-applications/

7

Gendered flexibility paradox

Introduction

The previous chapter showed that flexible working can lead to work encroaching on private life. This encroachment can take shape in terms of time, that is, working longer (unpaid) overtime or working during 'free time', and mental or cognitive space, that is, thinking about work when not at work, impacting one's capacity to fully relax and recover (Sonnentag, 2003; Sonnentag and Bayer, 2005). One pattern observed in the empirical evidence outlined in the previous chapter is that the pattern of the flexibility paradox, especially relating to overtime and long working hours, were more prevalent among men and women without children. Although we do see some patterns of the flexibility paradox among women with care responsibilities, in most cases, they were less likely to expand their working hours when they work flexibly.

This chapter aims to explain why these patterns occur. It argues that the weaker empirical evidence of the flexibility paradox found for mothers is largely due to the fact that these studies exclude an important part of the 'work' that is carried out in our societies, that is, namely unpaid domestic work. To quote Fraser, this is due 'to the inadequacy of androcentric definitions of work' (1994: 593). In other words, we cannot limit our analysis only to the measurement of paid work when examining the flexibility paradox. This is especially true when consider our original theoretical assumption of the flexibility paradox, that it is a manifestation of the subjectification of self to the capitalist model of homo-economicus as argued by Foucault (2010). Foucault argues that the pattern of subjectification is not limited to individuals exploiting their own labour as a form of entrepreneurship to maximise profits gained through the market. It also entails the need to invest in the human capital of the household, namely through one's children as a part of the formation of their human capital, in the form of caregiving.

In the next section, I will go into greater detail, using the works of Foucault and feminist theories of parenting such as that of Hays (1998) and Wall (2010), to explain why for women the pattern of the flexibility paradox may not necessarily be evident through the expansion of their working hours, but through the expansion of their hours spent in childcare and housework. Flexible working enables mothers to enact intensive parenting which is, as Wall (2010) notes, another way of perpetuating and reproducing the neo-liberal notions of self. I will then go onto present the empirical evidence of these patterns that show that women expand their childcare and housework when working flexibly, while men do not. In combination with the evidence found in Chapter 6, I argue that flexible working can in fact enable heterosexual dual-earning couples to 'do gender' (West and Zimmerman, 1987; Clawson and Gerstel, 2014), namely perform activities to adhere to their assigned gender roles engrained in our social norms (Chung and van der Lippe, 2020). In fact, it enables a more contemporary enactment of traditional gender roles in that flexible working enables women to carry out paid and unpaid work without disrupting the norm around who is responsible for housework/childcare nor the ideal worker norm.

Background context of the gendered nature of the flexibility paradox

Subjectification of self and the family

The model of homo-economicus is again the generalisation of the market exchange capitalist behaviour in all aspects of one's life, that is, 'generalising the "enterprising" form within the social body of social fabric' (Foucault, 2010: 241). In other words, internalising capitalism. Foucault argues that this type of enterprising behaviour extends to not only who you procreate with[1] but also shapes parenting styles. Foucault argues that parents make educational investments to ensure the development of 'abilities-machine' who will produce income in the future, through spending time with their children. He argues that this starts from a very early age of a child's life 'from the cradle' and is not only limited to simple educational activities but also includes affection as a form of investment. To put it in his words:

> [T]he mother-child relationship, concretely characterized by the time spent by the mother with the child, the quality of the care she give, the affection she shows, the vigilance with which she follows its development, its education, and not only its scholastic but also its physical progress, the way in which she not only gives it food but also imparts a particular style to eating patterns, and the relationship she has with its eating, all constitute for the neo-liberals an investment which can be measured in time. And what will this investment constitute? It will constitute a human capital, the child's human capital, which will produce an income. (Foucault, 2010: 243–44)

He goes on to argue that this investment will crystalise in physical income in the future, which will provide the mother with the satisfaction that her 'investment', that is, the affection, time and care she has provided to the child, has been successful. Through this, the interaction between the mother and child can be analysed in terms of investment, capital costs and profit on the capital invested. Although Foucault uses this analogy to prove how the economic analysis of investment–profit can be applied to all aspects of one's life in the neo-liberal capitalist society, he also points to an important aspect of the subjectification of self. Subjectification of self is not only observed by individuals' entrepreneurial behaviours as a worker in the labour market, that is, exploiting one's labour and other aspects of one's life (for example leisure, relationships) with a goal of maximising profit within the market. It is also observed in parents enterprising children, to ensure that the household can gain maximum profit now and into the future. This behaviour takes place in the shape of investing one's time, energy, and affection and ensuring the optimisation of activities for the child to enhance their competitive edge in the market, with future profit goals in mind. In this way, the household becomes a unit of production, similar to that of a firm (Foucault, 2010: 245).

Intensive parenting

Hays (1998) in her book exploring the cultural shifts around parenting that have occurred in the past decades argues that the culturally acceptable form of mothering in contemporary times is '*intensive mothering*'. Intensive mothering is '*a gendered model that advises mothers to expend a tremendous amount of time, energy, and money in raising their children*' (Hays, 1998: x). In this new cultural norm, parents, especially mothers, are considered to be more and more responsible for the behaviours and outcomes of children, including their mental and physical well-being, cognitive and academic achievements (Wall, 2010). Some of the earlier evidence came from theories such as the maternal attachment theory by Bowlby (1979), where it is argued that continuous and solicitous maternal attention especially in the early years of a child's life is crucial in ensuring the healthy emotional and psychological development of children. This development changed in the 1990s more towards the importance of parental engagement with children, the importance of providing the right and ample stimulation, that is, 'enrichment' activities (Craig and Mullan, 2011) in ensuring the optimal brain development and future intellectual potentials of children (Wall, 2010: 254). There has been a rise in the number of studies that note the importance of parents' time spent on 'enrichment' activities – namely childcare activities that relate to play, education and generally enriching a child's experience – on the cognitive and academic outcomes of children (for example Wilder, 2014; Cano et al, 2018; for a summary, see Chung, 2021a). Wall argues that this trend puts parents and caregivers in the role as engineers and programmers of children and their future, where the potential consequences of neglecting to give children ample input is portrayed as dire. Wall uses excerpts from parenting literature distributed in Canada and in the US to illustrate this phenomenon better:

Will a child lie and vegetate or blossom intellectually? Well, that depends on the seeds we plant during the first five years of a child's life. Simple things like talking, singing and reading to a child from the day of birth will have a lasting impact on her potential. Intelligence doesn't grow on trees, but it certainly grows on love and supportive stimulation. (Invest in Kids, 2001; excerpt from Wall, 2010)

Despite the popular belief that women spent more time with children during the 1950s or 1960s – when the conventional housewife architype was more prevalent, mothers, including mothers working full-time jobs, have increased their time caring for children in the past few decades. Dotti Sani and Treas (2016) examined parental time spent with children from 1965 to 2012 using the Multi-national Time Use Study,[2] which includes data from 11 different Western countries – such as the US, the UK, France, Italy and so on. Here, childcare time measures the more active engagement with children, rather than children being in a parent's presence (that is, children just being around the house while the parent is carrying out another activity like cooking or cleaning). The results of their analysis show that mothers doubled the time they spend with children from an average of 54 minutes per day in 1965 to 104 minutes per day in 2012. This again is despite the fact that mothers' employment rate and working hours have also increased significantly over the same period. Fathers also increased their time almost four-fold from a mere 16 minutes daily in 1965 to 59 minutes by 2012. This increase in parenting time was mostly driven by the higher-educated parents. In 1965, mothers with different levels of education were spending an approximately equal number of minutes with their children. However, by 2012, the gap between those with and without tertiary education significantly increased to approximately half an hour per day – with tertiary-educated mothers spending on average 123 minutes with their children compared to the 94 minutes of their lower-educated counterparts. Similarly, fathers' time spent with children grew mostly for the higher-educated fathers – where the gap between the lower-educated and the higher-educated grew from three minutes to 24 minutes from 1965 to 2012. Similar results can be found in the UK Time Use study (Wishart et al, 2019) where it was found that parents with full-time jobs and in managerial/professional roles increased their time spent on interactive care more than others.

This increase in the time parents are spending with children is not a bad thing. This is especially true when we think of its impact on family well-being, for both parents and children (Chung, 2021a; Walthery and Chung, 2021). Fathers' increased involvement in housework and childcare is especially important when we think about its potential to change gender norms (Cunningham, 2001) and tackle gender inequalities in the division of labour both at home and in the labour market (Norman et al, 2014;

Norman, 2019). However, Wall (2010) sees a direct link between the rise of intensive parenting and the neo-liberal processes of self-subjectification or entrepreneurial self. She argues that 'the intensification of parenting … is intertwined with a neo-liberal rationality that emphasizes individual responsibility, self-management, risk, and control' (Wall, 2010: 253). In other words, the rise in the need for parents to spend more time enriching a child's development is related to a growing trend that makes the individual (and their family) responsible for any labour market and societal risks they incur. This is echoed by the observations of others who have written about the millennial generation (those born between early/mid-1980s to mid-1990s) (Harris, 2017; Petersen, 2019), who have been at the centre of this intensive parenting boom. Harris (2017) argues that the millennial generation (and possibly xennials) have been born to evaluate every activity they carry out in terms of its investment value for future potential profits. He argues that the millennials grew up with parents with a keen interest in optimising every aspect of their child's life, including play dates with friends, which helped shape the children's view of the world. In other words, such intensive parenting culture is not only limited to shaping norms among parents of what the right type of parenting is. It also paves the way for nurturing the growth of new generations of workers who will have the neo-liberal rationality of entrepreneurial-mindset embedded into them from birth. These workers will equate any problems they experience in their lives (such as job or income loss) as individual failures[3] and are more likely to exploit themselves when given control over their work.

Intensive mothering and gender norms

Studies that evidence the increase in intensive parenting show that the phenomenon is not only limited to mothers, as fathers are also increasing their involvement in childcare, especially the non-routine enrichment care (Craig and Mullan, 2011; Walthery and Chung, 2021). However, a large share of the childcare responsibility, particularly relating to the routine day-to-day care of children, still lies with the mother (Wishart et al, 2019; Walthery and Chung, 2021). Although the question of who takes on a larger share of housework and childcare can be explained by who has the time to do them, who brings in more income/resources into the household, and who is better at it, the most important factor is who society expects to do them (Bianchi et al, 2000; Hook, 2010). Women do more housework and childcare because our societal norms still dictate that women are mostly responsible for these tasks, while men should focus on being the breadwinner. Although, we see some progress in the way in which societies feel about women taking part in breadwinning, there is still a general assumption across the world that it is the mother's responsibility to provide childcare, especially for preschool children (Scott and Clery, 2013; Knight and Brinton, 2017; Chung and Schober, 2018; Taylor and Scott, 2018). A large proportion of the population still believes that children suffer when mothers work. According to the European Value Study of 2017, although only 9 per cent support this statement in Denmark, 24 per cent believe this to be the case in the UK, 32 per cent in Germany, and more than half the population in many Eastern and Southern European countries like Poland and Italy.[4] This is why we find that even when women earn more money or work longer hours than their male partners, they still end up doing more housework and childcare (Brines, 1993; 1994; van der Lippe et al, 2010; van der Lippe et al, 2018). In sum, the intensification of parenting in fact generally presents itself in our society as cultural pressures put on mothers to increase their time and energy on childcare. In the next section, I will explain why these assumptions matter when we look at how the flexibility paradox plays out across genders.

Gendered flexibility paradox

Flexible working and the expansion of unpaid work

A large number of studies (for example, Noonan et al, 2007; Kim, 2020; Kurowska, 2020) evidence how flexible working can allow working parents to play a larger role in housework and childcare by providing them with the flexibility and control over the temporal and physical boundaries between their work and home domains. For example, parents who work fixed-work schedules may not be able to do certain time-specific childcare and housework tasks, such as dropping off or picking up their children from school, cooking dinner or carrying out their bedtime routines. Flexitime can fit work schedules around such rigid family schedules, and allow the use of tag team parenting. An example of tag team parenting is when one parent does the school drop-offs but works till later, while the other works earlier and does the pick-ups. Such practices enable the extension of family time, allowing parents to care for their children without reducing their working hours (Presser, 1988; Craig and Powell, 2012). Working from home allows a certain level of blending or multi-tasking of work and non-work tasks (Schieman and Young, 2010), where work and housework or childcare can be done at the same time (Sullivan and Lewis, 2001; Powell and Craig, 2015; Andrew et al, 2020). What is more, workers with long commutes will have more time for housework/care when they do not need to commute (Peters et al, 2009; Allen et al, 2015; Bloom et al, 2015).

Boundary and border theorists argue that the flexibility between the borders of the work and home domain will result in different outcomes depending on the priority each domain takes in one's life and which domain the worker identifies most with (Arthur, 1994; Clark, 2000). However, it is not necessarily left to the individual to choose how they prioritise work and home spheres, since external demands and social norms heavily shape the worker's capacity to make real choices (Hobson, 2013). Capabilities approach theory argues that family-friendly arrangements do not necessarily help individuals achieve work-life balance, because certain contexts in which these arrangements are embedded can limit capabilities and 'real' choices individuals can make (Hobson, 2011; Javornik and Kurowska, 2017; Yerkes and Javornik, 2019). These contexts can include both institutional factors at national and organisational levels, societal normative factors – namely work and gender cultures, as well as the family and individual context, that is, one's situated agency as a certain gender or ethnicity (Hobson, 2011). Thus, using this theory, we can understand why a worker's capacity to utilise the flexibility and control in their work to better address work-family issues can be limited or supported by the context the worker is situated in (Drobnič and Guillén Rodríguez, 2011). Societal norms on gender roles in combination with the rise of the intensive parenting culture shape, or in a way limits, what workers do or can do when they are given the 'freedom' and control over their work, with men and women being constrained by these external forces in very different ways. Namely, freedom and control over work when you largely bear the responsibility of breadwinning for the family means that you will (have to) expand your work spheres more. This is especially true in light of the increased competition in the labour market and the rise in insecurity workers are facing in recent times (Chung, 2018; Chung, 2020c). Freedom over work when there are societal pressures that dictates that you are responsible for the general upkeep and the well-being of your family, and possibly more importantly the future outcomes of your children, it is likely that you will have to use the control over your work to meet household and childcare demands. What is more, these external contexts shape how others – namely your employers, colleagues, and co-residents, that is, your partner, children and other family members – expect you to use the flexibility and the control over your work, reinforcing these gendered patterns.

Empirical evidence of the gendered flexibility paradox

Several studies (for example, Sullivan and Lewis, 2001; Singley and Hynes, 2005; Hilbrecht et al, 2013; Lott, 2019; Kim, 2020; Kurowska, 2020) show that flexible working is likely to be used by women to meet care purposes and when they do work flexibly, they are likely to expand their time and energy spent on childcare/housework. Men, on the other hand, do not take up flexible working for care purposes and are unlikely to increase their involvement in childcare and housework when they work flexibly. Sullivan and Lewis (2001) interviewed 14 home-based workers and their partners to examine the gendered patterns of working from home. They found that childcare was rarely brought up by men as the motive for working from home, whereas for women it was the main or the original reason for doing so. When working from home, the blurred boundaries between work and family life led to more housework and childcare for women. For men, it ended up resulting in over work, with work encroaching on family life. Men were able to keep stronger boundaries between work and family life, on the one hand, because of the choice they made to ensure that work was not impacted by family life when working from home. However, it was also due to the fact that their co-residents enabled this stronger boundary-keeping. Male teleworkers were able to focus on work because their partners usually worked part-time and were at home caring for children when the male teleworkers were working from home. When men engaged in housework or childcare, the male participants noted as 'helping out' their spouses who were seen as mainly responsible for these tasks. On the contrary, female teleworkers were usually alone at home without any spousal support available, making them need to combine both childcare and paid employment at the same time. This was largely due to the assumption from family members – including children – that when mothers worked from home, they were also available for caregiving and housework at the same time (see also Hilbrecht et al, 2008; Radcliffe and Cassell, 2014). In fact, other studies have shown that when men work from home, they work in a separate office spaces shielded away from children by their partners, while women tend to work in communal areas, for example on the dining room table, while multi-tasking childcare (Huws et al, 1990; Andrew et al, 2020).

Such patterns of behaviours have also been found in quantitative studies using large-scale representative data. For example, Kim (2020) examined how flexible working – both flexitime and homeworking – relates to parental-child interactions using the longitudinal data from the Early Childhood Longitudinal Survey-Birth Cohort (ECLS-B) in the US. He found that working from home was associated with more frequent non-routine parent-child interactions but only for mothers and not for fathers. However, fathers', especially fathers in dual-earning households, access to flexitime was associated with greater daily routine interactions with children. Lott (2019) examines how homeworking relates to parental time in childcare and overtime using the German SOEP data – again a large-scale household longitudinal panel data representative of the German population. Her results show that women who were working from home tended to spend three hours more on childcare per week compared to mothers who did not work from home. Fathers, in comparison, worked longer overtime hours when working from home – an increase of about three hours per week – with no significant increase of childcare hours.

Although she found that mothers working from home also worked longer overtime, it was by about an hour or so. Recent quantitative evidence also shows how mothers are also more likely to multi-task care and paid-work tasks compared to fathers. For example, during the first lockdown of the COVID-19 pandemic in the UK (April–May 2020), more than half of mothers' working hours at home were done while multi-tasking childcare. Fathers also multi-tasked somewhat but it was significantly lower at around a third of their time (Andrew et al, 2020).

Exploitation model and traditionalisation of gender roles through flexible working

Hilbrecht and colleagues (2013) interviewed 18 professional mothers working in a Canadian financial corporation who were working from home. They show that the intensive parenting culture ideology prevalent in Canadian society meant that these mothers ensured that they fitted work around their children's school and leisure activities, that is, prioritising their family domain's demands/temporal boundaries against that of other domains. This was the case despite the fact that these mothers all had higher-status professional jobs, where the work devotion schema and ideal worker norms are prevalent (Blair-Loy, 2009; Schieman et al, 2009; Glavin and Schieman, 2012). Not only were they prioritising family demands above work demands, these women were also using their time saved from working from home, that is, not having to commute, and sacrificing their leisure time to ensure they met both demands of motherhood and paid work without reducing time spent on either demands. Several studies show that access to flexitime and working from home arrangements can enable mothers to maintain their working hours and stay employed after childbirth (Chung and van der Horst, 2018; van der Lippe et al, 2019; see Chapter 4 for more details). Many also note the importance of access to flexible working as key in ensuring women's access to and capacity to stay in lucrative high-paying jobs (Goldin, 2014; Fuller and Hirsh, 2018). In this sense, flexible working can be seen as a helpful tool facilitating women's capacity to meet both the demands coming from work and home spheres. However, it also means that flexible working does little to disrupt the gendered division of housework and childcare. In fact, flexible working demands that mothers use their freedom and control over their work to meet the demands of work and family even if this means sacrificing other domains of life – such as leisure and sleep (see also, Schulte, 2015; Armstrong, 2018; Wishart et al, 2019). A good example of this is a mother who uses flexible working arrangements to perform two full-time roles, that of a full-time worker and a stay-at-home mother, within the limits of 24 hours a day. She will do the morning routine childcare (namely preparing breakfast, monitoring getting dressed, preparing the school bag/

lunch and so on), drop her children off at school by 9am, work till 3pm when she picks them up again, and helps them with their homework, prepares dinner and carries out the bedtime routine and so on. To fulfil her full-time working hours, she will work again at 8pm for another two to three hours (or some wake up at 5–6am to work a couple of hours before the children wake up), in addition to checking her emails, taking phone calls while multi-tasking childcare and housework tasks between 3pm and 8pm. They do all of this while their male partners work nine-to-five at the office, coming home for dinner (or later when commuting), many citing the lack of flexibility in their work to do otherwise. Even when fathers work from home, they shut themselves in the study/separate office space for a solid block of time working uninterrupted. Many women work some sort of variation of this (see, Armstrong, 2018; Young, 2018), where they are able to fulfil their 'duties' as a mother and a worker without disrupting neither the traditional gender roles nor the male-breadwinner based idea of 'the worker' (namely, someone who does not have any other responsibility outside of work), by sacrificing her rest and leisure time.

Kurowska (2020) explores how homeworking relates to the 'total necessary work' – that is combining both paid and unpaid domestic working hours. She shows that homeworking increased the number of total necessary work for women but not for men in countries like Poland where gender norms are traditional. This effectively means that it crowds out other types of activities for women, namely sleep or leisure (see also, Kossek et al, 2006; Schulte, 2015). Such crowding out of leisure and other domains can also be observed in other studies like that of Lott (2019) where mothers working from home increased both their working hours and their childcare hours.

Flexible working for women resulting in them forgoing leisure and other domains in their life to squeeze in as much childcare and housework, with minimal disruption to paid work, is the basic premise of the 'exploitation model' put forward by feminist scholars. Sullivan and Lewis argue that teleworking and other types of flexible working 'perpetuates the exploitation of women in terms of both paid work and the domestic burden of responsibility … subject to demands from both family and employer, and subject to control by their husband' (Sullivan and Lewis, 2001: 124–5). Thus, flexible working enables employers and male partners in heterosexual relationships to have easier access to the female labour market potential and the additional income associated with it without having to address the issues around housework and childcare, that is, the unequal division thereof. It also relieves governments the need for a more social response to the demands of working families. In a way, flexible working enabled the 'freeing up' of mothers' labour for free. In other words, the expansion of flexible working, or introducing policies such as the right to request flexible working at the national level, is a way to meet working parents' demand or ensuring female labour market potential, without the government (or organisations) having to provide other types of family policies, such as public childcare or generous parental leaves for both parents (Lewis et al, 2008). It also allows women's human capital to be freed up to work without disrupting the masculine work environment (Acker, 1990; Berdahl et al, 2018). Women are taking part in the labour market built for male workers, for example, in the 1950s, when men did not have any other responsibilities outside of work because of the support their wives gave them, rather than the labour market transforming significantly to enable better labour market participation for women. Similarly, flexible working does not disrupt the gender normative assumptions or the power dynamics within households that determine who should be the person mainly carrying out housework and childcare, but rather enables the traditional gender roles to remain. Flexible working can maintain or increase the traditional division of labour within households enabling heterosexual couples to 'do gender' (West and Zimmerman, 1987; Fleetwood, 2007;Clawson and Gerstel, 2014) in that they are able to fulfil the social normative roles prescribed within societies, that is, the so-called traditionalisation of gender role theory of flexible working (Chung and van der Lippe, 2020). In fact, it fosters a more contemporary form of traditional gender role by 'enabling' women to carry out both housework and paid work without asking men to be more involved in housework or childcare.

Class variations or arrangement variations?

A question arises whether the gendered patterns of flexible working and the traditionalisation of gender roles through flexible working can be observed across all social classes, or if this is a phenomenon largely enacted by middle-class, higher-educated professional couples. Much of the qualitative evidence for the gendered patterns of flexible working looks at couples in professional occupations (for example, Hilbrecht et al, 2013; Young, 2018). This is despite the fact that higher-educated workers, on average, are more likely to have an egalitarian view of gender roles (Knight and Brinton, 2017), and due to homogamy (Kalmijn, 1991) higher-educated workers marry one another. As we saw in the previous section, higher-educated fathers in professional or managerial jobs are also more likely to spend and want to spend more time with their children (Dotti Sani and Treas, 2016; Wishart et al, 2019). In this sense, you would expect the higher-educated to be less likely to fall into the trap of traditionalised gender roles through flexible working. However, the intensification of mothering is especially noticeable among higher-educated mothers/mothers in high-skilled occupations. What is more, fathers in higher-skilled occupations may also be more likely than others to adhere to the ideal worker norm/work devotion schema and likely to increase their overtime hours when boundaries between work and family life are blurred (see Chapter 6). Workers with lower education generally hold more traditional gender roles attitudes (Scott and Clery, 2013; Knight and Brinton, 2017) and prefer a more traditional division of labour (Stanczyk et al, 2017). However, workers in lower-paid occupations may experience stricter restrictions at work and lack resources, such as financial resources, that enable them to perform such gender roles (Roy et al, 2004; Tubbs et al, 2005). This is why we sometimes see a more equal division of housework in practice for these groups of workers despite their gender role attitudes (Lyonette and Crompton, 2015).

Clawson and Gerstel (2014) comparing the outcomes of flexible working of higher- versus lower-paid occupations in the US through a qualitative approach conclude that despite their gender role attitudes, it was the workers in lower-paid jobs who had a more egalitarian outcome in terms of gender roles when working flexibly. This was largely due to their limited capacity to do gender/perform a more traditional division of gender roles, because of the need for the mothers, as well as the fathers, in lower-income families to generate household income. With Cara Booker, using the UK Household Longitudinal Study data (Chung and Booker, forthcoming) we examined how class relates to the division of housework and childcare across different occupational groups, focusing on dual-earning heterosexual co-resident couples with children. We found that the arrangements with more boundary blurring potential – such as a lot of schedule control or homeworking – tended to result in a more traditional division of labour compared to other arrangements such as flexitime, especially for childcare. This pattern was especially noticeable for mothers in low-medium occupations compared to those in higher-paid/skilled occupations. Flexitime, on the other hand, was used more as a tool to divide housework more equally among couples, especially those in low- and medium-skill level occupations. Similar results are found by Kim (2020) using large-scale data in the US. His analysis shows that the positive association between mothers working from home and their increased parent-child interactions was more pronounced among low-income mothers than high- and medium-income mothers. He explains this as largely owing to the fact that lower-income mothers do not have other resources to meet their demands of childcare, compared to mothers in higher- and medium-income households. On the other hand, his study also shows that flexitime, for example, had more potential to result in a more egalitarian division of housework. Actually, when we look at Clawson and Gerstel's (2014) work more carefully, we do find that the differences lie not only in the class but the type of arrangements workers of different occupational classes were able to use. More specifically, workers in lower-paid jobs were more likely to use flexitime with similarities to shift work, while workers in higher-paid occupations had access to working time autonomy, where they had more freedom over when and possibly how much they worked. In other words, the tendencies for the gendered flexibility paradox to take place may not necessarily depend on class, but on the boundary blurring potential of the different flexible working arrangements that workers have access to.

Gendered nature of flexible working and access to flexible working

The gendered pattern of flexible working is largely guided by the expectations of society of what women will and should do when they gain more control over their work. However, as a vicious cycle, these patterns also feed into what people believe flexible working will result in for men and women, consequently shaping how people provide and reward/ stigmatise flexible working of men and women. Recent experimental studies (for example, Brescoll et al, 2013; Munsch, 2016) have shown that women, especially mothers, are less likely to gain access to flexible working arrangements, even when the arrangements are not used for care purposes. What is more, there was an assumption behind mothers' use of flexible working, where they were more likely to be stigmatised for its use compared to men (see also Chapter 8). For fathers, on the other hand, there seems to be a 'progressive badge of merit' (Gerstel and Clawson, 2018) where they are generally looked upon favourably for using flexible working for care purposes.

Similarly, I (Chung, 2018; Chung, 2019c) have examined data from across 30 countries in Europe to compare workers' access to flexible working arrangements across workplaces, sectors and occupations with different gender compositions. I found that workers in female-dominated workplaces or sectors, compared to those that were either male-dominated or where both genders were equally represented, were less likely to have access to flexible working arrangements that give workers more control over their work. This pattern has been observed in many other countries such as the US and Sweden (Jaffee, 1989; Glass, 1990; Adler, 1993; Magnusson, 2019). What is more, even when women contradict the expectations of employers and are productive due to flexible working, they are less likely to gain any income premiums (Lott and Chung, 2016; Magnusson, 2019), and rather experience negative career consequences (Chung, 2020b). Again, this is largely down to the expectations people hold regarding how men and women will use the flexibility in their work. In other words, especially in countries where traditional gender norms are prevalent, even when fathers take up flexible working for care purposes, there is a general expectation that the fathers will still maintain their work devotion/protect their work spheres and prioritise it over family time/care roles. On the other hand, people expect mothers to use the control over their work for care purposes, even when it is explicitly requested for other more performance-enhancing purposes and even when they increase their performance outcomes. This issue of stigma and its impact on one's career and income is the topic we will be looking into in the next chapter.

Conclusion

In this chapter, I argued that there is a gendered pattern in the way the flexibility paradox results in the expansion of work – that although for men it may result in the expansion of paid working hours, for women it results largely in the expansion of unpaid hours. This is why scholars have argued that flexible working can reinforce traditional gender roles (Fleetwood, 2007; Clawson and Gerstel, 2014; Chung and van der Lippe, 2020) – by making men work longer in paid work, and making women do more housework and childcare. What is more, for men when the flexibility and control over one's work resulted in long working hours, this meant that work encroached on one's family life. For women, having flexibility and control over work meant that they were able to or expected to squeeze in as much childcare and paid work into their lives as possible, increasing the amount of 'total necessary work' they carried out – crowding out leisure and sleep. This exploitation model of flexible working, that is, that flexible working enabling easier exploitation of women both at the workplace and at home, was confirmed through a number of empirical studies. I further show that the gendered paradox patterns are more evident when workers have more rather than less control over their work, that is, with arrangements that allow for more boundary blurring such as teleworking/homeworking or working time autonomy. Although many women did see flexible working as an opportunity to meet both demands of family and work, I argue that these behaviours cannot necessarily be seen as choices women make (see also, McRae, 2003). These choices are constrained by the contexts of intensification of parenting, which is another way in which the subjectification and the enterprising of self takes place within the household. It is also constrained by our current societal gender norms which push men to be mainly responsible for breadwinning and women to be responsible for caregiving while also contributing to breadwinning. What is more, these external contexts shape how others – namely your employers, colleagues, and co-residents, that is, your partner, children and other family members – expect you to use the flexibility and the control over your work, possibly reinforcing these gendered patterns. These assumptions of how men and women will use their freedom over their work – which domain they will most likely prioritise – will then shape how flexible working is stigmatised or rewarded. This is one of the topics in the next chapter. The importance of external contexts in shaping the practices of flexible working also means that when social norms and contexts change, such gendered patterns may also disappear. This is something we will be discussing in Chapter 9.

Notes

[1] Foucault argues that those with a certain level of 'good genetic make-up' would want to have children with someone whose genetic make-up is as good as their own to ensure that the child will have low risks and do well in society. He further argues that to do this, one would have to make an investment – work harder, have sufficient income and social status – to be able to meet a spouse or partner to co-produce the new human capital, namely your child, whose human capital is of a certain standard themselves (2010). He also notes that he is not saying this as a joke.

[2] This data is based on time diaries, where individuals are asked to keep a diary of their primary (and sometimes secondary) activities across a time-diary day in 15-minute or so intervals.

[3] Actually as the rise in most pregnancy books will show, the optimisation processes happen even before birth, or possibly even before conception.

[4] Author's own calculation using the European Value Study data of 2017. https://europeanvaluesstudy.eu/

8

Flexibility stigma and the rewards of flexible working

Introduction

In Chapter 5, we explored the issues around the manifestation of the subjectification of self – specifically around passion at work, and the issue of passion exploitation – to possibly explain why individuals are likely to overwork when working flexibly. The idea of how passion can lead you to work long hours when given more autonomy at work is generally based on the idea that you work longer hours to meet your goals, your passion. In other words, longer working hours is driven by your inner need to succeed and wanting to achieve a more positive notion of self and self-fulfilment. Flexibility stigma is different, although ultimately stemming from the same cause – the *entrepreneurial self*-culture and the ideal worker culture. It is embedded in guilt and the negative connotations of self when you fear that you have moved away from the ideal worker image or that you are not fulfilling it as rigorously as you should be. Flexibility stigma also stems from the assumptions of others of what flexible working can result in for different groups of workers, again shaped by societal norms such as gender norms and intensive parenting cultures.

Some scholars (Rudman and Mescher, 2013) argue that men are likely to experience double stigma when using flexible working arrangements for care purposes – namely, flexibility *and* femininity stigma. Flexible working for care purposes makes men be perceived as going against the ideal worker image and against the male-breadwinner image. However, as we discussed in Chapter 7, there are underlying assumptions behind men and women's flexible working practices. Namely, the idea that women primarily use flexible working to meet family demands – and would prioritise family/care demands when boundaries between work and private lives are blurred. Men are expected to use it for performance-enhancing purposes – and are expected to prioritise work demands when boundaries are blurred. Women already experience income and career penalties once they become mothers (Budig and England, 2001; Budig and Hodges, 2010) due to the underlying assumptions around mothers' capacity to work and be productive. When mothers work flexibly, this may be seen as a signal that they are further prioritising their family/care demands. This can explain why it is mothers who work flexibly who experience further stigmatisation and career penalties where motherhood penalties are compounded by flexibility stigma – namely the double-whammy stigma. In contrast, men are expected to (or have the capacity to) maintain stronger boundaries between work and family when working flexibly, or if there is blurring of boundaries between the two spheres, that work will encroach on family life. This way, men may experience a bonus when working flexibly, similar to the fatherhood bonus that has been found in previous research (Hodges and Budig, 2010).

This chapter explores the definition of flexibility and femininity stigma, and provides some empirical evidence of the prevalence of these stigma in our societies. We also aim to explain who is likely to hold this stigmatised view of flexible workers, and who is more likely to suffer from it with a special focus on gender differences.

Flexibility stigma and its prevalence

Defining flexibility stigma

Williams et al (2013) define flexibility stigma as the discrimination workers face when using various types of flexible working arrangements for family responsibilities. Stigma can be defined as attributes that discredit an individual as a 'less desirable kind ... reduced in our minds from a whole and usual person to a tainted, discounted one' (Goffman, 1990: 12). Stigma can arise from an abomination of the body – for example, disability, blemishes of the individual character – for example, arising from mental disorder, imprisonment, addiction or unemployment, or tribal or group identity stigma – that is, stigma towards a group of members within the same lineages/family such as nations, race and religion. Flexibility stigma stems from the fact that working flexibly can be perceived as a blemish in the individual's character. Or that the societal assumption behind flexible working for care purposes makes workers deviate away from 'normal' or ideal worker image (Williams, 1999) of someone who works perpetually, long hours and without any other obligations outside of work. In short, not working long hours in the office and not sticking to the nine-to-five regime, especially to address care responsibilities, may stigmatise the worker as someone who does not or cannot devote themselves to work and is not as committed or productive as other workers. This is why flexible working can lead to negative career outcomes.

Flexibility stigma can be conceptualised in various ways. Rudman and Mescher (2013), for example, distinguish between two types – the poor-worker stigma and the negative career outcomes of flexible working. The poor-worker stigma refers to views around flexible workers' work capacity – namely that workers who work flexibly are not as productive, and those who work flexibly are not as committed to the company or motivated in their work compared to those who do not work flexibly. This is essentially the stigmatised ideas *against* workers taking up flexible working arrangements because their working patterns or assumed devotion to work does not adhere to what is considered as the ideal. Although the flexible worker themselves may think this way due to the internalised ideas of what a 'good worker' looks like, it is more likely a perception people hold against flexible workers. The poor-worker stigma can be distinguished from perceptions of what workers think the consequences of flexible working is in relation to one's career, due to such stigmatised views. This refers to the belief that those who work flexibly will suffer from negative consequences regarding their promotion or other career opportunities. This is something that is more likely to be experienced by the flexible worker themselves, be it from direct experience or from others around them.

Prevalence of flexibility stigma

Much of the existing empirical studies that examine flexibility stigma have focused on the stigma workers face when they reduce their working hours (working part-time) (for example, Epstein et al, 1999; Stone and Hernandez, 2013), or take career break/parental leave (for example, Coltrane et al, 2013; Rudman and Mescher, 2013). Some look at more broadly defined work-family arrangements (for example, Cech and Blair-Loy, 2014) but only few studies (for example, Munsch, 2016) look specifically at the stigma towards workers working flexitime and teleworking/working from home. The reduction of working hours and taking time away from work results in reduction of work – which can be seen as a signal that you are prioritising (temporarily) other aspects of your life outside of work. Thus, it is clear why the take-up of such arrangements makes workers deviate away from the work devotion schema/ideal worker status. However, for the arrangements that provide workers more control over when and where they work, the deviation away from the ideal worker norm may not be as evident. As we explored in Chapter 5, these arrangements may have been introduced to enforce the ideal worker culture rather than deviate away from it (Mazmanian et al, 2013). In addition, as we showed in Chapter 6, such flexible working arrangements may allow for a better devotion towards work rather than reducing it. Despite this, there is still evidence that using flexitime and working from home results in negative perceptions towards workers' capacity and commitment (Leslie et al, 2012; Brescoll et al, 2013; Munsch, 2016; Chung, 2020b).

Figure 8.1 shows the prevalence of flexibility stigma through looking at workers' thoughts on flexible workers, and what flexible working results in, using data from the 2011 UK Work-Life Balance Survey (see for more info Chung, 2020b). As we can see, a large proportion of workers in the UK hold flexibility stigma, with 35 per cent believing that flexible workers create more work for others, and 32 per cent believing working flexibly decreases

Figure 8.1: Proportion of individuals with flexibility stigma by gender and parental status (children <12)

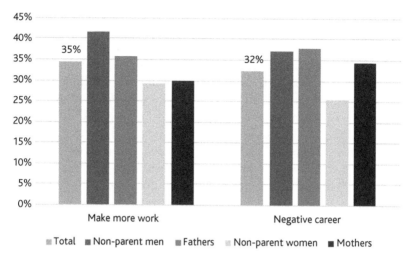

Source: Chung (2020b), WLB2011 Core (weighted averages)

Figure 8.2: Proportion of individuals who have experienced negative outcomes of flexible working arrangements by gender and parental status (children <12)

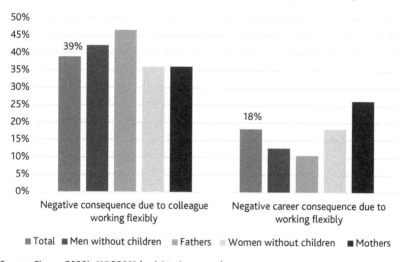

Source: Chung, 2020b; WLB2011 (weighted averages)

chances for promotion. Figure 8.2 presents the experiences of workers themselves or their colleagues working flexibly. On average, 39 per cent of workers (of those who have had someone in their work environment use flexible working) report that they have experienced some sort of negative outcome – for example, having to do more work/more pressures on others, problems with communication – due to colleagues working flexibly. Eighteen per cent of all those who used any flexible working arrangements report having experienced a negative career outcome due to it.

Although it is one of the most representative surveys of the British population, the work–life balance survey is more than a decade old, thus, it is important to examine more recent data on flexibility stigma. This is especially the case because the right to request flexible working in the UK has been expanded quickly to cover all workers as of the summer of 2014, specifically to tackle the negative perception towards flexible workers. The 36th wave of the UK British Social Attitude Survey (BSA) was conducted in the summer/autumn of 2018 (for more information about this survey, see Curtice et al, 2019). The survey asks all employees whether they think working flexibly has had or would have an impact on their employer's perception of them as an employee. Half (52 per cent) of those surveyed did not think there was/would be any impact, yet 22 per cent believed that there will be/has been a negative impact, while 26 per cent believed there will be/or has been a positive impact. The survey also asked: 'Do you think asking for a flexible working arrangement would have any impact on your career prospects or likelihood of promotion?', whereby 29 per cent responded that there definitely or probably would be a negative impact, and only 18 per cent believed there definitely or probably would be a positive impact, with 52 per cent believing there would not be any. The authors of the report note that comparing the results from 2012, there were no large shifts in both of these perceptions. Similarly, comparing the BSA results to the 2011 WLB survey results, we do not see a large shift in the attitudes despite the changes in the regulations on flexible working.

These surveys are limited in that they ask respondents directly whether they have negative stereotypes about flexible working, or whether they feel like flexible working can lead to negative career outcomes. Such self-reported perceptions may be limited in capturing the unconscious bias people have against workers who work flexibly either due to social desirability bias or because people themselves may be unaware of the biases they hold or have experienced. To overcome this limitation, Munsch (2016) ran an experimental vignette study to compare how people felt about workers working flexibly compared to those who do not. She specifically focused on flexitime and flexiplace (working from home) to see whether flexible workers were penalised in terms of five different areas – that is, how likely the respondent was to support the worker, the degree of respect and admiration one had for the worker, how likeable they were, how committed the respondent believed the worker was, and finally how likely the respondent would recommend the worker for promotion. She shows that participants were less likely to give high scores on all five elements measured to workers who had requested flexible working arrangements.

This effect was stronger towards those who had requested to work from home compared to those who had requested to work flexitime. What is more, those who had requested working from home arrangements for childcare purposes were seen more favourably compared to those who had requested it for other reasons, in this case for environmental reasons.

Another way of examining flexibility stigma is to see how flexible workers fare in terms of gaining career penalties and premiums in reality, especially in the longer run. In other words, when we see that flexible workers experience career penalties, compared to those who do not, even when we take other relevant factors into account, this is evidence of stigma against the work and the contributions made by those working flexibly. In an experimental study carried out in a Chinese call centre (Bloom et al, 2015), it was found that those working from home were less likely to be promoted compared to those who were working in the office. This effect was even more noticeable once they took into account the increase in performance found among the workers working from home. The authors note that the evidence is consistent with the 'out of sight, out of mind' phenomenon, and not being visible had led many workers to return back to the office to avoid the penalty workers experience when working from home.

Flexibility stigma and gender

Femininity stigma

Rudman and Mescher (2013) argue that when men use flexible working arrangements they experience 'femininity stigma' – they deviate away from the male-breadwinner image *and* from the ideal worker image when working flexibly for care purposes. Through their experimental study, they show how participants associate men taking up leave (for childcare or parental care purposes) with more feminine traits (that is, communal and weak) and less with masculine traits (that is, agentic and dominant). They also show how such associations have led the participants to penalise these workers, rather than reward them, as evidence to show that men taking up leave will be penalised for their transgressions.

However, the conclusions of the empirical studies examining the negative impact flexible working can have on men and women's careers using survey or administrative data are not as clear-cut. Cech and Blair-Loy (2014) in their analysis of academics in STEM subjects found that women and parents of young children are more likely to believe that flexible working results in negative career consequences, yet the gender difference disappeared when comparing mothers and fathers. Coltrane et al (2013), examined the wage penalties of mothers and fathers that stopped working or reduced their hours for family reasons. They came to the conclusion that there are no statistical differences between the two groups.

Rethinking the gendered stigma

Reducing working hours and taking up leave is largely done by women (Costa Dias et al, 2018a) and may explain why such patterns of behaviour are linked to less masculine characteristics. When we consider teleworking and flexitime, the gendered nature of flexibility stigma may look rather different. Men and workers in male-dominated workplaces are more likely to have access to and use arrangements that provide workers more control over their work, compared to women and workers in female-dominated workplaces (see Chapter 3, the end of Chapter 7, and Golden, 2009; Chung, 2019c). This is because men are usually in higher-status jobs which generally come with more control over one's work (Schieman et al, 2013), and because employers may perceive men to be 'trusted workers' without the need for close supervision (Kossek et al, 2005; Williams et al, 2013). Employers may assume that women will use the flexibility in their work to conform to their gender roles, meaning restricting work to facilitate family demands (Lott and Chung, 2016). In other words, because of the gendered assumptions employers have over work identity and devotion, and how men and women will use flexibility in their work differently, women may be more likely to suffer from or fear negative career outcomes due to flexibility stigma when taking up flexitime and teleworking.

The gendered nature of flexibility stigma and its consequences may be more apparent during parenthood. Parents may be subject to stigma more than non-parents given their responsibility as care givers and given employers' assumption of their devotion towards work and capacity to adhere to the ideal worker culture. Of mothers and fathers, it is likely that mothers will pay a larger penalty and thus may face a larger stigma when taking up flexible working arrangements. This is because the workers' parental status may be more apparent for women, due to pregnancy and maternity leave. Further, traditional gender norms that still exist in today's society shape how employers, co-workers, but also family members, neighbours and even children, assume that women will (have to) do the bulk of the care and thus may not be able to adhere to the ideal worker norm. On the contrary, fathers are expected to increase their work intensity when becoming a father because of the male-breadwinner ideas embedded in our societal norms, thinking that fathers bear the responsibility of ensuring the financial security of the household. In fact, many studies provide evidence of this motherhood penalty (Budig and England, 2001) and fatherhood bonus (Hodges and Budig, 2010), which show that women face discrimination when becoming mothers in job search and in pay, while men benefit from their parental status receiving higher pay (Correll et al, 2007). In other words, already existing biases against certain groups of workers will influence how their flexible working will be viewed – whether it will be considered performance-enhancing or reducing. In this sense, I argue that women/mothers and other workers in disadvantaged positions – such as disabled, minority ethnic groups, LGBTQ+ workers – are more likely to face a 'double-whammy stigma' when working flexibly. These workers already deviate away from the 'ideal worker' image prevalent in hegemonic masculine organisations (Berdahl et al, 2018) and suffer from unconscious biases against their work capacity and performance. Flexibility stigma may compound such existing biases, where when disadvantaged workers work flexibly it is more likely to lead to negative career outcomes. In comparison, those who are more able to adhere to the ideal worker norms – for example, able-bodied heterosexual men with a supportive partner, – may be more likely to hold stigmatised views against flexible workers.

Evidence of the gendered flexibility stigma

Looking back at Figure 8.1, we can see that both gender and parental status matter in who is likely to hold stigmatised views against flexible workers and who is likely to experience negative consequences due to these views. Men were more likely to agree to both flexibility stigma statements, especially regarding the poor-worker stigma. Of men, men without children were more likely than fathers (41 per cent versus 36 per cent) to believe that flexible workers make more work for others. In a multivariate analysis where other factors such as occupation, sector and other individual and family characteristics were taken into account, I found that men were 1.6 times more likely than women to hold negative views against flexible workers – namely that flexible workers made more work for others (Chung, 2020b). Similarly, men were significantly more likely to have reported that they have directly experienced negative consequences due to colleagues working flexibly compared to women (36 per cent). However, in this case, fathers were more likely to say this compared to men without children (47 per cent versus 42 per cent). This result also held true even when other factors were taken into account. Mothers were more likely to think that working flexibly would lead to negative outcomes compared to women without children (34 per cent versus 25 per cent). Also, again women, especially mothers (26 per cent) are more likely to have expressed that their careers have taken a hit due to flexible working compared to women without children (18 per cent) or men both with and without children (11 per cent and 13 per cent respectively). Again these results hold true even when we control for other factors (Chung, 2020b). As expected (detailed results can be found in Chung, 2020b) in addition to parents, those with other care responsibilities and disabilities were also significantly more likely to have experienced negative career outcomes when working flexibly. This confirms the earlier assumptions that workers who may already be party to unconscious bias against their work capacities are those most likely to be the ones to face career penalties when working flexibly.

Yvonne Lott and I used the German SOEP (Lott and Chung, 2016) to examine how flexible schedules – that is, flexitime and working time autonomy – led to income premiums for men and women. We argue that because flexible working leads to increased working hours (overtime) and work intensity (Kelliher and Anderson, 2010), which has been shown to lead to increased productivity (Beauregard and Henry, 2009; Kelliher and de Menezes, 2019; Boltz et al, 2020), it could lead to income premiums as well. We found that flexible working does lead to income premiums partly due to the overtime the workers carry out, and for some it led to additional income on top of this. However, this was only true for men. This could be partially explained through the fact that men were more likely to increase their overtime hours when working flexibly. However, on closer inspection we found that even when women, especially mothers, increased their overtime hours when working flexibly, they were not compensated with additional income. For mothers, it seemed that they were working longer overtime hours in exchange for the possibility to work flexibly without being compensated even for the additional hours they carried out.

These results are mirrored in Glass and Noonan's (2016) study that examined the additional income gained by workers when working overtime when working from home, separating those who did those overtime hours in the office (or on the employer's premises) versus those who did those hours at home. They used the National Longitudinal Survey of Youth, which follows the life course of individuals born in the 1970s across time in the US. They concluded that the overtime done in the office was rewarded significantly more than the hours done at home. They showed that this gap was especially poignant for women rather than men. This again highlights the fact that when women work from home, managers are likely to assume that they are unable to carry out work as effectively as they do in the office, while for men it is assumed that they will be able to have stronger boundaries between the two spheres, influencing how the hours worked at home is compensated.

There is also evidence for a fatherhood bonus when requesting flexible working arrangements. Munsch (2016) shows that fathers were evaluated more positively than men without children and women with children when requesting teleworking even when requested for childcare purposes. Interestingly enough, in her study she did not find any evidence of a further motherhood penalty with flexibility stigma. Female workers who requested flexible working for childcare purposes were perceived more favourably compared to those who requested flexible working for environmental reasons. Brescoll et al (2013) argue that rather than just gender, the status of the worker also makes a difference. They found that lower-status working men requesting flexible schedules for childcare purposes were seen more favourably by managers compared to higher-status men requesting the same policy. On the other hand, higher-status men requesting flexible schedules for career progression purposes were also seen favourably by managers. They do not find a similar pattern for women, arguing that 'motherhood status is so strong in employment decision making that neither high-job status nor career justification for a flexibility request can modify it' (Brescoll et al, 2013: 382). This again evidences how our gender norms shape not only the outcomes of flexible working, but also access to such arrangements and how it is perceived by others.

Conclusion

Another manifestation of the flexibility paradox and the entrepreneurial-self culture can be found in the prevalence of flexibility stigma – namely the negative connotation towards those who work flexibly to meet family demands. As this chapter has examined, although we do see a slow decline in the perception that flexible working hinders the work of others or that it can lead to negative career outcomes, it is still prevalent in many of our societies. This prevalence of flexibility stigma also explains why workers end up working harder and longer when working flexibly, to overcompensate for the negative connotations they may experience (see also Kelliher and Andersen, 2010; Mazmanian et al, 2013). Changes in legislation including the expansion of rights to flexible working has not changed the prevalence of flexibility stigma much in the UK. What has shifted these perceptions, however, was the COVID-19 pandemic when workers were forced to work from home by law due to national lockdown regulations across countries. Such changes in the way flexible working was introduced as well as the extent to which it was used has changed the attitudes of both workers and managers, which we will examine in greater detail in Chapter 10.

The chapter further shows that flexibility stigma may be gendered in that men are more likely to hold negative views against flexible workers, while women who work flexibly may experience stigma and thus rightfully be more likely to fear the negative consequences of flexible working more often. These results can be understood in combination with the findings of Chapter 7, where we discussed how societal norms around men and women's roles shaped how men and women do, and are expected to, use flexibility in their work. Namely, there are societal beliefs that women, especially mothers, will or should use the flexibility in their work to meet family demands, and that they will or should prioritise family demands foremost. These assumptions around women's capacity and willingness to put family first was so strong to the point that mothers were penalised, or not compensated to the same degree as men were, when working flexibly. This was even the case when mothers worked longer and harder when working flexibly. On the other hand, men are likely to adhere to, and are expected to adhere to the work devotion schema, presenting themselves as the ideal worker – working long hours, putting work demands above that of family (Williams et al, 2013; Berdahl et al, 2018). This explains why many men may feel that workers prioritising family roles or workers balancing work with other aspects of their lives through flexible working is disruptive to the workgroups or organisations, hindering their day-to-day operations. I argue in this chapter that it is not only women who are at risk of this double-whammy stigma. Other disadvantaged workers towards whom managers or co-workers may hold unconscious bias regarding their work capacity and productivity may also be more likely to experience negative career outcomes when working flexibly. There was evidence of this for those with other care responsibilities and disabled workers (Chung, 2020b). More evidence is needed to explore this question for other groups such as minority ethnic or migrant workers, LGBTQ+ workers, and workers of other protected characteristics.

In the chapter, long-hours presenteeism-based work cultures and traditional gender norms were presented as some of the key underlying factors explaining why flexibility stigma exists in society and why it may impact women more than men. This raises an interesting question. As we know that work cultures and gender norms vary across the world (Hofstede et al, 1991; Chung and Schober, 2018), does this mean that flexibility stigma, and the flexibility paradox and its gendered outcomes, is only applicable to certain countries? This is the question we explore in the next chapter, Chapter 9, where we investigate the role of national contexts.

The importance of contexts

Introduction

In the previous chapter, we ended with the question whether flexibility stigma exists across all countries, and whether in all countries women will be the ones who suffer more from its prevalence. Given that norms around the 'ideal worker' are different across countries, and as countries differ in the extent to which traditional gender roles exist, we can expect some variations across countries. Flexible working is not used in a vacuum, and the socio-economic, cultural and institutional context in which it is used matter. As we have discussed in the previous chapters, according to capabilities approach theories, a person's capacity to use the 'freedom' given to oneself is limited by the context in which that individual is embedded (Hobson, 2011). The same could be found if we examine Foucault's (2010) theory of the subjectification of self and the rise of the homo-economicus which enables the flexibility paradox to occur. The crux of the argument lies in the context of widespread neo-liberalism and the shifts found in societal norms – and the individual's own identity – towards one that privilege capitalist market exchange values above all else. However, there are a variety of capitalisms (Hall and Soskice, 2001) and neo-liberalistic ideals are not as prevalent across all countries. In fact, examining some of the evidence of the flexibility and autonomy paradox, we see that most previous studies are from countries that are typically considered liberal countries (Esping-Andersen, 1990). The question arises then whether we would not see similar patterns in other countries where norms around work and work-life balance are very different. Similarly, we can expect to find variations in the degree to which the gendered flexibility paradox occurs across countries. One main reason why we expect to find and do find gendered patterns of the flexibility paradox was largely due to the patriarchal societal structures with strict gender norms around men and women's roles. Thus, in countries where such traditional gender norms do not exist, the gendered flexibility paradox may also not occur.

Due to the scope of the book, I will not be able to go into greater detail on the variance across organisations and sectors which is the focus of other studies and projects[1] (for example Kelly et al, 2011; Kelly et al, 2014; Kelly and Moen, 2020; van der Lippe and Lippényi, 2020; van der Lippe and Lippényi, 2021). However, much of the conclusions drawn from this chapter could be directly applicable to the organisational level in terms of understanding under which context flexible working can benefit both workers and companies. Put differently, the findings of this chapter can help us understand what changes we need to make at both company and national levels to ensure that flexible working 'works' for both workers, companies and for the society.

In this chapter, I first provide some theoretical framework to help us understand the role of key context factors in shaping flexible working practices. I start off with cultural norms around work and gender, as these were highlighted as key drivers of the flexibility paradox, flexibility stigma and its gendered outcome. However, socio-economic and institutional contexts also help shape flexible working practices. This includes national policies that shape the discourse around work-life balance, and institutions that shape worker's bargaining powers – both collectively and individually. I will then present empirical evidence of the importance of national contexts. Here, I present how national contexts shape the provision of flexible working arrangements at the company level, the take-up and access to flexible working at the individual level, the prevalence of flexibility stigma, and finally the outcomes of flexible working. This evidence is critical in helping us find potential solutions necessary to ensure that flexible working does not lead to unintended negative consequences – which is the focus of the final chapter of this book, Chapter 11.

Which contexts matter?

Of the different national contexts identified in the literature as key in shaping flexible working practices (for a summary see Chung, 2020a), here I present three key contexts – namely cultural normative context, institutional context and economic context – namely the labour market and economic conditions of the country. In sum, they relate to cultures around work, work-life balance, gender roles, and the negotiation power and insecurity of workers – gained or lost through union strength, collective bargaining or through labour market and economic conditions.

Work centrality

A key context that helps us understand why the flexibility paradox happens, or why the freedom over one's work leads to further or enhanced exploitation of one's labour, is our work culture and how work is prioritised in one's life. As examined in previous chapters, neo-liberalistic notions of self, the prevalence of the ideal-worker and long-hours work culture, and work taking priority over all else in life are some of the driving forces of why flexible working leads to long working hours and work spilling over to and encroaching on family life. We can expect that in countries where there is a more balanced notion of work and private life, and where all workers expect and are expected to have a good work-life balance, the flexibility paradox and stigmatised views against flexible workers will be less prevalent. There are various ways in which we can measure work and work-life balance cultures in societies. Some studies have done this through measuring the work ethic or work centrality of the country (for example, den Dulk et al, 2013; Chung, 2014). Here work centrality indicates how central work is to one's life in a given society (Van Oorschot, 2006) measured through asking respondents how much they agree to statements such as: 'Work should always come first, even if it means less spare time' or 'Work is a duty towards society' (some of this is examined in Chapters 1 and 5). We could expect that in countries where work is and is expected to be central to one's life, flexibility stigma against those who take up flexible working for care purposes to be more prevalent. This is again because in these countries workers are expected to devote themselves to work without having other responsibilities outside of work. This may then impact the way flexible working arrangements are provided, or taken up. Namely, employers may not feel a need to provide family-friendly flexible working arrangements, and even when they do workers will hesitate in taking them up due to stigmatised views around its take-up. We are also likely to see more evidence of the flexibility paradox, where flexible working is more likely to lead to long working hours and increased levels of work-family conflict, in work-centric cultures. Although not measuring work cultures directly, some scholars (for example, Präg and Mills, 2014) used the affluence of a country – namely GDP per capita – to indicate society's preference towards leisure and work. This is based on Mincer's (1962) theory that as countries become more affluent, people's preference towards leisure over paid work time increases – and accordingly work becomes less central to one's life.

Gender norms

As we examined in Chapter 7 when we discussed the gendered flexibility paradox, gender norms around men and women's roles are important in explaining why we find gender discrepancies in the outcomes of flexible working. Gender norms also influence how and for whom flexible working is stigmatised and leads to negative career outcomes – as examined in Chapter 8. Such gendered patterns in the outcomes of flexible working will be more evident in countries where gender roles are more traditional, especially in relation to men's breadwinning roles and women's caregiving responsibilities. On the other hand, in countries where gender roles are more egalitarian and men and women are expected to take on similar roles in the household and labour market – for example, where men are also expected to be involved in childcare and housework as much as women, and women are expected to be responsible for breadwinning as much as men – we would not expect clear gendered patterns in the outcomes of flexible working. In Kurowska's (2020) study of how homeworking increases 'necessary work', that is, paid and unpaid domestic working hours, we see that the discrepancy between men and women is more visible in Poland where gender norms are more traditional. However, in Sweden where gender norms are more egalitarian, she finds that men and women increase the amount of 'necessary work' at a similar rate when working from home. Gender norms can also shift employers' and co-workers' assumptions around women's flexible working. Stigmatised views around women's flexible working is largely based on the idea that women will prioritise family responsibilities when working flexibly. Thus, in egalitarian societies where both men and women are expected to prioritise work and family in a similar manner, it is unlikely that women will be stigmatised more. Due to this, we expect gender norms of a society to be key in explaining why we see the gendered flexibility paradox and stigma in some countries, but not in others (see also, Lott, 2015). In addition, societies with egalitarian gender norms may be those where a more balanced view around work-life may be prevalent. As both men and women take on dual roles in housework and paid work, both men and women will be unlikely to privilege work above other aspects of one's life. This entails that egalitarian gender norms may also help reduce work-centric values in societies, which can help reduce flexibility stigma for both men and women, and reduce the likelihood of the flexibility paradox to occur.

Family and social policy

National level institutions can help shape social norms around work, work-life balance and gender roles in a country. Scholars have argued that institutions, laws and policies shift the norms and culture in society and change the way individuals and organisations behave (DiMaggio and Powell, 1983; Künemund and Rein, 1999; Van Oorschot and Arts, 2005). For example, when the government provides generous family policies at the national level, it can change the norm around what the company should provide as family-friendly benefits (den Dulk et al, 2013). In countries with generous family policies, the access to and the use of flexible working arrangements are likely to be seen as part of the general terms of employment rather than 'a gift' that needs to be reciprocated (Been et al, 2017). The capabilities approach also argues that national policies can change the norms prevalent in societies in terms of what are acceptable work-family reconciliation practices for individuals (Hobson and Fahlén, 2009; Hobson, 2011). For example, when there are generous paternity-leave policies, it enables fathers to take a larger role in childcare and housework without being stigmatised for deviating away from what society considers as the role of men. Similarly, generous family policies at the national level will shape cultural norms around work-life balance – namely, where having a good work-life balance becomes the norm rather than the exception. This can help reduce stigma against those who use flexible working for care purposes which can help enhance workers' access to flexible working arrangements. Such a change in norms can also help ensure that flexible working does not lead to the encroachment on private lives. What is more, family policies can help shape norms around roles of men and women in society (Hook, 2006; Korpi et al, 2013). This can shape whose flexible working is stigmatised (more), and the outcomes of flexible working – for example, whether flexible working will lead to longer working hours or more involvement in unpaid domestic work and for whom.

Workers' bargaining powers

In addition to cultural normative views around work, work-life balance and gender roles, the insecurity and negotiation power of workers are other key factors that can explain why workers are unable to expand their private or leisure time when given more freedom and control over their work. As we examined in Chapter 1, the context in which the flexibility paradox takes place is one of the worker's declining bargaining power and the rise in employment and income insecurity among workers (Chung and Mau, 2014; van Oorschot and Chung, 2015).

According to the power resource theory, strong trade unions can not only protect workers in their own trade union or company, but can also ensure the strong protection of workers in general by providing 'contagion from the left' (Korpi, 1989: 316). Unions also influence workers' power by shaping national level policies and levelling up the general working conditions of workers in general, ensuring the better provision of family-friendly policies (Berg et al, 2004; Lyness et al, 2012; Chung, 2018). Strong unions can also help workers take up existing policies (Budd and Mumford, 2004; Seeleib-Kaiser and Fleckenstein, 2009) by providing protection against negative outcomes or the stigma/discrimination against workers using flexible working arrangements especially for care purposes. Thus, we can expect in countries where workers have stronger bargaining power – namely where there are large trade union memberships or where collective bargaining power of unions are strong – stigma against flexible working to be weaker, and flexible working to be less likely to lead to longer hours of work. In fact, a number of unions across Europe have been active in promoting flexible working for care purposes and tackling some of the negative stigma surrounding its use, highlighting the potential problems of blurring of boundaries (for example, ETUC, 2015; TUC, 2017).

Economic and labour market conditions

Workers' bargaining power is also shaped by the economic and labour market condition of the country. When the economy is under strain and there is a greater supply of labour than demand – namely high unemployment, workers will have weaker negotiation power over employers (see also Schor, 2008). Under such conditions, not only are employers less likely to provide family-friendly flexible working arrangements, but stigmatised views against workers who use flexible working for family-friendly purposes may also be more commonplace. Under such conditions, workers may also feel the need to enhance their own competitiveness within the labour market and prioritise enhancing their performance rather than facilitating private life demands when working flexibly. This will then result in workers working harder and longer when boundaries between work and private life is blurred, and is more likely to result in work encroaching on private life. Even when using flexible working for care purposes, workers may end up having to work harder or longer to avoid negative career consequences, which in times of high unemployment rates may be more consequential (see also, Chung, 2009; Kelly and Moen, 2020). On the other hand, when demand for workers outstrips supply – namely, low unemployment rates, employers may use family-friendly flexible working arrangements as incentives to help recruit and retain workers (Aryee et al, 1998; Batt and Valcour, 2003; Chung, 2009; den Dulk et al, 2013). Flexible working, even for care purposes, is less likely to be viewed with negative connotations under such contexts. Similarly, flexible working is less likely to lead to negative career outcomes – as employers may be keener to support workers' work-life balance demands when there is a shortage of workers in general. This can help workers to use flexible working for better work-life balance.

Prevalence of flexible working

One final factor I want to explore is what happens when flexible working becomes widespread and becomes more of a 'norm'. Would it change how it is viewed, stigmatised and consequently the outcome of flexible working? This is especially important when we consider the impact of COVID-19 when working from home became the norm (see Chapter 10 for more). What is more, we are increasingly seeing politicians and policy makers, policy stakeholders arguing for making 'flexibility the norm' in the future (Casalicchio, 2021; Stewart, 2021).

The widespread use of flexible working can help reduce biases against flexible workers for several reasons. First, it is due to self-interest (Sears et al, 1980). When flexible working is widespread, workers may be using the arrangements themselves or will be likely to use it in the future, and therefore may have a more favourable view towards flexible workers. Second, similar to what is found in intergroup contact theory (Pettigrew, 1998) the larger the number of workers that use flexible working arrangements, the more likely the workers are to have come into contact with someone who has used it. Similarly, managers are more likely to have experienced managing workers using flexible working practices. Although not all experiences may be positive, the more positive or neutral experiences can help reduce prejudiced bias against flexible workers. This is what happened during the COVID-19 pandemic, which we will explore in Chapter 10. When flexible working is used predominantly by a smaller group of workers, especially when that group is one that already suffers from biased views against their work capacities, for example mothers, it may lead to increased biases against flexible workers in general – for example it will be considered a 'mother's arrangement' (Young, 2018). This is similar to what has happened for part-time work (Fouarge and Muffels, 2009; Chung, 2020b). Despite the empirical evidence of part-time workers doing more work than others (Durbin and Tomlinson, 2010), and being more productive per hour (Künn-Nelen et al, 2013), part-time workers are considered to be less productive and less motivated. This is largely due to the biases against mothers' work capacity which makes up the majority of part-time workers. Thus, when flexible working arrangements become more widespread across groups of workers of different statuses and labour market positions, those working flexibly are less likely to be singled out and penalised/stigmatised. In sum, the larger the proportion of workers working flexibly, stigma against flexible workers is likely to be reduced. This is likely to result in more workers using flexible working to meet work-life balance needs, and a reduction in the likelihood of the flexibility paradox to occur.

Empirical evidence of the impact of national contexts

In this section, I will summarise studies exploring how national contexts shape flexible working practices – namely its provision, access and outcomes. I present the results of my own empirical analyses supplemented with that of others.

Provision of flexible working[2]

Using the European Company Survey (ECS) of 2009, I examined (Chung, 2014) how national contexts helped shape the provision of flexitime across 27 European countries (EU member states). Results show that one of the most important factors that is associated with the likelihood of a company providing flexitime to its workers, and the likelihood of providing it to a larger group of workers, was the work centrality of the country (see also, den Dulk et al, 2013). Similarly, the affluence of the country measured as GDP per capita was important (see also, Präg and Mills, 2014). The family-friendly nature of the labour market measured through female labour market participation rate, and generosity of family policies, was also found to be significant in explaining the provision of flexitime by European companies. This echoes findings of other studies using similar approaches (den Dulk et al, 2013; Kassinis and Stavrou, 2013). In countries where there is higher union density and where collective bargaining coverage rates are higher, companies are more likely to provide flexitime and more likely to provide it to a larger group of workers (see also, Berg et al, 2013). However, it is worth noting that these variables become insignificant when the more dominant variables – such as work centrality or GDP per capita – are included in the model. This could also be understood in terms of mediating relationships, where industrial relations and family policies may impact work cultures, which then has a more direct impact on the provision of flexitime.

Use and access to flexible working

Next I examine access to and use of flexible working arrangements as perceived by workers from across 30 European countries in 2015 using the EWCS (see also Chung, 2018; Chung, 2019a). Here, I look at workers' access to flexitime, working time autonomy (which is having more control over one's work), teleworking (working at home or in a public space like a café at least several times a month), and homeworking (working at home at least several times a month). Detailed descriptions of the variables used both at the individual and national levels can be found in the Appendix. Detailed analysis results are in Table A9.1. In countries where family policies are generous, especially when there is support for both parents to take part in the labour market through the provision of public childcare, are those where workers have better access to and are more likely to use flexible working arrangements. Similarly, in countries where there are more women taking part in the labour market, workers had better access to/used flexible working arrangements. It is important to note that these factors mattered in ensuring access to flexible working not only for women but also for men. This confirms previous studies (for example Been et al, 2017) that country-level policies can shape norms around family-friendly policies to make it more of a right rather than a gift, which enables better access to company-level policies such as flexible working. I also examined the relationship between generous paid leave for parents with access to flexible schedules (that is flexitime and working time autonomy) (Chung, 2019a). Results show that there is a U-shaped curve. Countries with very meagre or very generous levels of leave are those where the access to flexible schedules is low. Workers had the best access to flexible schedules in countries where parental leave was about a year. Such differences in the outcomes between childcare and paid leave relate to some of the policy goals these family policies aim to meet. Childcare can be considered a 'work-facilitating policy' (Misra et al, 2011), policies provided by the state that encourage women's labour market participation and where both partners are encouraged to take part in paid employment. Previous studies have shown that such policies are positively associated with ('crowd in') the access to (family-friendly) flexible working policies (see also, Chung, 2009; Lyness et al, 2012; den Dulk et al, 2013). Parental leave, on the other hand, can be considered a 'work-reducing policy' (Misra et al, 2011), policies that encourages parents to provide care themselves, while not leaving the labour force altogether. Although parental leave is technically 'gender neutral', it is mostly mothers who take this up due to existing gender norms and gender pay gaps (it makes more financial sense for the second earner to take leave in most cases). These policies can 'crowd in' the use of (family-friendly) flexible working only to a certain degree and then 'crowd out' – meaning countries that have very generous leave policies do not tend be associated with the widespread use of flexible working (Chung, 2019a). This is similar to the findings found for women's employment patterns and leave provisions (see Misra et al, 2011).

Confirming existing studies (Berg et al, 2004; Chung, 2009; Lyness et al, 2012; Präg and Mills, 2014; Chung, 2018), Table A9.1 shows that in countries where workers' bargaining powers are stronger, workers have better access to flexible working arrangements. Here, bargaining power is measured through high collective bargaining coverage and union density rates and low unemployment rates. The importance of workers' bargaining power in explaining access to flexible working arrangements was also found at the organisational level (Seeleib-Kaiser and Fleckenstein, 2009; Chung, 2018) – where the existence of a (strong) union at company level significantly influenced workers' access to flexible working (see also Chapter 3).

As expected, the most significant factors explaining workers' access to/ use of flexible working in a given country was the cultural normative views around work and gender roles. In countries where there are progressive views towards men and women's roles in society are those where workers have better access to all four types of flexible working arrangements (namely, flexitime, working time autonomy, teleworking, homeworking). On the other hand, in countries where work is believed to be more central to one's life are those where workers are less likely to have access to flexible working arrangements. Gender norms at the national level is one of the strongest factors explaining the cross-national variance in the access to/use of flexible working arrangements across Europe. However, it is important to note that gender norm is highly correlated with other national level variables, especially childcare coverage, female labour market participation rates and even union bargaining power variables (Table A9.3). This indicates that these contexts go hand in hand, with one influencing the other. Generous public childcare provisions and shared parental leave (for example well-paid earmarked paternity leave) shapes the way people think about men and women's roles in childcare, housework and breadwinning (Nepomnyaschy and Waldfogel, 2007; Hobson and Fahlén, 2009; Bünning, 2015; Andersen, 2018). In other words, family policies, workers' bargaining power and other institutions may be key in shaping normative views around gender roles and work, which can be a more direct cause of the provision of flexible working.

Flexibility stigma

Next, I examined the variance in the extent to which flexibility stigma exists in different countries. I examined the Flash Eurobarometer of 2018 which includes questions on flexibility stigma perceptions of workers.[3] First the survey asks the extent to which respondents agree to the statement: 'Making use of such flexible working arrangements is/was badly perceived by colleagues' (Figure 9.1). We see a large cross-national variation, with almost half of all respondents in Greece agreeing to this statement, while only about one in eight respondents believed this was the case in Denmark. The UK holds a position of being somewhat in the middle with approximately 29 per cent of respondents saying this was the case. The survey also asks: 'Making use of such flexible working arrangements has a negative impact on one's career (promotion, bonus, type of work allocated, and so on)' (Figure 9.2). Here again in Greece, but also Romania and Luxembourg, 44 per cent of all those surveyed agreed that flexible working leads to negative career outcomes, while unsurprisingly those mostly in Northern European countries such as Finland, Sweden and Estonia that number is less than 15 per cent. The UK again stands somewhat in the average position with just under a third of its respondents believing that flexible working leads to negative career outcomes, mirroring the results found in the 2011 WLB and 2018 BSA surveys in the previous chapter.

Next I examine whether cultural norms, institutions and socio-economic factors can explain the variation in the degree to which people hold stigmatised views around flexible working. Here, it is important to note that the two questions used here, rather than measuring people's biases *against* flexible workers, captures the perceived negative *consequences* of flexible working. One of the most important factors I wanted to examine is how widespread use of flexible working can shape the extent to which flexible working is stigmatised in a society. Examining Figure 9.3 and Table A9.2, the countries where there are more workers using schedule control arrangements (that is, flexitime or working time autonomy) (correlation -0.71 significant at the 0.001 level) or where there are more workers working from home (correlation -0.58 significant at the 0.001 level), are those where people are less likely to think

Figure 9.1: Proportion of individuals agreeing to the statement 'flexible working is badly perceived by colleagues' across European countries

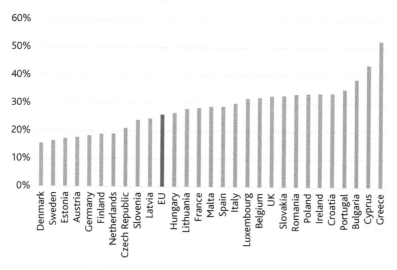

Source: Eurobarometer 2018 (weighted averages), author's calculation

Figure 9.2: Proportion of individuals agreeing to the statement 'flexible working has/had a negative impact on one's career' across European countries

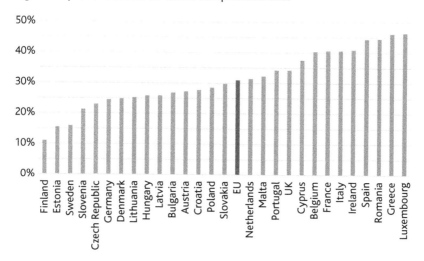

Source: Eurobarometer 2018 (weighted averages), author's calculation

Figure 9.3: Relationship between prevalence of flexible working (in 2015) and prevalence of flexibility stigma (in 2018)

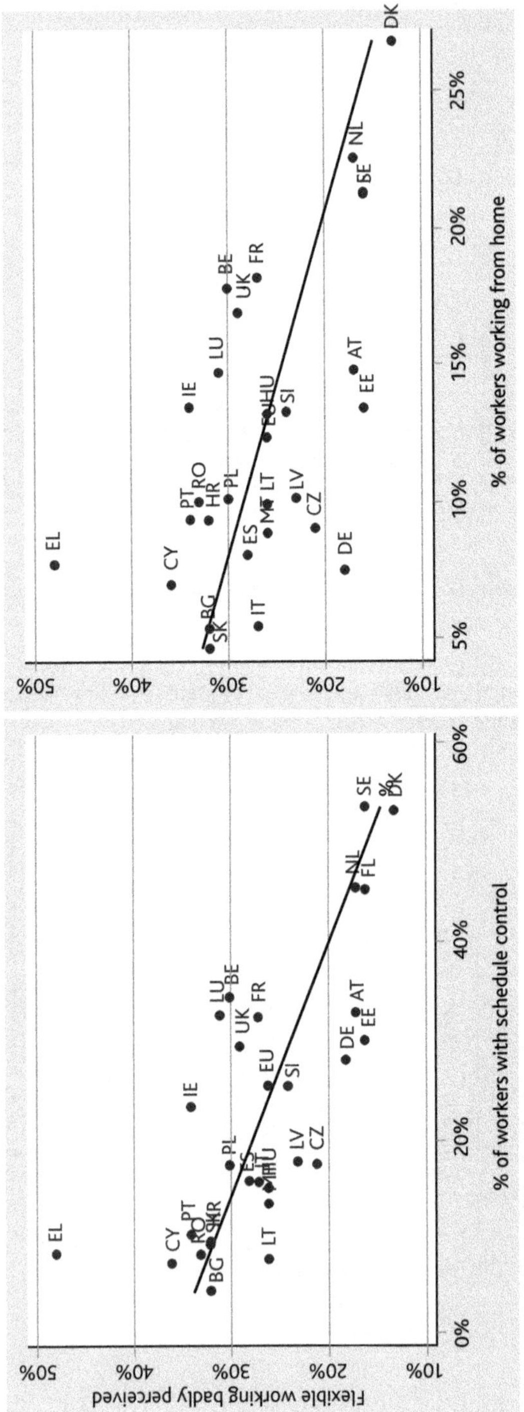

Source: EWCS, 2015 and Eurobarometer 2018 (author's calculation)

that flexible working is badly perceived by colleagues. Similarly, but to a lesser extent, the countries where schedule control arrangements are widely used are those where workers are less likely to think that flexible working has a negative impact on one's career (correlation -0.36 significant at the 0.05 level). However, we can also assume that this may be largely due to a reverse causality. Namely, people do not take up flexible working arrangements when they fear the consequences for their career, and know it will be perceived negatively by colleagues. Despite the fact that there is a significant time lag between the two variables (the use/take-up of flexible working data was gathered three years prior to when the data on stigma perceptions were captured), knowing that cultural norms do not shift rapidly (with the exception of large shocks and crises like COVID-19) we cannot exclude this possibility.

I also examined other factors that may be of relevance in reducing flexibility stigma. The results of the correlation matrix is in Table A9.2, for the total population and for men and women separately. I find that in countries with generous family policies both measured in terms of family policy expenditure and childcare coverage rates, where there are more women in the labour market, progressive gender norms, and somewhat where there are stronger unions, are those where workers are less likely to feel that flexible working is badly perceived by colleagues. Thus, countries where in general there are policies at the national level to support working families better or workers' work-life balance issues better, and there are more progressive views on men and women's roles in society, overall people are less inclined to believe that flexible working is perceived badly by others. Stronger unions can also help by providing workers better protection from discrimination and provide better working conditions (Fleckenstein and Seeleib-Kaiser, 2011) which can also help shape perceptions towards a number of family-friendly arrangements, including flexible working arrangements. On the other hand, in countries where there is high unemployment and in cultures where work is more central to people's lives, are those where workers are more likely to feel that flexible working is badly perceived by others. This is most likely due to the fact that when there is high unemployment, there is higher competition across workers for jobs and possibly an increased sense of insecurity which may increase the fear of deviating away from the ideal worker image. Similarly when work is central to one's life, it is not surprising that people hold negative views around workers working flexibly possibly for work-life balance purposes. On closer inspection we can see that many of the national contexts, such as family policy variables, collective bargaining coverage, explain the variance of men's flexibility stigma more than that of women. This could be linked to the fact that countries with generous family policies, especially with generous public childcare, generally promote the dual earning as well as dual-caring roles, meaning they focus on promoting men's role in care giving (Korpi et al, 2013). As we observed in Chapter 8, men are more inclined to hold negative views towards flexible workers. Family policies may thus help reduce these views of men by enabling a better more balanced view of work and private life.

Cross-national variation in the perception that flexible working leads to negative career outcomes is not significantly associated with any national contexts I examined with the exception of female labour market participation rates. In countries where there are more women in the labour market, people are less likely to believe that flexible working leads to negative career outcomes. Examining this closely, we see that access to flexitime/schedule control, unemployment rates, and to a certain extent access to working from home and family policy expenditure, also explain the variation across countries in the extent to which men agree to this statement, whereas this is not the case for women. We expected that national policies would impact women's positions more than those of men. However, rethinking the implications of the results, it does not fully contradict our assumptions. The stigma men hold influences the negative consequences women have to face (Chung, 2020b), possibly more than what women think. This is especially true if we consider that men are more likely to be in the position of power/supervisor roles making decisions about women's careers (Anker, 1997). In other words, national level policies as well as prevalence of flexible working influencing men's views around flexibility stigma may help support women's careers and use of flexible working.

Outcomes of flexible working[4]

As we have seen, national level institutions, culture and labour market and economic conditions help explain how widespread flexible working is in a country. These factors and the prevalence of flexible working then explain the extent to which flexible working is stigmatised in a country. Thus, it is not surprising that such national contexts shape the outcomes of flexible working. This is the main focus of the analysis (Chung, 2021c) where I explore which national contexts moderate the relationship between flexible working and work-to-family conflict. Work-to-family conflict is the conflict individuals feel at home due to the demands from the work spheres. Here, rather than examining the different types of work-family conflict separately – as I have done in Chapters 4 and 6 – I combined them in a single index,[5] as has been done in many previous studies (Kelly et al, 2011; Glavin and Schieman, 2012). It combines the extent to which individuals agree with the following five statements: in the past 12 months did you … 'keep worrying about work problems when you are not working?', 'feel too tired after work to do some of the household jobs which need to be done?', 'find that your job prevented you from giving the time you wanted to your family?', 'how often have you worked in your free time to meet work demands?' and finally, 'In general, how do your working hours fit in with your family or social commitments outside work?' All variables are coded so a higher score entails a higher level of work-to-family conflict.

The results (Figure 9.4 and Table A9.5) show that in countries with generous childcare policies, where there are more women in the labour market, and gender norms are more progressive, are those where the positive association between flexitime and work-family conflict is weaker. This result may be interpreted as where there are more family-friendly work cultures or where gender roles are not as traditional/strictly divided – the nature of flexitime can change, allowing it to be used in a more family-friendly manner or reduce the negative consequences that may arise. This may also entail that in these countries, we may not necessarily expect the flexibility paradox and its gendered outcomes to occur. Additional analysis shows that generous family policies seem to moderate the negative outcomes of flexitime especially for women. In countries with very generous family policies, women with access to flexitime feel lower levels of work-family conflict compared to those without flexitime access. Whereas, in countries with very meagre levels of family policies, women with access to flexitime feel higher levels of work-family conflict compared to those without flexitime. Similarly, although the significance level is just above the traditional $p<0.05$ level, work-centred cultures and workers' weak bargaining powers (as measured by low collective bargaining coverage and union density) also moderate the relationship between flexitime and work-family conflict. Similar results are found for teleworking (Table A9.6). In other words, flexitime and teleworking is associated with higher levels of work-family conflict. However, this is especially true in countries where work is central to people's lives and workers have weak bargaining powers. This means that in such societies, we can expect the flexibility paradox to occur more frequently, possibly to a larger group of workers to a larger degree. This can potentially explain why we see so many case studies of the flexibility paradox outcomes in countries like the US, the UK (for example, Kelliher and Anderson, 2010; Mazmanian et al, 2013) where we know workers' bargaining powers are weak, family policies are not generous and work centrality norms prevail. On the other hand, in countries such as Denmark or Sweden where gender norms are more progressive, family policies are also generous and there are more women in the labour market, workers' bargaining powers are strong, the flexibility paradox may not be as evident.

Finally, I examined whether the widespread use of flexible working practices may result in flexible working enhancing workers' work–life balance rather than resulting in the flexibility paradox. In the previous section, we found that as flexible working becomes more widespread, the stigma against flexible workers decreases. Similarly, results show that in countries where flexitime is widespread it is less likely to be associated with work-family conflict (see also, Kelly et al, 2014; van der Lippe and Lippényi, 2020). The

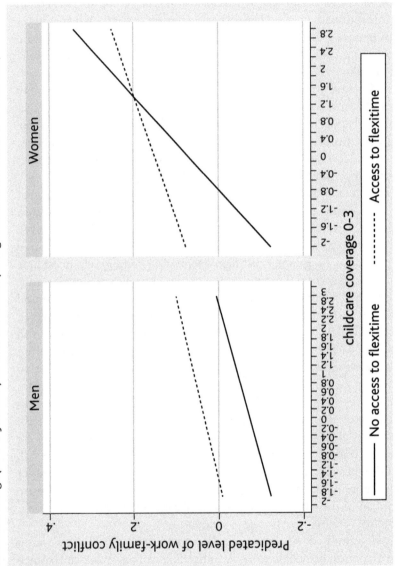

Figure 9.4: The association between flexitime and work-family conflict across countries with different levels of childcare coverage (for 0–3-year-olds) for men and women (having controlled for a number of covariates)

Source: Chung, 2021c

Note: childcare coverage is standardised.

prevalence of flexitime was also one of the most important factors explaining cross-national variation in the association between flexitime and work-family conflict. This can mean, on the one hand, that the widespread use of flexitime can be one of the most important ways to tackle the negative (unintended) consequences of flexible working. However, as we know from the previous section and other studies (for example, den Dulk et al, 2012; Lyness et al, 2012; den Dulk et al, 2013; Kassinis and Stavrou, 2013; Präg and Mills, 2014; Chung, 2019a), national institutional and cultural contexts largely shape the prevalence of flexible working. Thus, the prevalence of flexible working may be more of a mediator. Namely that national family policies and cultural norms shape the use of flexible working practices, and when flexible working is widespread it can potentially result in positive outcomes not only in terms of reducing stigma around its use but also ensuring it leads to positive work–life balance outcomes.

Conclusion

Flexible working is not used in a vacuum and the contexts in which it is used can shape its outcomes. As outlined in the previous chapters, it was posited that contexts such as cultural norms around the devotion towards work and gender roles enable the flexibility paradox and its gender patterns to occur. This chapter's goal was to understand whether changes in institutional and cultural contexts can then possibly alter the outcomes of flexible working. Finding out under which contexts we can stop the flexibility paradox occurring, and reduce stigmatised views towards flexible workers, will help us find solutions to ensure that the unintended consequences of flexible working are eliminated.

I found that in cultures where work is not so central to one's life and where progressive gender norms prevail are where companies provide and workers have better access to flexible working arrangements. I also found that national institutional contexts – such as generous national level family policies and workers' strong bargaining positions – also help shape the widespread use of flexible working practices. In fact, it is likely that national institutions help shape the cultural norms around work, work–life balance and gender roles, which can be crucial in determining the provision of flexible working arrangements at company level, and workers' take-up of these arrangements. The prevalence of flexible working as well as the other national institutional and cultural contexts were also important in explaining the extent to which flexible working was stigmatised in a society, and the extent to which flexible working was likely to lead to higher levels of perceived work-family conflict. Although institutions and cultural norms also help shape the outcomes of flexible working, their influence seems to be more by guaranteeing the more widespread use of flexible working arrangements. Widespread use of flexible working arrangements decreases the likelihood of flexible working for family purposes being stigmatised by others, which then helps ensure that the flexibility paradox patterns do not occur as much.

The results of these analyses tell us one thing. The flexibility paradox and its gendered outcomes are not inevitable. In fact, many of the studies that evidence patterns of the flexibility paradox and the gendered outcomes of flexible working have been based in countries such as the US and the UK where we know the ideal working culture prevails and gender norms are traditional. This means that, on the one hand, we may not find the same degree of paradoxical outcomes of flexible working in certain countries like Sweden, Denmark or other countries where family policies are generous, workers' bargaining powers are strong, and cultural norms around work are more balanced with other aspects of one's life, and gender roles are more egalitarian. It is not surprising that these countries are those where flexible working is more widespread across the society (see Chapter 2). It can also mean that when contexts change, the flexibility paradox may no longer prevail (Kelly et al, 2011).

Although sudden changes in cultures and institutions are unlikely to occur, we have seen what happens when flexible working becomes the norm recently. This is namely the COVID-19 pandemic and the large-scale homeworking that followed due to national government-led lockdowns to contain the spread of the virus. This is the topic we will be examining in the next chapter, Chapter 10, where I examine whether we see large changes in the flexibility paradox and flexibility stigma during the pandemic. The results presented in this chapter leads us to another important point. Through changing the contexts in which flexible working is introduced, we may be able to tackle some of the negative outcomes it can lead to for workers, resulting in good outcomes for companies and society as a whole as well. This is what I will be exploring in the final chapter, Chapter 11, where I outline what we need to do next and provide key recommendations for policy makers both at the (inter)national level, company level, and for individual workers.

Notes

[1] There are two projects I would highly recommend readers to look at. The first one is the Work, Family & Health Network (WFHN) in the US led by an interdisciplinary team of researchers, including Erin Kelly and Phyllis Moen, which ran an intervention study of American workplaces to improve the health of workers and their families, while benefiting employers. More about this project can be found here: https://workfamilyhealthnetwork.org/

The other project I would recommend on the importance of organisational-level context is the project funded by the European Research Council Advance Grant namely Sustainable Workforce by Tanja van der Lippe which gathered surveys from 11,000 workforces across nine countries. For more information: www.uu.nl/en/news/5-important-findings-from-sustainable-workforce-research

[2] Detailed results can be found in Chung (2014).

[3] For more information about the 2018 Flash Eurobarometer on work-life balance see: https://data.europa.eu/euodp/en/data/dataset/S2185_470_ENG

[4] This is largely based on the results from Chung (2021c). Detailed analysis tables and results can be found in the paper and the accompanying online appendix.

[5] A principle components analysis of these variables resulted in a one-factor solution, indicating that the variables can be considered to represent one underlying latent factor. The Cronbach alpha was 0.70 indicating internal consistency.

10

COVID-19 and flexible working

Introduction

One of the key findings drawn from the previous chapter was that as flexible working becomes more widespread, people are less likely to hold stigmatised views against flexible workers, and it is less likely to lead to negative outcomes in terms of work-life balance. The results were based on cross-national studies which meant that although we do see strong associations we cannot guarantee the direction of the relationship (for example, which came first, stigma or prevalence of flexible working?). We also cannot be certain if the more widespread use of flexible working or changes in contexts are the real causes or if it has to do with something else we failed to observe.[1] In other words, the question arises whether we would see positive changes to flexible working practices in countries like the UK and the US if we were to change some of the contexts. These are difficult questions to answer given that cultures, policies and the take-up of flexible working do not usually change rapidly enough for us to properly answer them.

Then the COVID-19 pandemic happened and provided us with a very unique experimental opportunity to answer some of these difficult questions: What happens if a large group of workers starts working from home? How would this sudden rise of flexible working change stigmatised views towards flexible workers? How would this change the flexibility paradox patterns we have observed previously? How would this change the gender dynamics of the outcomes of flexible working? Just to clarify, I am not making light of the devastating impact the pandemic had in terms of not only deaths but the health, mental health and economic impact it has had on millions of families. However, given the scope of this book, the COVID-19 pandemic provided us with a once in a lifetime opportunity to better understand how (drastic) changes in contexts may change much of our existing understanding about the nature and outcomes of flexible working. This chapter aims to explore these questions by summarising key studies carried out during the pandemic. The conclusion shows that the widespread use of flexible working helped change the perception towards flexible working to be more positive. However, given that our work culture, work-life balance and gender cultures remained as is, many of the flexibility paradox patterns also remained. This provides us with evidence that the widespread use of flexible working alone may be insufficient to tackle the flexibility paradox phenomenon.

COVID-19 context

COVID-19 global context

COVID-19 is a severe acute respiratory syndrome coronavirus 2 (SARS-CoV-2) first identified in December 2019 in Wuhan, China. The World Health Organization declared the outbreak a Public Health Emergency of International Concern in January 2020 and a pandemic in March 2020. At the time of writing the pandemic is still ongoing but already it has been considered one of the deadliest pandemics in history, with more than 250 million cases confirmed and over 5 million deaths attributed to the COVID-19 virus across the globe (based on www.worldometers.info/coronavirus, as at 11 November 2021). To contain the virus many governments across the world enforced a lockdown, especially at the beginning of the pandemic. Many went into subsequent lockdowns during 2020/21 where many countries suffered from the second/third + spikes in numbers due to new mutations.[2] Across the world, many governments asked people to not leave their house unless for emergency reasons, asking many to work from home if possible. This led to a sharp rise in workers working from home during the pandemic (Buffer, 2020; Eurofound, 2020). Furthermore, governments closed schools and other childcare facilities – the move to online learning during these periods meant that there have been significant changes in the care and housework demands faced by parents. It is impossible to go into greater detail about the government policies of several different countries in this chapter, due to limited space. However, given that I will be examining data gathered from the UK to better understand the issues around the flexibility paradox during the pandemic, I present some key contexts of COVID-19 for the UK.

COVID-19 context in the UK

The UK has had over 9 million cases and over 142,000 deaths (data from worldometers.info, as at 11 November 2021), reaching one of the highest per capita cases and deaths among the larger industrialised countries. The UK government announced its first full-scale lockdown measures as of 23 March 2020. Lockdown measures included asking the public to work from home if possible, and to stay at home with the exception of essential travel for food and medical issues. All non-essential retail shops and all leisure and hospitality sectors, such as pubs, restaurants, hotels and gyms, were shut during this period. These lockdown measures were eased over the course of the summer where many of the sectors were partially open under COVID-19-related restrictions. With the lockdown, the government announced the closure of schools and other childcare facilities as of 20 March 2020, with the exception of childcare facilities for key workers such as those working in the health and social care sectors, retail and transport, and essential government workers. From 1 June 2020, schools were reopened but limited to three year groups: Reception, Year 1 and Year 6. Nurseries and other childcare facilities for preschool children were allowed to open from this time. Schools returned fully in September 2020 (Hill, 2020). The UK had its second national lockdown in November 2020 although schools remained open during this period. The UK went through a third nationwide lockdown in January 2021. On 22 February 2021 Boris Johnson, the UK's Prime Minister at the time, announced his 'one way road to freedom', which included plans for children to be back in school from 8 March 2021, with small incremental changes relaxing social distancing rules until 21 June 2021 where all legal limits on social contacts were planned to end (BBC, 2021). Although there were some delays, the UK eased the majority of its restrictions by July 2021.

The UK government introduced the Job Retention Scheme as of 20 March 2020 alongside the enhanced lockdown measures in place. The Job Retention Scheme provides 80 per cent of wages of employees up to £2500 a month. Initially introduced until July 2020, the scheme was further extended to autumn 2021. Despite these efforts, 2.7 million people claimed unemployment benefit during March to July of 2020, and there was a record number of 7.5 million people away from work during the month of June 2020 according to Official Statistics (King, 2020). Furthermore, the UK had the worst economic recession over the first COVID-19 lockdown period with an economic decline of 20.4 per cent during April and June 2020 compared to previous periods, effectively wiping out 17 years of economic growth (Nelson, 2020; ONS, 2020f).

Flexible working during the pandemic

The prevalence of working from home during the pandemic

Before the pandemic, only few workers were able to work from home on a regular basis. For example, in the EWCS of 2015 only about 8 per cent of the surveyed workers across Europe said they worked from home at least several times a week. During the pandemic, July 2020, close to half (47.9 per cent) of all workers surveyed were working from home exclusively (33.7 per cent) or partially (14.2 per cent) (Eurofound, 2020) across 27 European countries. Figures shows that the rise in homeworking was higher for women compared to men. While in the 2015 survey, a similar proportion of men and women responded that they were working from home (Chung and van der Lippe, 2020), during the pandemic, 50 per cent of women were working from home while only about 45 per cent of men were able to do so. A similar result was found for the UK. Prior to the pandemic, more men were working from home compared to women (Chung and van der Horst, 2020; ONS, 2020a). During the pandemic, slightly more women (48 per cent) compared to men (46 per cent) were working from home (ONS, 2020d). This provides some hope that employers may have relaxed their assumptions of workers' ability and willingness to carry out their work when working from home. Although more conclusive evidence is needed, this change in attitude may have benefitted the more disadvantaged workers who were unable to work from home previously – for example women and mothers.

Having said that, the COVID-19 pandemic did not do much in reducing the gap in access to homeworking across occupational groups. As we have seen in Chapter 3, prior to the pandemic, higher-educated workers in higher-status occupations had better access to flexible working arrangements that gave workers control over when and where they worked (Chung, 2019a). Despite some changes (ONS, 2020d) (Figure 10.1), it was white-collar workers in the top three occupational groups – namely, managers, professionals and associate professionals and technicians, that were able to work from home. Even during the lockdown periods, those in the lower-paid jobs – such as skilled trades occupations, caring leisure and other services occupations, were less able to do so (ONS, 2020d). However, it is still worth noting that even in occupations where one would think it is impossible to carry out work from home, many workers were able to do so. For example, many health care professionals moved towards an online video and telephone consultation system during the lockdown periods.[3] As schools were closed, the majority of education was carried out via online home-learning systems – meaning teachers were also able to/had to work from home. One major improvement we see during the pandemic was the access to homeworking found for workers working in

Figure 10.1: The proportion of workers who were able to do any work from home in the reference week in April for the UK (per cent)

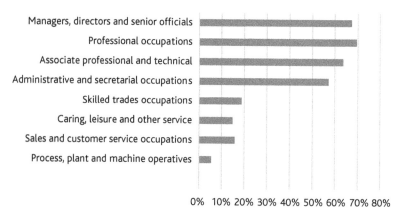

Data: ONS (2020d)

administrative and secretarial occupations. Although the nature of the work they carry out is not at odds with homeworking, many of these workers did not have access to homeworking prior to the pandemic (only one in ten worked from home based on the 2019 data). Administrative and secretarial occupations have seen one of the largest gains in access to homeworking with more than half (57 per cent) working from home in April 2020, most of whom did so because of the virus (86 per cent) (ONS, 2020c; ONS, 2020d). This pattern can partly explain why we see a large increase in women's homeworking during the pandemic, given that the majority of those in administrative and secretarial occupations are women. Such changes may have occurred despite managers' concerns regarding women's, especially mothers', capacity and commitment towards work when working from home (see Chapters 7 and 8). When given the choice between no work being carried out during the pandemic versus allowing workers to work from home, managers chose to do the latter.

Changing the perception towards flexible working

The pandemic has provided a good natural experimental setting to see how large-scale homeworking can change the perception towards flexible working. In fact, during the pandemic, not only was homeworking used more frequently, but also, more workers were working at home full-time (five days a week). Most importantly, it was not done at the request of the worker but enforced by the government or employers. As we will see later, this has largely shifted the way people think about flexible working.

Managers' perception

To understand changes in managers' perception towards homeworking, we conducted a survey of over 750 UK managers (those with a supervisory role of at least one person) between 24 July and 11 August 2020 (Forbes et al, 2020). We found that the majority of managers surveyed responded that working from home increases productivity (58 per cent) and concentration (51 per cent), and motivation (54 per cent), with significant changes in these perceptions compared to before the COVID-19 outbreak. For example, while 49 per cent of managers agreed that working from home is a performance-enhancing tool prior to the pandemic, 68 per cent believed this was the case during the pandemic. Stigma against flexible workers has decreased as well. Although we do not have information about managers' perception before the COVID-19 pandemic, in the summer of 2020, only 23 per cent of managers disagreed that flexible workers are just as likely to be promoted as those who do not work flexibly, and only 11 per cent agreed that flexible workers are less committed.

Similar findings could be seen in surveys conducted by other groups such as the Chartered Management Institute (CMI) or the Chartered Institute for Personnel Development (CIPD). In their surveys of managers across the UK, most managers reported no significant changes in productivity when workers were largely or partly working from home, with many noting that they have seen increases in productivity of those working from home (CIPD, 2020; CMI, 2020). For example, according to a CIPD survey, using data gathered between December 2020 and January 2021 of over 2,100 managers, 33 per cent of managers saw an improvement in productivity due to homeworking, while 38 per cent reported no significant change (CIPD, 2021).

However, it is also important to note that in all surveys, managers also voiced concerns over managing a workforce that largely worked from home. These included issues around collaboration and communication, providing sufficient support including digital and other infrastructure to work from home. For example, in the CIPD survey of managers, 26 per cent of managers reported issues around difficulties in staff interaction and cooperation as a problem of large-scale homeworking (CIPD, 2021). However, the most commonly voiced concerns of managers were around workers' isolation (44 per cent of all managers in the CIPD survey) and well-being, including issues around workers' lack of clear boundaries between work and non-work spheres leading to boundary blurring and long-hours work (CIPD, 2020; Forbes et al, 2020; CIPD, 2021; RSPH, 2021). This shows that even managers themselves have seen evidence of the flexibility paradox – blurring boundaries, long working hours – occurring even during the pandemic even when flexible working was an enforced policy rather than a 'gift' given to workers.

Employees' perception

To understand workers' own experiences of working from home during the pandemic, we gathered data from 1,160 individuals across the UK between 22 May and 15 June 2020 (Chung et al, 2020b) – a period when workers generally were asked to work from home due to social distancing measures. As we can see in Figure 10.2, as expected, managers' support towards workers working from home has increased drastically. According to those who were working from home during the COVID-19 lockdown, 90 per cent responded that their managers were supportive of homeworking (up from 50 per cent before the lockdown). This increase has been seen across all groups in our data, but the largest increase comes from mothers (76 per cent), many of whom did not feel that there was much management support prior to the lockdown (38 per cent agreed that managers were supportive prior to the pandemic) (Chung et al, 2020b). However, it is worth noting that mothers were still the least likely to say that their managers were supportive of their homeworking, compared to women without children, and men both with and without children. Despite some improvements, managers' bias towards mothers' homeworking capacities (Munsch, 2016) may not have been completely alleviated.

We also see in Figure 10.2 a slight reduction in employees' perception that working from home negatively impacts colleagues (from 15 per cent pre-pandemic to 13 per cent during the pandemic), and that it can lead to negative career outcomes (from 16 per cent to 10 per cent) among those who worked from home during the lockdown. However, we do not see such changes in flexibility stigma perception among those who were not working from home, although for both groups this perception was not as prevalent compared to what we have seen in previous data (see Chapter 8). This may be because we are asking for retrospective information about how respondents thought of these issues before the lockdown during the time we as a society had been experiencing homeworking on a mass scale for the past two to three months. This experience may have already shaped people's beliefs on flexibility stigma, changing what they remember as their perceptions were prior to the lockdown. Another positive change is that employees are less likely to say that there is a long hour work culture at their workplace – namely those who agree that you need to work long hours to succeed in the workplace. Although we do not see a big change it is moving in a positive direction.

Although the findings from the survey sheds some light on the changes in the perception towards flexible working of workers in the UK, given the small sample size and due to the sampling procedure, we cannot guarantee that the data represents the overall working population of the UK. Thus, to support the findings I have examined the data from the most recent survey of employees carried out by the UK department of Business, Energy, and Industrial Strategies – namely, the Employee Rights and Experience Survey of 2020. The survey was carried out between 14 May and 8 June 2020, and covers close to 6,000 employees across the UK. It is one of the largest and most representative surveys of UK employees and their working conditions. Although the survey asked workers to think about pre-COVID-19 periods of work when things were 'normal', we expect workers to have been influenced by the large-scale homeworking that was in place during the period of the data collection and can provide us with information about the changes in the perception towards flexible working during the COVID-19 pandemic.

In this survey, respondents were asked the degree to which they agreed with different statements on flexible working. Twenty-six per cent of individuals agreed that flexible working makes more work for others, a significant decline from the 35 per cent who agreed to this statement in 2011. Twenty-eight per cent agreed that flexible workers are less likely to be promoted – again a sizeable decrease from 32 per cent in 2011. What is more, of those who

Figure 10.2: The perception of management support and impact of working from home before and during the COVID-19 lockdown (per cent)

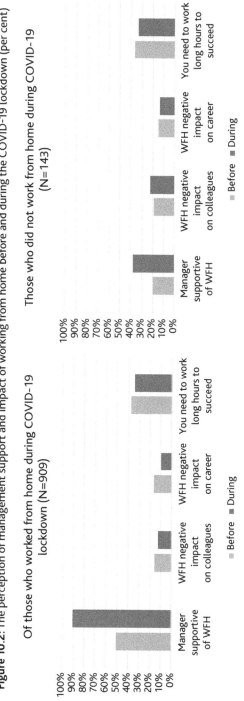

Source: Chung et al, 2020b

worked flexibly 88 per cent noted a positive outcome of working flexibly while 44 per cent (also) noted a negative. Some of the most significant positive outcomes noted by workers included improved work–life balance (86 per cent), making the workplace a better place to work (67 per cent), and increased productivity (57 per cent). Some of the negative outcomes included lack of social interaction (11 per cent), difficulty communicating with team (7 per cent), reduced income (7 per cent) and working more than the contracted hours (7 per cent).

Outcomes of flexible working during the pandemic

Given that homeworking was not carried out as a request from the workers themselves, and due to the positive experience managers had (for example improved productivity) in managing workers who were working from home, we saw that the stigma against flexible workers decreased during the pandemic. The question then remains whether we will still see the same type of flexibility paradox we found evidenced in Chapter 6 during the COVID-19 pandemic. As we have seen in Chapter 9, the large-scale expansion of flexible working is associated with positive outcomes, or less negative outcomes (van der Lippe and Lippényi, 2020; Chung, 2021c). Thus, on the one hand, given that flexible working was widespread during the pandemic, we would expect to see less of the flexibility paradox patterns of long-hours work and less of the gendered patterns of flexible working outcomes, that is, leading to more of a traditionalised division of housework and childcare. However, despite the changed context we may also find that the flexibility paradox outcomes still remain especially given that much of the other contexts such as work and gender cultures did not change. Actually, given the sharp rise in care demands (and home-schooling demands) parents had to face, we may even see a further traditionalisation of gender roles through flexible working during the pandemic. Similarly, given the rise in insecurity during the pandemic, we are also likely to see the blurring of boundaries leading to encroachment of work on private lives. We examine these questions in the following section.

Long-hours work

There are many reports of workers working longer rather than shorter hours when working from home during the COVID-19 pandemic. For example, Bloomberg along with NordVPN teams analysed the patterns of work using data from across ten different countries (Austria, Belgium, Canada, Denmark, France, Italy, the Netherlands, Spain, the UK and the US) of the amount of time workers were logged onto their Virtual Private Network (VPN) system. VPN systems allow workers to log on remotely to company servers, and for many workers they need to be logged on to do their work or access their emails and so on. The results show that in March–April 2020, workers on average logged on to their VPN longer compared to pre-pandemic times in all countries analysed with the exception of Italy. This was up to two to three hours more in countries like Canada, the UK and the US. By January 2021, some countries such as Belgium, Denmark, and to a certain extent Spain, workers' VPN connection hours have gone back to pre-pandemic figures. However, in Italy the number has risen, and in Canada, the UK and the US, the increased number of working hours found in the early stages of the pandemic remained the same (Meakin, 2021; Osborne, 2021).

However, these figures do not necessarily mean that workers have been working during the entire time they were logged onto the VPN systems – although the same could be said about workers sat in front of the computer in the office in pre-pandemic times. To overcome this issue of 'idle time', an analysis carried out by Atlassian examines VPN activities of workers focused more on direct interactions with user interfaces, such as creating a document, updating a ticket and so on. Not to say all 'productive' work entails such engagement – that is, thinking time counts as working hours – such an approach allows us to possibly discount time where workers are logged on to the VPN systems yet maybe doing other 'non-work'-related tasks. The data was gathered from countries across the world, such as Japan, South Korea, India, Israel, Turkey, Spain, Germany, France, Ireland, Sweden, the UK, the US, Canada and Australia (Friedman, 2020). Even using this method, they found that workers on average worked longer during the pandemic periods compared to pre-pandemic times. The only exception to this was South Korean workers who were already working very long hours during pre-pandemic times. The long-hours work that workers were carrying out were largely due to workers starting work earlier (before 9am) than they would have normally, and more so working later in the evenings (past 6pm) than they had during pre-pandemic times. However, the study also found that in most countries, workers were engaging less during the day than they did pre-pandemic times. In other words, workers working from home were working longer in part due to the blurring of boundaries between work and family life. Whereas before the pandemic, when workers were working largely from the office, they would have had a stricter border of time and space between work and non-work spheres, that is, starting work in the office at 9am, ending around 5–6pm and travelling back home. During the pandemic, workers started work early – possibly because of the lack of commuting and preparation times, took a bit longer during lunch times (possibly to include a walk or some other non-work activity), but ended up working until late. This may especially happen because people were no longer allowed to socialise during the lockdown, leaving workers without much else to do in the evenings. However, this may be an indication that the flexibility paradox still remained during the pandemic. Similar patterns were found in the ONS Time Use study examining parental working time during the pandemic (ONS, 2020g). Now without such clear boundaries, work was happening at all times of the day with work leading to encroachment on non-work spheres.

Blurring of boundaries

Blurring of boundaries between work and home life have been found to be the most cited negative outcome of working from home in our own survey of workers in the UK (Chung et al, 2020b). For example, close to two thirds of working parents in our data responded that they had experienced it. This pattern may have been inevitable for some workers with childcare responsibilities, where during the day they had no option but to carry out childcare, home-schooling, and housework (such as cooking) while working. Flexible working was used as a tool for many mothers to be able to maintain their working hours during the lockdown, carrying out both unpaid/care work and paid work. For example, in the ONS Time Use study, it was observed that many parents were working early in the morning – before 9am, and then again late in the evening between 6pm and 11pm during the lockdown periods to free up the afternoon for childcare, especially home-schooling (ONS, 2020g). In our managers' survey, many managers noted the use of flexible working in terms of *when* work is conducted as a strategy used to ensure working parents were able to carry out work – as this quote from a manager illustrates when asked about the most significant challenge of managing home workers (for more, see Forbes et al, 2020):

> 'The most significant challenge of managing home workers ... mostly revolved around childcare issues and having to be more flexible to accommodate those members of staff with children. So I'm allowing people to start work earlier then log off in the middle of the day if they need to, and I'm allowing staff to work later if they need to. My approach is to be flexible to their needs whilst simultaneously making sure the business needs are covered from 9–5 as well.' (Male line manager in a large health and social work sector)

However, this meant that parents, and especially women who were mainly responsible for childcare during the pandemic, were 'working' – that is, both paid and unpaid work – throughout the pandemic without many breaks. They were using the flexibility in their work to squeeze in as much work and family care/housework demands as possible – as this quote from a social worker in an article in *The Guardian* illustrates (Walter, 2021):

Their idea of flexibility is just to say I can catch up on the office work in evenings and weekends. As a social worker you always have to work extra hours anyway. This just meant that I was working for hours in the evenings and weekends. In the end I collapsed. I burned out. I was signed off sick for a month. (Maria – social worker from Shropshire, *The Guardian*, 28 February 2021)

In this way, flexible working during the pandemic could be seen as the ultimate 'exploitation tool' (Sullivan and Lewis, 2001; Hilbrecht et al, 2008) – as it was used to ensure workers were able to maintain their workload without any altercations in times of crisis where they were faced with an enormous amount of family care demands. However, the blurring of boundaries and increase in working hours was not something that was limited to working parents. More than half of non-parents in our survey noted that they had experienced this blurring of boundaries during the first lockdown in the UK (Chung et al, 2020b). In addition to this, more than a quarter of those surveyed noted that they had also experienced increased workload/hours and work-related stress while working from home during the first lockdown in the UK. This is illustrated in the quotes from workers when asked about the negative experiences of working from home: "I just feel unable to escape from work, I have no privacy, it has invaded my home and intrudes on every aspect of my life" (Woman working in medium-sized professional scientific technical activity sector company); "Burnout with little space away from work, worse to my mental health" (Woman working in large higher education sector).

For workers without children or any other additional care roles, working from home may have meant that they had fewer distractions which may have exacerbated the expansion of work during lockdown – as mentioned by our manager's quote: "The biggest challenge has been ensuring the team maintain a good work/life balance as initially when they moved to working from home they would switch on the laptop to work if there was nothing in TV" (Female senior manager in a medium-sized real estate sector).

Such patterns of flexible working leading to longer hours, or work encroaching on non-work spheres, both in terms of time but also in terms of mental space, may especially be evident during the pandemic due to the rise in economic and employment insecurity. Many countries have seen a significant economic decline, with the World Bank estimating that the economic activities in advanced economies will shrink by 7 per cent in 2020, with the EU zone shrinking by 9 per cent.[4] The UK, for example, has been reported to have seen the largest economic decline in 300 years (Douglas and Hannon, 2021), where its GDP has shrunk by 9.9 per cent in 2020 but many other countries not far behind – France (8.3 per cent), Italy (8.8 per cent), Germany (5 per cent). The economic decline was accompanied by high levels of unemployment with young workers having experienced higher risks of losing their jobs (Dias et al, 2020; TUC, 2020) and expected to face higher unemployment going forward (Resolution Foundation, 2020). I argued in the previous chapters that one of the driving causes of workers working longer and harder is due to the need to keep a competitive edge within the organisation and in the labour market, with subjective insecurity driving some of these behaviours. What is more, the work and work–life balance culture remained largely the same during the pandemic. Based on this, it is not surprising to see the flexibility paradox being even more prevalent during the COVID-19 pandemic, despite the more widespread use of flexible working, when flexible working was not the choice of workers but enforced by companies and the state. Similarly, we can expect this to continue in post-pandemic times especially before the economy fully recovers.

Reduction of hours

Unlike what we have seen earlier, there have also been many reports showing a decline rather than an increase in working hours/work intensity among women and mothers during the COVID-19 pandemic across several countries (Collins et al, 2020; Petts et al, 2020; Fuller and Qian, 2021). For example, Collins and colleagues (2020) examining the US Population Survey data compared the working hours trends of parents with different age group children – preschool, primary, and secondary – from February (pre-COVID-19 lockdown) to April (when schools were closed and home-schooling was in full swing). They found that the gender gap in working hours between mothers and fathers grew significantly during this period, especially for parents of primary and preschool children, largely due to the reduction in mothers' working hours. Fathers' working hours on the other hand did not change much, with the exception of fathers of children between 12 and 17 whose hours have had a slight (1.2 hour) reduction. The authors note that this pattern of working hours especially seen during the months of April can be attributed to the increased burden put on parents due to loss of childcare and demands for home-schooling. This assumption has been confirmed by Petts and colleagues (2020) who use data from over 700 couples in the US to examine parental involuntary job loss and reduction in working hours. They conclude that for those with young children, loss of full-time childcare was associated with the job loss of mothers but not fathers. Parental participation in home-schooling led to adverse effects on employment again for mothers yet not fathers. This leads us to our next point – whether this increase in gender gap in employment and working hours is evidence of the gendered paradox in play during the pandemic. Namely, has working from home led to more housework and childcare only for women, and not for men even during the pandemic? Or could we see changes in the gendered paradox patterns due to the rise in flexible working and the reduction in flexibility stigma?

The division of household labour and childcare

Has the COVID-19 pandemic and the rise in homeworking proved to be a great leveller in terms of unequal division of unpaid work among heterosexual couples? This has been the ongoing debate in many countries. Many reported the pandemic 'led to a profound shift in parenting roles' (Topping, 2020) with evidence from across the globe of more fathers being involved in childcare than before the pandemic started (Andrew et al, 2020; Carlson et al, 2020; Craig and Churchill, 2020; Hipp and Bünning, 2020; Prados and Zamarro, 2020; Yerkes et al, 2020; Zamarro et al, 2020; Dunatchik et al, 2021). However, there are also concerns about moving back to a more traditionalised division of labour or 'moving back to the 1950s' (Chung, 2020d; Summers, 2020). There have been reports that women (still) bear the larger brunt of the additional housework, childcare and home-schooling brought on by the pandemic and lockdown. This additional housework burden impeded women's ability to take part in the labour market (Petts et al, 2020; Prados and Zamarro, 2020; Fuller and Qian, 2021) with signs that homeworking men did not in fact pitch in as much as they were expected to (Collins et al, 2020; Hipp and Bünning, 2020).

In this section, I will examine whether the gendered paradox of homeworking persisted during the COVID-19 pandemic. Thus, do we still see women doing more housework and childcare, and men doing more paid work when working from home or do we see changes in this dynamic? There are several reason as to why we expect to see changes during this period. First, working from home and other flexible working measures have been widespread during the pandemic, and was encouraged or enforced by managers and the state. This also resulted in a large positive shift in the perception towards flexible working both among workers/co-workers and managers. Given that the stigma around flexible working for care purposes was one key reason why men were less likely to work in this way, we expect changes in the attitudes towards flexible working to have influenced the way fathers used flexible working. What is more, due to the sheer volume of housework, childcare and home-schooling parents needed to carry out during this period (Andrew et al, 2020; ONS, 2020b; ONS, 2020e) it may have been inevitable for fathers to also take a larger part in childcare. The fact that many workers worked from home exclusively also meant that many saved time they would have normally spent on commuting. Studies have shown that there is a gender gap in commuting times of mothers and fathers, where mothers' commuting time reduces post-childbirth while it increases for fathers (Joyce and Keiller, 2018). This implies that it was especially fathers working from home that may have gained additional time by not commuting during the pandemic.

There is evidence that fathers have been spending more time on childcare compared to pre-pandemic times. For example, based on the ONS Time Use survey (ONS, 2020e), parents or other adults living with children spent 35 per cent longer on average providing childcare in March–April 2020 compared to the previous data gathered in 2015. It was especially developmental care time (namely enrichment care) that increased, from 24 minutes to 64 minutes a day, an increase of 169 per cent. Non-developmental care time reduced, largely due to not having to take children to school and other activities (ONS, 2020g). Men have increased their time spent on childcare proportionately more so than women, by 58 per cent compared to data from 2015. Yet, it was women who were still largely in charge of caring for children. Mothers with children under the age of 18 were doing an average of three hours and 18 minutes of childcare per day, while for men, it was limited to two hours (ONS, 2020g). This gap was even larger among parents with young children, with men merely providing just over half of what women were doing. Women living with a child aged under five years, for example, spent on average four and a half hours on childcare, while men spent on average two hours 29 minutes (ONS, 2020g). In fact, these figures show a larger absolute gap compared to 2015 data (Wishart et al, 2019) due to the significant increase in the amount of time women were spending/had to spend on childcare during the pandemic.

There is some evidence that it is especially fathers who were working from home that have increased their time spent on childcare and housework. Looking at our data from the UK of dual-earning co-resident heterosexual couples (Chung et al, 2020a; Chung et al, 2020b), we found that when fathers worked from home, couples were more likely to say they were sharing cleaning/laundry, routine childcare (generally looking after children), and to a certain extent home-schooling children (Chung et al, 2021). What is more, fathers who were working from home exclusively (compared to those going into work fully or partially) were up to 3.5 times and 3.6 times more likely to say that they were spending more time carrying out routine childcare and home-schooling during the pandemic compared to before (Chung et al, 2020a). It is worth noting that UK fathers did not spend much time providing routine childcare in pre-pandemic times, with less than half of fathers reporting doing any routine care on a weekday based on the 2015 Time Use Survey (Walthery and Chung, 2021). In addition, routine childcare and home-schooling are the two areas where parents experienced increased demand for their time during the pandemic (Morris, 2020; ONS, 2020b; ONS, 2020g). Thus, on the one hand, it makes sense that fathers were spending more time doing these childcare activities during the pandemic, but also on the other hand, fathers taking a larger role in home-schooling and routine care activities may have provided additional relief for working mothers. We found similar evidence from across the world regarding fathers' homeworking and increased involvement in housework and childcare (Carlson et al, 2020; Collins et al, 2020; Hipp and Bünning, 2020; Prados and Zamarro, 2020; Dunatchik et al, 2021). For example, looking at parents in the US, Carlson and colleagues (2020) found that mothers and fathers who were exclusively working from home (in April 2020) were 2.9 and 2.4 times more likely respectively to say that they were doing more childcare during the pandemic, compared to parents who were either not working from home, or doing only some of their work from home. Using data from the US, Prados and Zamarro found that when fathers worked from home, they were 15 per cent more likely to report that parents were equally sharing childcare (Prados and Zamarro, 2020), although the same could not be said based on data capturing mothers' perceptions. Dunatchik and colleagues (2021) examined data collected by *The New York Times* in April 2020 (Morning Consult and The New York Times, 2020) to examine how parental remote working related to the division of housework and childcare during the pandemic in the US. They conclude that fathers' remote working increased the amount of unpaid domestic work done by fathers, especially when both parents were working remotely. Homeworking fathers carried out a relatively equal share of housework. However, the same could not be said about childcare, especially home-schooling children during the pandemic – which was left as the mothers' remit even when fathers were home.

Despite some variation, we could infer that the capacity to work from home during the pandemic may have enabled couples to juggle the increased care and housework demands better by possibly distributing it somewhat more evenly. This may have helped mothers to continue to work during the lockdown periods (Petts et al, 2020). In this sense, we could potentially say that the gendered paradox patterns we have observed in pre-pandemic times, where fathers did not increase their childcare hours when working flexibly, were less visible during the pandemic period. However, in our UK data, we also found that women who were working from home during the pandemic had increased the amount of housework and childcare they were carrying out even further compared to pre-pandemic times (Chung et al, 2020a). Similar results were found using the UKHLS COVID-19 data sets (Benzeval et al, 2020), in the US (Carlson et al, 2020; Dunatchik et al, 2021) and Germany (Hipp and Bünning, 2020) where mothers who were working from home increased the amount of unpaid work they were carrying out. In other words, we cannot say that the gendered paradox was fully eliminated during the COVID-19 pandemic. As many empirical studies have shown, unpaid domestic work – especially childcare and home-schooling – largely remained a women's remit even during the lockdown periods, especially for women who were working from home.

Given that men and women had very different starting points in terms of the amount of time they spent on housework and childcare, this increase in time spent on housework and childcare meant that women's work has been impacted more. For example, a time-diary study carried out by the Institute of Fiscal Studies in the UK during the first lockdown period has shown that 47 per cent of mothers' working hours were interrupted by childcare or housework during the pandemic (Andrew et al, 2020). Fathers' working hours were also interrupted but far less so – 30 per cent of their working hours. What is more, as we saw in the previous section, there has been an increase in mothers extending their working hours to make up for lost time during the day due to housework and childcare – working early in the morning and late in the evening (Chung et al, 2020b). Such an increase in multi-tasking, long-hours work (especially when we consider unpaid work as well), and boundary blurring has meant that we have seen unprecedented levels of mental health problems especially among mothers (Banks and Xu, 2020; Prados and Zamarro, 2020; Oxford University, 2021; RSPH, 2021). Such pressure led to many mothers leaving their jobs or reducing their working hours significantly (Petts et al, 2020), or others planning to do so in the future (McKinsey, 2020b).

Conclusion

The COVID-19 pandemic has led to profound changes in the way flexible working was carried out throughout the world. It has led to an steep rise in workers working from home, due to social distancing measures in place. Due to such large-scale use of flexible working we also saw changes in the perception towards it. We saw significant reductions in stigmatised views towards flexible workers and increase in positive perceptions of flexible working, such as many managers responding that it leads to increased productivity. These changes in attitude can potentially explain why, unlike pre-pandemic times, flexible working led to an increase in childcare involvement of fathers during the pandemic. However, we also found that much of the other flexibility paradox phenomenon remained the same during the pandemic despite changes in contexts. For example, we still saw the expansion of work and work encroaching on family life when workers worked from home. We also found that mothers working from home ended up increasing their housework and childcare hours even further, resulting in high levels of multi-tasking of care/work tasks. This explains why we see high levels of stress and mental health problems for mothers during the pandemic, with many leaving the labour market or having to reduce their hours to cope. In other words, the flexible working practices during the pandemic were not necessarily immune to the paradoxical outcomes we have observed in previous years. This provides us with evidence that the widespread use of flexible working alone may not be enough to tackle the problems of the flexibility paradox. Without disrupting norms around work, work–life balance and gender roles, without changes to workers' bargaining powers, we are unlikely to see the flexibility paradox disappear.

Then what do we need to do to remove the flexibility paradox? In addition, what do we expect to happen in the next coming years in terms of flexible working patterns and the implications on workers' well-being and gender equality? These are some of the questions we will be asking in the next chapter.

Notes

[1]   Economists call this 'confounders', and if you ever attend an economics conference you can just shout 'confounder!' and everyone would nod approvingly. That and endogeneity. You're welcome.

[2]   For details on this see COVID-19 Government Response Tracker based at the University of Oxford: www.bsg.ox.ac.uk/research/research-projects/Covid-19-government-response-tracker

[3]   For more info see: www.bma.org.uk/advice-and-support/Covid-19/adapting-to-Covid/Covid-19-video-consultations-and-homeworking

[4]   www.worldbank.org/en/news/press-release/2020/06/08/covid-19-to-plunge-global-economy-into-worst-recession-since-world-war-ii

11

Conclusion: Where do we go from here?

Introduction

This book set out to explore flexible working in a more critical way, asking the question whether flexible working actually provides positive outcomes for workers in terms of work–life balance, workers' well-being and gender equality as many expect it to. The results of the previous chapters show that paradoxically rather than improving workers' work–life balance, flexible working increased feelings of conflict between work and family. The reason behind this phenomenon was explained through the flexibility paradox, that flexible working can lead to further exploitation of workers' labour. This exploitation pattern is gendered. Men expanded their employment hours, namely overtime hours, to fulfil their ideal worker and breadwinner masculine image. Women expanded their unpaid working hours, namely increased time spent on housework and childcare adhering to the social norms around their roles as caregivers. What is more, due to these gendered patterns of flexible working or more so the assumptions behind such patterns, women end up being penalised further when working flexibly despite the fact that they are also likely to work longer and harder on their paid work when working flexibly.

However, I have also shown that the take-up and outcomes of flexible working largely depends on the contexts in which it is used. The way we think about work, work–life balance, and gender roles, workers' bargaining power and insecurity all help shape the outcomes of flexible working. The book also showed that as flexible working becomes more widely used, we see a shift in the attitudes towards flexible working – namely through the decline in flexibility stigma. The pandemic has provided us with some evidence of this, where the large-scale introduction of homeworking has led to profound changes not only in the perceptions towards and practices of flexible working, but also partly the gendered outcomes of flexible working. However, we still see signs that the flexibility paradox still exists, given that many other cultural normative and institutional factors remain largely the same during this period, and because the pandemic has given rise to higher levels of insecurity among workers which may exacerbate the problem.

In this chapter I would like to answer some remaining questions and provide some recommendations, or dare I say solutions, that can help us tackle the flexibility paradox, and enable managers, workers and policy makers alike to use flexible working better. First, the chapter starts off by responding to important questions – whether we will see a rise in flexible working in the future, post-pandemic, and for whom?[1] How this, and the changes that occurred during the pandemic, change our understanding of the flexibility paradox – namely, how flexible working relates to workers' work-life balance, well-being, and gender equality. This will provide us with some key issues that need to be addressed. The second part of the chapter responds to these issues by providing recommendations for the state including international governmental organisations, companies and managers, and individuals and families based on the evidence gathered in this book. In general, the key message of this chapter is that it is not flexible working or giving workers more control over their work that is the problem, but the general work culture and social norms around work and gender roles that need to be fixed. We need to dismantle the long-hours presenteeism work culture and find new definitions and new ways of measuring productivity and commitment, and tackle biases against disadvantaged workers' capacity to work. We further need to dismantle the gender normative views around whose responsibility it is to provide income, and whose responsibility it is to provide care. Without such changes and reflections we cannot expect flexible working to fulfil the goals it is meant to achieve.

Future scenarios of flexible working

Are we going to see a rise in flexible working?

In Chapter 2, I argued that despite legislative changes and accelerated development in technologies that enables more workers to work remotely, there has not been such a great rise in homeworking/remote working in most countries in the past decade. However, it seems that the COVID-19 pandemic has accelerated the process of shifting companies into remote working in the coming future. We can say the flexible working or homeworking genie is out of the bottle and is unlikely to go back in again.[2]

In our survey of workers during the first lockdown in the UK, a remarkable 76 per cent of all mothers and 73 per cent of fathers surveyed responded that they would like to work flexibly to spend more time with their children in the future. In addition, approximately two thirds of all respondents who were not parents, both men and women, also responded that they would like to work from home after the COVID-19 lockdown has ended (Chung et al, 2020b). A YouGov survey of almost 5,000 workers across the UK, gathered in September 2020, shows that more than half (57 per cent) of workers would like to work from home after the pandemic has ended, about a third of whom wanted to work from home 'all the time' (Smith, 2020). Similar results are found in other studies across the world (Buffer, 2020; 2021), where despite the problems workers experienced while working from home, very few want to go back to the office especially on a full-time basis. This, if I may remind everyone, is despite the fact that most of us were working in the office/workplaces full-time prior to the pandemic. In fact, in a survey conducted by *The Times* in the UK in early 2021, not only did the large majority of the 2,000 workers surveyed want the possibility to work from home, half of those surveyed responded that they would look for a new job if their bosses did not allow flexible working after lockdown (Clarence-Smith, 2021).

The changes in the preferences and attitude towards flexible working is reflected also in manager surveys. Three quarters of the managers in our survey collected in July and August 2020 in the UK responded that they expect more working from home requests to be supported, and more than 70 per cent believe that more requests for other types of flexible working practices will be supported (Forbes et al, 2020). In our and other surveys, we also see signs of managers expecting flexible working to become more widely available across all levels of jobs, and expect that there will be more support, including technical support, provided to workers to better enable homeworking (CMI, 2020; Forbes et al, 2020; CIPD, 2021). In a report by Chamber of Business and Industries UK and Price Waterhouse Coopers (PWC) in October 2020, 88 per cent of company managers surveyed responded that the pandemic has resulted in a greater shift towards remote working (Makortoff, 2020). In a YouGov survey of managers in June 2021, only one in five said that they expect workers to come in five days a week after the pandemic is over (Nolsoe, 2021). This pattern of homeworking being more embedded into jobs and organisations as a norm in the future can also be evidenced through a large number of companies removing office spaces especially in areas where real estate prices are high, such as London (Thomas, 2021). For example in the PWC survey in October 2020, three quarters of those surveyed responded that they were reviewing removing and restructuring office spaces (Makortoff, 2020). In fact by the beginning of 2021, we have seen many companies reporting plans to have their office spaces removed – for example HBSC reported removing up to 40 per cent of their global office spaces (Makortoff and Farrer, 2021). We also see many companies introducing (mandatory) working from home policies for their workforce – for example BP asked its 25,000 workers to work from home (at least) two days a week (Ambrose, 2021). In other words, many companies may shift to large-scale homeworking as a response to budget cuts (or rental and office running costs) necessary due to the impact of the pandemic and economic pressures. Similar practices have already been seen in organisations, including in the public sector, due to organisations cutting down on their office spaces in central parts of major cities[3] as a part of budgetary cuts and austerity measures (Lyonette et al, 2016).

These initiatives and the growth of flexible working is not necessarily limited to countries where flexible working and homeworking was commonplace prior to the pandemic. For example, in Korea where homeworking was barely used prior to the pandemic, not only has there been a steep growth in the use of homeworking practice during the pandemic, but there are also reports of the growing popularity of homeworking among managers and workers alike. According to a survey of managers and employees in Korea in September of 2020 (Lee, 2020), half of the companies surveyed responded that they offered homeworking opportunities to their workers during the pandemic, with two thirds of workers who worked from home having had a positive experience of it. In their report in December 2020, the Bank of Korea reported that teleworking is likely to continue, with companies hoping to achieve positive performance outcomes with its implementation (Bank of Korea, 2020).

Having said this, we also see reports of CEOs demanding a return to the office as soon as possible – both Goldman Sachs CEO David Solomon, JPMorgan CEO Jamie Dimon[4] called for their employees to return to the office, the former calling remote working an 'aberration'. Yet, there are also reports of employees revolting against such demands – such as Apple employees revolting against the Apple CEO's demand for workers return to work.[5]

In sum, after the large-scale natural experiment of flexible working that has taken place during the pandemic, it is likely that companies will be increasing flexible working, especially working from home options for their staff in the future. These changes are not necessarily driven by the demands coming from their workforce alone but from managers' and companies' demand for efficiency, increasing productivity and cutting costs.

Will flexible working be accessible for everyone in the future?

A question remains whether flexible working and homeworking will be something all workers will have access to and all companies will embrace. As we have seen in the UK ONS figures in Chapter 10, despite the rise in homeworking across the workforce during the pandemic, there were clear variations across occupations. High- and medium-skilled white-collar workers had more access to homeworking, while pink- and blue-collar workers had limited access. Obviously, there are certain occupations whereby it is not possible to carry out the work from home – for example bus drivers, retail shop-floor workers, social care workers. However, even in such occupations, other types of flexible working such as flexitime or self-rostering systems are still possible (Thornthwaite and Sheldon, 2004; Kossek et al, 2019), and have been used during the pandemic as part of social distancing measures. What is more, we have seen that many pink-collar jobs that were once thought not possible to be carried out remotely were not only possible, but were also done remotely with improved performance outcomes – for example health care services and a wide range of educational services.

The bigger issue that determines who gets access to and utilises flexible working or flexibility in their work will most likely be the position of the workers and the companies. For example, in a survey of companies across Korea in January 2021, up to 57 per cent of companies reported having used teleworking during the pandemic. However, there were large discrepancies across companies of different sizes; while 76 per cent of large companies used teleworking, only 47 per cent of smaller companies did so (Jung, 2021). What is more, there were discrepancies in the length of time teleworking was used during the pandemic with larger companies implementing it for a longer period of time compared to small and medium-sized companies (SMEs). SMEs may not have the capacity or resources available to introduce a full-scale working from home or other types of flexible working practices and may resort to informal practices. Similarly, workers in lower-paid jobs may not necessarily benefit from the rise in teleworking, be it due to the lack of incentives from companies to introduce such policies to retain and recruit workers, or due to managers still not fully trusting workers to be able to carry out their work flexibly/remotely without compromising productivity. What is clearer is that during the pandemic, many women – especially in administrative secretarial roles, as well as those in more associate professional roles (see Chapter 10) – were able to access homeworking, who were unable to do so in previous times. Whether this pattern remains will be crucial in not only shaping the future of flexible working but gender equality patterns in the future.

Another question that arises is whether the degree of freedom afforded to workers when they work flexibly will be the same. Previous empirical research shows that those in more privileged positions are given a greater degree of flexibility and control when working flexibly (Clawson and Gerstel, 2014). On the other hand, flexible working arrangements provided to lower-paid jobs or in disadvantaged positions may be limited in the degree of flexibility and control they have over their work. What is more, teleworking, for example, may increase the level of managerial control over one's work. For example, we have seen a rise in companies using camera/computer software surveillance systems on workers working remotely during the pandemic (Connolly, 2020). This may be especially used against those towards whom managers are already biased against, again disadvantaging marginalised workers, and this can limit these workers' capacity to be productive when working from home further. I would like to remind managers that even in routine jobs we have evidence that flexible working can result in positive performance outcomes (Bloom et al, 2015; Boltz et al, 2020). What is more, based on the economic theory of control (Falk and Kosfeld, 2006) and the high-performance work systems approach (Appelbaum et al, 2000), these surveillance systems may hinder rather than encourage the good performance outcomes flexible working practices can bring. Finally, whatever surveillance system managers introduce, workers will find a way to beat the system.

Will flexible working help tackle gender equality in the future?

How will flexible working change the patterns of gender equality in the future, especially in light of the fact that we have seen a steep rise in gender inequality in the labour market due to the pandemic and lockdown measures (Collins et al, 2020; Collins et al, 2021; ONS, 2021a)? Will the potential rise in flexible working help reduce these patterns of gender and other types of inequality or exacerbate it?

As we saw in Chapter 4 (Chung and van der Horst, 2018; Fuller and Hirsh, 2018; van der Lippe et al, 2019), flexible working can help women reduce their likelihood of moving out of the labour market or moving into part-time jobs after childbirth and help them stay in higher-paid lucrative jobs (Goldin, 2014). Thus, the expansion of flexible working opportunities for all workers would be a very welcome step in the right direction in possibly tackling some of the gender inequalities caused by the pandemic. Similarly, the expansion of flexible working could also benefit other disadvantaged workers – such as workers with informal care responsibilities, or disabled workers – who may benefit from flexible working in a similar way through removing barriers into work. When flexible working becomes the norm and more workers take it up, we are likely to see the bias against flexible workers reduce, and see shifts in attitudes towards flexible working. Flexible working is more likely to be considered a performance-enhancing measure, not only a work-family or diversity measure – as we have seen happen during the pandemic (Forbes et al, 2020). Such changes in the perception towards flexible working can help achieve gender equality, on the one hand, by reducing the biases mothers face when working flexibly, and on the other, by helping fathers take up flexible working for care purposes. Fathers' flexible working for care purposes can enable a more equal division of unpaid work between partners as we have seen during the pandemic, which can further help reduce gender inequality patterns in our labour market.

However, this expansion of flexible working may also lead to unintended negative impact for gender inequalities and workers' well-being if it is done without any reflection on our existing gender norms and work culture. Despite the changes we have seen in the behaviours of homeworking fathers in relation to childcare and housework, women still not only took up the bulk of the tasks, but also increased their time in these roles when working from home. In other words, despite some improvements, we can still expect to see gendered patterns of flexible working where it is likely to expand the unpaid housework and childcare hours of women more than men. This can reinforce the unequal division of housework among heterosexual couples. It can further lead to negative career consequences for women – due to the reinforcement of how flexible working will be used and how it will be evaluated by managers. This may especially be the case in countries like the US, the UK, Korea, where the working culture is that of an ideal worker norm (Acker, 1990; Berdahl et al, 2018) which equates long-hours work to a sign of commitment, performance and motivation of workers. As we saw in Chapter 9, in such contexts, flexible working and its blurring of boundaries between work and family life is more likely to lead to an encroachment of work on other spheres of life (Glass and Noonan, 2016; Lott and Chung, 2016) and increase competition among workers, where workers end up working everywhere and all the time (Mazmanian et al, 2013; Eurofound and the International Labour Office, 2017). Given the rise in insecurity we are seeing and likely to see in the near future due to the economic shocks felt across societies due to the pandemic (Chung and van Oorschot, 2011), it is likely that such blurring of boundaries and expansion of work due to flexible working will continue, despite the larger expansion of flexible working. In such scenarios, women may be left vulnerable given their limited capacity to expand their working hours due to their already existing demands of unpaid work compared to men. This may in fact exacerbate the gender gap in labour markets.

Another pattern of home working we need to be cautious of is where we end up with a two-tiered system where women with care demands, and other disadvantaged workers, end up working from home while other workers go back to the office. There is already evidence of remote workers not receiving the same level of compensation for their work efforts due to presenteeism culture and out of sight, out of mind-based reward systems (Bloom et al, 2015; Glass and Noonan, 2016; Cristea and Leonardi, 2019). We have further seen CEOs perpetuate this presenteeism culture by noting how those who are motivated will return to the office, and those who stay at home are not as committed to the workplace.[6] Thus, if women/disadvantaged workers are the only ones working from home, it will increase rather than decrease labour market inequalities by penalising those working from home.

What are the implications of flexible working on workers' well-being?

The expansion of work and blurring of boundaries between work and family life due to the rise in flexible working will have significant implications for workers' well-being in the future. The multi-tasking that we have seen from home workers during the pandemic may not happen as much in post-pandemic times, given that schools and childcare places are open again. However, it is likely that workers, especially mothers, may be multi-tasking various paid and unpaid domestic work activities not necessarily due to preferences but out of necessity (and others' expectations) of needing to meet the demands of both work and family. Such multi-tasking has been shown to be detrimental for workers' well-being outcomes (Craig and Brown, 2017;

Dunatchik and Speight, 2020). Workers' inability to detach themselves from work, mentally and physically, while working from home can also cause problems not only for well-being but also for productivity (Sonnentag, 2012).

What is more, there are concerns regarding issues around isolation and other mental and physical well-being issues – such as muscular-skeletal issues due to lack of proper office equipment (RSPH, 2021) – that can arise when workers work from home on a longer-term basis. One of the key negative outcomes of homeworking, mentioned by both managers and workers, was the isolation people felt. Work friendships constitute an important part of people's lives and influence their happiness especially in countries where workers tend to work long hours (Berman et al, 2002; Schawbel, 2018). In a study prior to the pandemic of almost 2,000 workers across the UK, on average, workers spend about 40 minutes talking to colleagues about non-work related issues during their eight-hour workday (Vouchercloud, 2016). Although this could be seen as a sign of time not being well spent at work, it is also an indication of how much we rely on work as a source of socialisation. Workplace friendships improve work collaboration, feelings of commitment to the organisation, and contributes to one's happiness (Berman et al, 2002; Schawbel, 2018). Thus, an increase in flexible working where more workers work different time schedules and in different locations/at home can lead to a reduction in the socialising carried out among work colleagues which can impact workers' well-being.

However, flexible working can reduce sickness and absenteeism among workers (see Chapter 4) as well. In fact, ONS reported that in 2020 the UK has seen the lowest levels of sickness and absenteeism since 1995 to 1.8 per cent, despite COVID-19 accounting for a large number (14 per cent) of all occurrences. Much of this could be attributed to large-scale homeworking. When large groups of workers work from home it can reduce the exposure to germs. Not needing to commute on a day-to-day basis can also help reduce any issues around injuries and physical fatigue caused by commuting. However, working from home and other types of flexible working can also help reduce sickness and absenteeism because workers may feel more able to carry out, at least parts of, their work if they do not need to go into the office and commute, or work during the schedules which feel more right for them (Bloom et al, 2015; Wood, 2021). On the one hand, this can raise potential problems with workers feeling more obliged to work when sick when given the opportunity to work flexibly, given that they may still be able to carry out the work. This may lead to negative consequences for workers' well-being and health especially in the longer term. On the other hand, this also raises an interesting issue around whether and how the rise in flexible working can potentially increase the labour market participation of workers with disabilities and long-standing health issues (Jones and Wass, 2013; Warmate et al, 2021). In other words, the ability to work from home and having control over one's schedule may be able to enhance the labour market participation capacity of many workers who were unable to take part in the labour market fully due to barriers of work in the office and in commuting (Jolly, 2000; Ryan, 2021). More research is needed to explore this further.

What do we need to do? Policy recommendations for governments

Better rights and protection for flexible workers

One important change needed in our legislation to ensure flexible working does not lead to self-exploitation and negative career outcomes that further increase the inequalities in our labour markets is to enhance the right to flexible working, to make it a norm rather than an exception. The current right to request flexible working in the UK and in the EU Work-Life Balance directive, for example, is insufficient in ensuring workers access to flexible working in that the request can be rejected by managers for a number of reasons. What is more, the request and reasons arguing for why flexible working is needed lies on the onus of workers.[7] The EU directive in their non-legislative element stating the need for protection of workers who work flexibly from possible career consequences and penalty provides better legal protection for workers. However, even this may not be enough to eradicate flexibility stigma and its impact, especially on mothers and other disadvantaged workers, and workers' tendency to work longer hours due to such stigma. The Dutch right to flexible working, which has stronger legislative basis for workers to work flexibly with the onus on managers in having to explain why a job cannot be done flexibly – for example due to business constraints, potential negative impact on profits – is a better way forward. Yet it is also not enough to ensure that flexible working rights are protected for all workers, especially for those without the strong bargaining positions many workers in the Netherlands enjoy. Instead, the method used by the Finnish government providing a legal basis for workers to decide when and where they work, with a guaranteed minimum (50 per cent or more), may be a better option to ensure that flexible working becomes the norm. The Finnish government's approach (for more information about this and other countries' policies see Chapter 2) of exploring the changes necessary in employment law regarding the place of work and hours of work is also a necessary step for governments. This is especially true if we do not want the rise in flexible working to result in the (possibly unintended) exploitation of workers' labour. Despite its problems, clear working boundaries provided by office-working during nine-to-five schedules, which our current labour laws are based on, provide us with clearer indications of what constitute as long hours and overtime work. This ensures better protections of workers, and their health and safety. These mechanisms ultimately help protect companies and managers from misusing workers, which can result in costly outcomes for companies and society as a whole. For example, burnt-out or injured workers cost not only the company, but also the national health care systems, and impact the family's well-being which are all costs to the society. Flexible working and the blurring of boundaries that comes with it can make much of the current protective mechanisms in our labour laws meaningless. For example, working time regulations restricting maximum working hours becomes difficult to enforce when the definition of what constitutes working hours becomes blurred. We need new mechanisms to ensure that workers have ample rest and recovery away from work – which is critical to ensure a healthy and productive workforce. Again these are necessary steps to protect workers not only from managers but possibly from themselves and the long-hours/competition work cultures that can develop when boundaries between work and non-work are unclear.

The EU right to disconnect currently being discussed in the European Parliament (European Parliament, 2021) is an interesting development and is a welcome step in the right direction to protect workers. The right states that employers should not require workers to be available outside their working hours and co-workers should refrain from contacting colleagues for work purposes. The right further states that EU countries should ensure that workers who invoke their right to disconnect are protected from victimisation and other repercussions and that there are mechanisms in place to deal with complaints or breaches of the right to disconnect. Finally it states that remote professional learning and training activities must be counted as work activity and must not take place during overtime or days off without adequate compensation. Similarly in 2021, Ireland passed a Code of Practice on the Right to Disconnect.[8] Three rights are enshrined in the code: 1) the right of an employee to not have to routinely perform work outside their normal working hours; 2) the right not to be penalised for refusing to attend to work matters outside of normal working hours; and 3) the duty to respect another person's right to disconnect (for example by not routinely emailing or calling outside normal working hours). In 2021 Portugal also passed a law to protect remote workers, which states that employers may face penalties for contacting workers during out of office hours. The new regulation also states that employers are forbidden to monitor workers working from home. Finally, companies have to help pay for expenses incurred by homeworking, such as higher electricity and internet bills, which will be tax deducted.[9] Again the key message these labour laws convey are that we need to protect workers' right to time for recovery and rest, and the need to engender a work culture that understands that such recovery times are crucial in order to achieve productivity in the longer run, without incurring social costs.

Reshaping normative views around work-life balance and gender

Another issue governments need to address is around changing the normative views around work-life balance and gender roles. Results found in Chapter 9 shows us that the flexibility paradox can be attributed to our norms around work and work-life balance. Based on the analysis results, we can potentially change the family-friendly culture of the country by introducing generous family policies at the national level – such as generous public childcare. This can make family-friendly working conditions the norm rather than the exception (Been et al, 2017) which can help reduce flexibility stigma, and remove patterns of the flexibility paradox. However, we should also be careful as certain family policies may reinforce the gendered flexibility paradox. Long and generous maternity leave, for example, act to reinforce traditional gender roles in our society by ensuring that mothers are put in charge of children in the first years of the child's life, reinforcing these roles into the future (Budig et al, 2012). 'Gender neutral' parental leave policies with low-income replacement rates and part-time childcare provision do little to change these traditional gender norms as well (Korpi et al, 2013). Given the gender pay gap in all societies (World Economic Forum, 2020), this 'gender neutral' leave will be taken up by mothers. Similarly, part-time childcare still leaves much of the childcare duties to mothers. To change this, we need policies to ensure that fathers take part in childcare from the early years of a child's life. Studies have shown that when fathers take up leave, especially in the first year of a child's life and without the mother, it is likely to result in a more equal division of childcare and housework in later years (Nepomnyaschy and Waldfogel, 2007; Tanaka and Waldfogel, 2007; Norman, 2019). In fact, as we have shown in the previous chapters, in countries with a more generous paternity leave, men are likely to show similar patterns of behaviours as women when working flexibly (Kurowska, 2020). Thus, governments should introduce well-paid earmarked 'daddy leave' for fathers (or second parents) to be taken up in the first year of a child's life, where if the father (and second parents) do not take up the leave allocated, they lose it. Such policies can help change gender norms around whose responsibility it is to care so that flexible working does not end up reinforcing the traditional gender division of housework and paid work, and reduces the likelihood of women being penalised when they work flexibly.

In addition, governments may think about requiring companies to report the use and take-up of family-friendly benefits as done for the gender pay gap in the UK.[10] Provisions at the national level, even those enshrined in law, may not necessarily lead to 'real access' for workers (Chung and Tijdens, 2013). This is especially the case given the variation in workers' negotiation positions and level of protection provided at the company level, and due to the fear of retribution or career penalties once such policies are taken up (Hobson, 2013; Chung, 2018). Thus, it would make sense for governments to ask companies to report on the take-up of policies such as shared parental leave/ earmarked daddy leave and family-friendly flexible working arrangements. This can help make these take-ups key targets companies and line managers are encouraged to meet, and help companies think about key pathways to meet these targets.

Changing the long working hours culture

Governments also need to tackle the long-hours work culture prevalent in many of our societies if we want to ensure that flexible working results in positive outcomes. Many of the problems of flexible working noted in this book relate to our current work culture that privileges work above all else, and equates long-hours work with productivity and commitment of workers. Without a significant change to our work culture, it is impossible to fully eradicate the flexibility paradox. What is more, when boundaries between work and private life becomes blurred, it will become harder to protect workers' time away from work as work is likely to encroach on their private time. Only through drastically changing the norm of how much of our lives we should dedicate to work (by changing the full-time working norm), can we help ensure that flexible working does not end up with workers working all the time and everywhere.

This is why I suggest a national collective move towards shortening the full-time working hours norm – for example through the introduction of a four-day week – is critical to help protect all workers (Chung, forthcoming/2022; see also, Haraldsson and Kellam, 2021). The four-day-week idea is that the full-time standard, which is currently around 36–40 hours in most countries, should move to a four-day, 30–32-hour-week standard without a reduction in pay workers receive – that is, not part-time work. This is largely based on the need to provide workers with more time to 'recover' from work and enable engagements in a wide range of activities that generate social value outside of paid employment – such as care for children and elderly relatives. The four-day week has been shown to increase productivity (Booth, 2019; Pang, 2019). For example, Microsoft Japan has reported a staggering 40 per cent increase in productivity after the launch of its four-day-week experiment (Paul, 2019). The four-day week has also been gaining support from both managers and workers due to its potential to tackle the climate crisis (Knight et al, 2013) and solve the ongoing issues around workers' well-being and gender equality (Stronge et al, 2019; Coote et al, 2020). Long-hours work has been largely the culprit of women being excluded from the most lucrative jobs (Cha and

Weeden, 2014; Goldin, 2014), and men's long hours prohibit them from taking a more active role in housework and childcare (Craig and Mullan, 2011; Walthery and Chung, 2021). Thus, making a four-day week a norm can enable better divisions of housework and care, and remove stigma against workers who can only work shorter hours, reducing some of the key barriers in achieving gender and other social equality, including those relating to the flexibility paradox. Especially in light of the COVID-19 pandemic, there has been serious discussions across countries, like the UK, Iceland, Korea, Spain, India, New Zealand, in using a four-day-week approach in addressing issues around gender equality, workers' deteriorated mental health, and rejuvenating the tourism and hospitality industries that have been hit the hardest.[11] Although it is possible to leave such a move to a four-day week to be introduced at the company level, a national move to a four-day week is crucial for the following reasons. First, it can help shape the norm around working hours to provide companies, especially those without the capacity to be reflective around their working practices, to use their workforce more effectively. It provides a nudge for companies to value their workers' time, think about what is a more efficient use of it by making additional working hours more costly for companies to use (as in the current case for long-hours work due to overtime premiums that are protected by labour laws in many countries). Second, given that the cost of workers working long hours results in costly outcomes for the society, which in some cases companies do not need to bear – for example the cost of health outcomes especially for those who have left the labour market or the cost of reduced family well-being due to the breadwinner working long hours – a national move towards a four-day week also reflects the need to consider these costs at the larger societal scale. Third, a national move to a four-day week provides workers with a stronger basis for their 'right to time'. Given that our current cultural norm around work performance and commitment still largely centres around long-hours work in the office,[12] it will be difficult for workers to ask to work shorter hours through a more individualised negotiation process, especially in industries where long-hours cultures are strongly embedded in its system. Such individualised approaches will only result in the exclusion of workers who are unable to take part in the long-hours work culture increasing the inequalities among workers (Cha and Weeden, 2014; Goldin, 2014). A national introduction of four-day week provides workers with a legal basis to use their limited resource of time as they wish outside of work. This allows for a more collective approach to re-examining working hours where the debates centre not only around productivity and efficiencies at work, but also around the basic human rights of individuals for rest, leisure, care and other types of activities that provide social value. Such an approach may be the best way to ensure that the expansion of flexible working does not result in workers working or being expected to work all the time and everywhere.

Recommendations for companies and managers[13]

Redefining productivity and KPIs

The foremost important change companies need to make when introducing flexible working is to redefine and set up new measures of productivity, commitment and success, and set up new key performance indicators (KPIs) for the company and the work group. At the moment, many companies rely on hours worked in the office visible to the line manager/supervisors as the key indicator of the value generated by the worker (Glass and Noonan, 2016; Cristea and Leonardi, 2019). These are artefacts of the industrialisation stage of capitalism, where hours worked in the production line were thought to be equated to outputs generated. Yet, when we consider that the current five-day, 40-hour week was introduced to enhance productivity in factories the 1920s,[14] even in such contexts, hours worked cannot be equated to output and performance (see also, Pang, 2019). The basic assumption behind the introduction of flexible working, especially for performance-enhancing purposes, is based on the notion that when workers have more control over when, where and potentially how much to work, they will work better. Then, for an effective introduction of such a policy, discussions around what 'working better' means and re-establishing the KPIs of the organisations and groups that go beyond hours spent in the office is required (Kelly et al, 2011; Kelly and Moen, 2020). This cannot just be a top-down approach, but would need to be led by group discussions with everyone involved to get a clear indication of what success means and what measurable goals should be set – for the individual and as a group – for people to achieve/prioritise when at work. Again as definitions of what constitute 'work' and 'at work' become blurred, the targets of what the company/group would like to or should achieve become more critical. As easy as it may sound, basing people's commitment and productivity on hours worked (and years leading to seniority) is currently being used by many organisations across the world for a reason – mainly because it is easy to administer and is a clear indicator. It is a clear indicator given that time is a limited resource we all have in common, and if someone is willing to allocate a large portion of it to work, it is assumed that this person is devoted to work more than anything else. However, such assumptions are more likely to make workers work longer with flexible working, with work encroaching on family life, again not necessarily generating any real value during this time. This cannot be beneficial for workers or the company.

Ensuring a clearer boundary between work and non-work spheres

Sonnentag and colleagues (Sonnentag, 2003; Sonnentag and Bayer, 2005; Sonnentag, 2012) present evidence of the need to detach mentally and physically away from work in order for workers to be more productive at work. This is necessary to be able to maintain their well-being, and to increase work engagement and proactive behaviours (such as initiative and pursuit of learning), ultimately impacting on job performance outcomes. This is also outlined in Alex Pang's book *Rest* (Pang, 2017), where he argues that deliberate rest is actually an integral part of productivity. He argues that through resting, including taking part in leisure activities away from work and sleeping, our brains process information that may be of great benefit for problem-solving during the workday. In other words, it is in the managers' and companies' own interests to ensure that workers are able to maintain a health boundary of time and space between work and non-work spheres and to protect workers' recovery periods. This is especially true when we also know that very long hours of work, without ample rest, can result in negative health outcomes (Dembe et al, 2005; Caruso et al, 2006), which can be very costly for a company (Health and Safety Executive, 2019). What is more, working long hours does not necessarily mean more productive outcomes (Parkinson and Osborn, 1957) and workers can end up making more mistakes when working very long hours, resulting in negative productivity (Pencavel, 2014). Again, it is in the company's interest that workers work shorter hours or at least stick to their contracted hours, with clearer boundaries between work and non-work life and have ample recovery periods.

As we observed in the previous chapter on COVID-19, blurring of boundaries between work and non-work has been noted as one of the key negative experiences of working from home during the pandemic voiced by both workers and managers. One key solution to ensuring that workers' flexible working does not result in work encroaching on private life will be to communicate clearly that this is not the goal of the company nor is it for the benefit of the company for workers to do so. Setting out clear guidelines as to when work is expected to be done, and when email replies are expected may also be of benefit – somewhat like a company-level policy of right to disconnect. How well this is implemented can be included as a part of the evaluation criteria for the team. The goal should be to have workers who are able to meet the agreed set of targets without having to work all hours of the day. In fact, workers who spend all hours of their day at work should be stigmatised as being ineffective and/or perpetuating a work culture that is not beneficial for the individual, the company or society. It could also be a sign that the person is not getting sufficient training and support to get the work done, or that targets are set inappropriately and need further evaluation. Having role models of 'good workers' that are able to work more efficiently by working focused shorter hours and with clear boundaries between work and private lives are needed, especially in top positions, to shift the norms around the notion of what constitutes an 'ideal worker' (Chung, 2021b).

Removing the stigma around flexible working for care purposes

Similarly, it will be useful to have role models in senior positions or from 'top performing' workers to shift the stigmatised ideas around flexible working used for care purposes. Flexible working, even when explicitly used for care purposes, can help improve performance outcomes for companies especially in terms of boosting loyalty, morale, reduce sickness absenteeism, and help worker recruitment and retention. However, workers will be weary of using such arrangements especially if there is a culture that still equates a worker using flexible working for care purposes as someone who is not productive and not as committed to the company. Highlighting the fact that it is for the company's benefit that workers use flexible working to achieve better work–life balance, and providing case studies of individuals who are able to achieve good performance outcomes while using flexible working for work–life balance, will be a good way to tackle some of these existing norms. Of these case studies, it will be crucial to highlight cases of men, especially senior men, who use or have used flexible working for work–life balance purposes to change the norms around who flexible working arrangements are for. As mentioned, it may be especially men who feel hesitant in taking up flexible working arrangements especially for care purposes. Men may fear a femininity stigma (Rudman and Mescher, 2013) – that they are not adhering to the ideal worker type by not working long hours in the office and not adhering to the male-breadwinner model of masculinity by not prioritising work above care. Providing guidance for workers is one thing, but providing role models of senior more established men within the organisation who use flexible working for care purposes may help remove the fear of being stigmatised as deviating away from the worker type that can succeed within the company. These role models will be especially beneficial for younger/junior men who may be potential fathers/carers. This can also help develop a positive notion of masculinity (Brandth and Kvande, 1998; Elliott, 2016). Such changes in the normative views around flexible working can help remove the stigma women have to face by allowing the idea that work–life balance does not have to come at a cost to performance outcomes. In addition, companies can ask line managers to report back on the progress made in terms of the take-up of flexible working and other family-friendly arrangements at the work-group level. Workers' work–life balance satisfaction can also be included as a KPI managers are evaluated against. Finally, there can also be policies at company level that ensure better access and protection for workers who use flexible working for work–life balance needs. Although not perfect, it can provide a sense of security for workers who can potentially face discrimination and unfair treatment in terms of career progression or work opportunities when using flexible working. It will further help workers not to exploit themselves but to use flexible working to better enable work–life balance. When such policies are drawn, companies should ensure the intersectional nature of discrimination and penalties which working-class people, women, minority ethnic or religion, disabled, LGBTQ+ community and people of other protected characteristics can face.

Recommendations for individuals and families

There are already a number of books written as self-help books for people who are working flexibly or for those who have more control over their working time and space. These include *Solo* by Rebecca Seal (2021) which was originally written for the self-employed solo workers mainly working from home, but its contents can easily be applicable for the 'entrepreneurial' employees working flexibly. The book touches upon issues around how to deal with isolation or boundary blurring. Similarly Kossek and Lautsch's (2008) book *CEO of Me* provides tips around boundary management for workers who work flexibly. Alex Soo-jung Kim Pang's book *Rest* (Pang, 2017) is one of my favourites, and provides a thorough insight into why you should take deliberate rest away from work seriously. It also provides useful tips on how to maximise your work productivity especially for those who have more control over when and where you work. This may be especially useful for those in occupations that require high levels of creativity and critical thinking. Brigid Schulte's book *Overwhelmed* (Schulte, 2015), another favourite of mine, similarly provides tips around time management, highlighting the crucial role of rest, leisure, love and play in ensuring that you are able to work and live better. I would especially recommend this book to working mothers, many of whom are suffering from the exploitation model (Sullivan and Lewis, 2001) – crowding out their 'play' time. My goal here is not to compete with any of these books, nor do I promise to provide detailed tips on how to better use flexible working for individuals in the short amount of space I have left in this book. Rather, I would like to focus on the key principles workers need to think about knowing what we have covered in the previous chapters of this book around the flexibility paradox. This includes the need to be mindful about blurring of boundaries, issues around multi-tasking and overwork tendencies that result from this blurring, issues around the gender inequality patterns of flexible working, and finally fighting the internalised capitalist notions of success and the importance of valuing rest.

Maintaining clear boundaries

One of the most difficult things I found myself as someone working in academia who has had control over when and where they work pretty much their entire working life, is to maintain clear boundaries between work and private life. As mentioned in the previous chapters, this was especially difficult because, as many academics and as we saw in Chapter 5 many other workers also believe, work was my passion and not only a way to make a living. Especially at times when there were no clear competing demands – read no children or care responsibilities – it was difficult to know when to stop working without the clear boundaries a nine-to-five office job can provide. This was exacerbated by the fact that academia has a notorious long-hours work culture, where established scholars brag about the long hours they put in at work. For example, when I was doing my PhD in Tilburg, the Netherlands (ironically the country with the one of the shortest average working hours in the world) my working day would easily span until 10–11pm at night, a habit I picked up doing my Master's degree in Korea where it was assumed that any serious academic would work at least 70 hours a week. It was only after my then PhD supervisor, Ton Wilthagen, advised me to stop work before dinner (around 6–7pm) and preferably start around 9am was I able to change my habits. He said if this more rigid nine-to-five schedule did not work for me after two to three weeks, I could go back to my old ways.[15] I became more productive when clear boundaries were set. This also gave me more time to spend on other activities, for example sports or leisure, and more time for thinking that went on the background while I was doing other activities. Parkinson's law states that 'work expands so as to fill the time available for its completion' (Parkinson and Osborn, 1957). In other words, when flexible working alongside technological developments 'enable' work to be done anywhere and all the time, we are likely to work anywhere and all the time. Some of us do it because we think this is a good/better way of working and makes us 'better workers'. However, as Parkinson's law notes, and as many studies on productivity and my own experience can attest to, you working long hours does not mean you are doing more. In fact, short focused hours can prove to be much more efficient in finishing a job (Pencavel, 2014; Pang, 2017) especially in the longer run. A good example of this was when my daughter was six months old and I was back at work full-time. Given her feeding and napping schedule, I had approximately 4.5 hours a day between 1pm and 5.30pm to work uninterrupted while she was at nursery. These hours were probably my most productive hours where I managed to finish off most work despite the constant grogginess I felt due to lack of sleep.

You might say, wait a minute, other people are productive during the eight to nine hours of work they do at their places of work. This may be true for some, but survey data shows that most people spend quite a lot of time doing other tasks during working hours. This includes reading the news, drinking coffee, checking social media, talking to their partners and/or colleagues, to the point that it is said that the average full-time worker in the UK only tends to their real work activities for less than three hours a day (Vouchercloud, 2016). This may have been a unique study, and three hours may be an overstatement. However, the point is that you may not be doing anyone any favours by expanding your working day when working flexibly. Rather, we may be more productive when we maintain clear boundaries of work, working shorter focused hours (see also Newport, 2016) which then provides us more time to focus on our private lives. One thing to repeat here is the studies by Sonnentag (Sonnentag, 2003; Sonnentag, 2012) which show that we need the psychological and physical detachment away from work to fully recover. This recovery period is crucial especially for those in demanding jobs, and is key to ensuring that you are able to be productive and creative during the time you spend at work. In other words, the rest and detachment periods are in fact a critical part of productivity (Pang, 2017; Pang, 2019). I noted earlier how managers now need to ensure that workers do not end up blurring the boundaries of work and non-work when workers work flexibly. However, flexible working in a way makes the workers managers of their own time (see also, Kossek and Lautsch, 2008; Seal, 2021). This means that workers themselves have to be much more aware of the consequences of long-hours work, and what the time and mental encroachment of work on private spheres can lead to. As Rebecca Seal says in her book, you need to be a better and kinder manager to yourself.

Gender division and housework, childcare

Then you may ask, isn't the great thing about flexible working having the capacity to be able to meet both work and private/family demands without having to sacrifice one or the other through the flexible boundaries and blending of the two spheres? I would then say, yes, absolutely, especially if you are a man. Please go ahead and have a conversation with your manager about flexible working to utilise it to engage more in childcare and housework. You will realise that this will not only benefit your children – in terms of their emotional and cognitive development – but it will also make you happier, more satisfied with your work–life balance (Walthery and Chung, 2021). Your relationship with your partner will also improve, reducing the likelihood of divorce or separation (Chung, 2021a). For women, many are already using flexible working arrangements to juggle work with childcare and housework by squeezing in some sort of work/housework activity in every minute of their day, effectively crowding out leisure and time for rest. For those women, we need to think about the implications of this for their well-being, their career, and gender equality not only for themselves but for our children in the future.

Going back to my own story when my daughter was young, I did mention I was productive during the 4.5 hours I was at work during the day. What I did not mention was that due to my obligation in feeling that I hadn't completed my full-time workload, I used to work from 8pm to 11pm to do the additional three hours of work I thought I needed to do. This was after a whirlwind of 3.5 hours where I was the main carer of my daughter – picking her up from nursery, feeding, bathing, and putting her to sleep. I don't think I actually did any real productive work during those three hours in the evenings. What is worse, for those years, I was resentful towards my husband who I felt wasn't doing an equal share of care, whose boss at the time would not allow for homeworking nor part-time working, which would have improved our lives tremendously. Given that he was commuting an hour each way to work, working a full eight-hour +lunch time job, he had limited capacity to be more involved.

First of all, being able to ensure that you are able to work (full-time or long hours) while doing a large bulk of housework and childcare tasks is not good for your health especially in the longer run (Chandola et al, 2019; Oxford University, 2021). As I argued in Chapter 7, flexible working enables women to take part in work while not demanding sufficient engagement of fathers and men in housework and childcare, and without sufficient policy support from companies or governments to address the demands of working parents (see also Lewis et al, 2008). In other words, flexible working frees up female human capital without disrupting the gender normative views around who should be responsible for childcare and housework, leading women to expand the effort in carrying out what effectively was a two-person job in the 1970s. Actually, mothers are expected to do even more childcare compared to the 1970s due to the rise in intensive parenting cultures, leading many women to experience high levels of stress and other mental health issues. To address this, we can firstly say although the flexibility in one's work can provide workers with the capacity to meet these demands, it does not mean you should do everything. It may be worth setting up clear boundaries for yourself, for your work and for housework/childcare, limiting the amount of time you spend 'working' – including unpaid care/ housework – to ensure you have time for leisure and recovery (see also Schulte, 2015). However, what is more important is to not fall back onto traditional gender roles when working flexibly. At the moment, the basic assumptions held by male partners, children, and even the female partners themselves is that when a female partner works flexibly they are able to carry out both housework/childcare and paid work. This needs to be disrupted. In other words, we need to have difficult conversations within the households to ensure that men do an equal share of housework and care, without relying on women to manage it all through flexible working or otherwise. We should also encourage men to have difficult conversations with their managers about adapting their work to ensure that they are able to provide an equal and meaningful contribution to the unpaid work, including mental load, needed to maintain a household. Despite men's hesitation in doing so, it is such hesitations that perpetuate flexibility stigma which exacerbates the career penalties women face due to the constrained choices they need to make (McRae, 2003). Only when men do an equal share of the housework and childcare and are also expected to use flexible working to address these demands, can we make meaningful changes in our social norms around gender roles. These changes can shape not only how this generation of workers and managers think about men and women's work but also children's expectations of what their parents' roles are and what their roles should be once they themselves become parents (Cunningham, 2001; McGinn et al, 2019). This can effectively shift the next generation's construction of gender. Only through this can we genuinely tackle the issues around the gendered flexibility paradox.

In addition to engaging men to do more housework, we as a society need to think about how much work – both paid and unpaid domestic labour – we are asking households to carry out. Through flexible working (and other measures) we are now asking both partners to take part in the labour market, without having to reshape 'work' which was built on the one-breadwinner model. In this model, the other partner takes on the reproductive work, namely all the supportive work that is needed so that the working spouse can fully focus only on work. Actually, work has become greedier in terms of the time and commitment asked of workers over the years (Coser, 1974). Childcare has also become even more complex in what parents are expected to do to prepare children for future labour market risks (Hays, 1998). In other words, we have managed to ask two partners to squeeze in what effectively used to be a three-or-more-people's worth of work without the expansion of how much time individuals have – 24 hours a day, 365 days a year. Flexible working may have enabled the freeing up of labour without disrupting the labour market norm of what companies and government should expect from workers – how much time and commitment they should give to companies – despite the changes in characteristics and other demands workers now need to face. In this regard, it is worth thinking again about demanding shorter working hours and for companies and governments to shift the norms around *who* workers are. The norm of 'the worker' is and should be someone with care, child, elderly, self and even pet care demands and responsibilities outside of work for their family, community and the larger society (Kelliher et al, 2019) rather than someone who can focus only on work.

Doing less

Finally I want to talk about the internalised ideas of self-worth and busyness. One reason why we see such an expansion of work – both paid and unpaid domestic work – when workers gain freedom over when and where and potentially how much they work, is due to our cultural norm around busyness. Busyness in modern-day society is considered a badge of honour presented as an indicator of superiority or achievement (Gershuny, 2005; Bellezza et al, 2017). It is not only a source of conspicuous consumption – to show others of one's position – but also can provide individuals with confirmation of self, of self-worth. As explored in Chapter 5, this may also be largely due to our internalised capitalism or subjectification of self – namely the neo-liberalist normative control over how we value ourselves and our use of time. We have come to prioritise work or investment of our time with a view towards its possible returns – for example enrichment educational activities with children resulting in better labour market outcomes for them. There has been a rise in groups that have formed to tackle these cultural shifts we see in modern-day society – such as the nap ministry,[16] which see rest as a form of resistance and sleep deprivation as a form of racial and social justice issue. The worry I have with flexible working enabling us to do more by shaping the boundaries between different elements of work and non-work lives is that we are doing too much without time for reflection. This is not to put the blame on the individual for doing this, especially knowing that we live in times of high levels of job insecurity and instability, wage stagnation, dismantlement of collective bargaining powers, and increasing levels of competition among workers with fewer and fewer opportunities especially for our youth (Costa Dias et al, 2020). However, for those with the privilege to work flexibly, have control over their work and are not in direct risk of job or employment loss, it is worth thinking of the bar we are setting for others (both at work and at home/parenting) when we utilise flexible working to stretch ourselves and our capacity to the max without much room left (see also, Chung, 2021b). I had dinner with Hans Pongratz, the scholar who put forward the self-exploitation theory of flexible working (Voß and Pongratz, 1998; Pongratz and Voß, 2003), where we reflected on our own working patterns. Were we hypocrites? Do we exploit our labour to the maximum through flexible working while criticising it? We did not have clear answers to that. However, he said after much reflection of his working life (to note, Hans was in his early 60s at the time this conversation took place), he asks himself, 'Can I keep working this way in ten years' time without becoming ill or burning out?'. I think this is a good way of looking at this, but maybe expand this to think about whether if others work at the same speed/performance level you currently achieve, whether it may make others sick, ill or burn out as well. Flexible working enables us to do so much, stretch us our day and energy to do as much as we possibly can, yet we need to reflect on whether this is sustainable for us as individuals and us as a collective. In other words, we need to think whether by being able to do so much, we are encouraging a continuous spiral of increased competition (Mazmanian et al, 2013) not only among ourselves but for others who may not have the liberty nor the job security to resist this trend. It may be good to actually perform the expectations many have of expanding our leisure time when gaining more control and freedom over your work. I know this is going to be difficult for those not in strong bargaining positions either individually or collectively (that is, living in countries with strong unions), but maybe this is the only way for us to not fuel the ever increasing spiral of competition. As many note (and I mentioned earlier), rest as resistance may result in more value production both at work and for society as a whole (Chung, forthcoming/2022). Deliberate rest can be an act of social justice.

Conclusion

This book was about flexible working. Although for the reader it may feel like I spent the past 200 pages arguing how bad flexible working can be for workers' well-being, gender equality and society, I want to make it very clear here that this is not what I want to say. In no way am I arguing for the withdrawal of flexible working practices nor am I arguing against its spread. The main take-home message is that flexible working can be a great enabler to make workers work better and more efficiently, enable better work-life balance and well-being, and achieve gender and other social equality. However, flexible working is not a panacea, but rather a sort of an amplifier. It is an amplifier in that it amplifies many of the problems we have in our society in terms of work culture and gender norms. Without a serious reflection of these issues, flexible working can actually reinforce many of the problems we face in society today. Flexible working is not used in a vacuum, and the context in which flexible working is used ultimately shapes what flexible working can result in. Thus, we need to be able to change the normative and institutional contexts in which it is used to ensure that flexible working meets the goals of workers, companies and society. More specifically we need to significantly disrupt the way we think about work, work-life balance, rest, time and gender roles. Otherwise, the expansion of flexible working can lead to further (self-)exploitation of workers and revert back to old gender roles which will result in negative consequences for everyone involved especially in the longer run.

Notes

[1] It is important to note that it is currently March 2021 where the UK and many other countries are still in (or yet again going into) lockdown with social distancing measures that requires workers to work from home if at all possible. I understand that the reader, you, may be reading this in the future (probably 2022 and beyond) where some of these questions are already answered!

[2] This is a quote from a webinar with Tiger Recruitment I did done in June 2020 with Bruce Daisley, host of the *Eat Sleep Work Repeat* podcast, CIPD Director David D'Souza and myself, which is a great summary of what to expect in the future of work in post-pandemic times, available here: https://tiger-recruitment.com/hr/watch-the-future-of-work-after-Covid-19/

[3] For example many council boroughs, such as Camden, and government departments such as the Home Office have reduced their office spaces significantly over the past years prior to the pandemic. With limited office space available, staff were encouraged to work from home at least one or two days a week, with many only going into the office one out of the five days they were contracted to work.

[4] www.theguardian.com/business/2021/jun/14/companies-keener-on-return-to-uk-offices-than-staff-surveys-say; www.forbes.com/sites/jackkelly/2021/04/28/jp-morgan-requires-employees-to-return-to-their-offices-by-july-striking-a-blow-to-the-remote-work-trend/?sh=139d715e4cdc

[5] www.businessinsider.com/apple-tim-cook-return-office-working-from-home-three-days-2021-6?r=US&IR=T

[6] www.forbes.com/sites/jackkelly/2021/05/13/weworks-new-ceo-says-uberly-engaged-employees-will-return-to-the-office-while-others-will-be-very-comfortableat-home/?sh=3394045a740f

[7] In the UK, at the time of writing (October 2021) there are plans for this to be changed as a part of the flexible working consultation. For more see: www.gov.uk/government/consultations/making-flexible-working-the-default

[8] www.gov.ie/en/press-release/6b64a-tanaiste-signs-code-of-practice-on-right-to-disconnect/

[9] https://www.euronews.com/next/2021/11/08/portugal-makes-it-illegal-for-your-boss-to-text-you-after-work

[10] From 2017 the UK government has asked all companies with 250 or more employees to report their gender pay gap, with a plan of how to tackle this issue. www.gov.uk/government/collections/gender-pay-gap-reporting

[11] For more, see coverages: www.theguardian.com/world/2021/mar/15/spain-to-launch-trial-of-four-day-working-week; www.independent.co.uk/news/world/asia/india-four-day-work-week-new-labour-code-b1800331.html; indianexpress.com/article/explained/new-labour-codes-india-four-day-week-7182376/; https://www.theguardian.com/world/2020/may/20/jacinda-ardern-flags-four-day-working-week-as-way-to-rebuild-new-zealand-after-covid-19 www.koreaherald.com/view.php?ud=20210217000870

[12] At the time of writing, a report was circulated in Goldman Sachs based on a survey of first year analysts outlining the very long-hours work culture (of over 100 hours a week), and the steep decline in well-being from nine (healthiest being ten) to a mere two. https://assets.bwbx.io/documents/users/iqjWHBFdfxIU/rim9z3X.NpYk/v0 Despite the junior associates and many others in Goldman Sachs demanding a change in the work culture to work 'only 80 hours a week', the CEO responded by saying, 'If we all go an extra mile for our client, even when we feel that we're reaching our limit, it can really make a difference in our performance', again emphasising the assumption that only through long-hours work, workers can achieve performance outcomes. www.theguardian.com/business/2021/mar/22/goldman-sachs-boss-responds-to-leaked-report-into-inhumane-working-hours

13 I also recommend managers take a look at the book by Gemma Dale (2020), and a recent report by CIPD (2021).

14 www.history.com/this-day-in-history/ford-factory-workers-get-40-hour-week

15 Another really important mentor of mine who takes work-life balance seriously is Wim van Oorschot. I wrote a whole chapter about this in Chung (2021b).

16 https://thenapministry.wordpress.com/

Appendix

Data used

European Company Survey 2013

To examine the provision of flexitime, the ECS of 2013 from the European Foundation is used. The ECS provides information at the establishment level on various workplace practices, ranging from working time to social dialogue. A representative sample of establishments with more than ten employees was gathered from 32 countries, including the EU28 member states and four candidate countries – namely, Iceland, Montenegro, FYROM and Turkey. Of those I only use data from the EU28 countries. The survey was conducted during February and March 2013 via telephone, with personnel managers of over 30,0000 establishments and employee representatives from 9,000 establishments being interviewed. This book makes use of the data from the manager survey, which covers a wider and more representative range of companies. The survey gathered data from approximately 1,000 companies per country, proportionate to the country size, using a disproportionate sample method to gather data from sufficient numbers of companies in each category of size and sector, resulting in just under 30,000 cases. Establishment weighting is used in this book: this allows the data to be more representative of the real composition of companies in terms of size and sector (with the exception of agriculture and fishing industries) as well as the size of each country. For more detail on the survey see: www.eurofound.europa.eu/surveys/european-company-surveys/european-company-survey-2013/ecs-2013-methodology

European Working Conditions Survey 2015

This EWCS data is gathered by the European Foundation and aims to provide information on a number of dimensions of working conditions for workers across Europe. Individuals across the European Union (EU28) and five candidate countries were included. In this book, for comparability issues, I use the EU28 member states. A random stratified sampling procedure was used to gather a representative sample of those aged 15 or over and in employment (minimum one hour a week) at the time of the survey and was conducted through face-to-face interviews. Approximately 1,000 cases are included per country with varying response rates. Of the total sample, I restrict the analysis to those in dependent employment, and further exclude those in the armed forces, and in agriculture/fishery due to the specific nature of these jobs. The analysis further excludes workers over the retirement age of 65, and when excluding all cases with a missing value in any one of the independent variables in the model results in just over 23,000 cases across 28 countries. For more information see online Appendix for the descriptive statistics of all variables including missing cases, and see: www. eurofound.europa.eu/surveys/european-working-conditions-surveys for more information on the data.

Variables: European Working Conditions Survey

Flexitime, working time autonomy and schedule control

The survey asks respondents the following question: 'How are your working time arrangements set?'. Here when workers responded as: 1) 'They are set by the company/organisation with no possibility for changes', it is considered as fixed schedules; 2) 'You can choose between several fixed working schedules determined by the company/organisation', I consider employer-oriented flexibility; 3) 'You can adapt your working hours within certain limits (for example flexitime)' is considered **flexitime**; and 4) 'Your working hours are entirely determined by yourself' is considered to be **working time autonomy**.

Teleworking/home working

The survey also asked regarding the place of work through the following question: 'How often have you worked in each location during the last 12 months in your main paid job?', with a number of options to choose from including: 1) Your employer's/your own business' premises (office, factory, shop, school and so on); 2) Client's premises; 3) A car or another vehicle; 4) An outside site (for example construction site, agricultural field, streets of a city); 5) Your own home; 6) Public spaces such as coffee shops, airports and so on. Respondents could reply that they work in this location: 'Daily', 'Several times a week', 'Several times a month', 'Less often' or 'Never'. I consider those who replied that they work in public spaces and/or their own home *at least several times a month* as those who **telework**, and those who work from home *at least several times a month* as those who **work from home** (homeworking). This data doesn't allow us to fully capture whether workers had the 'freedom to choose' to work from home or other public spaces to carry out their contracted or main working hours, or captures more the overtime work done at home in addition to the normal hours of work done in the workplace (see also Glass and Noonan, 2016). However, the response to this question provides us with an idea of the extent to which workers are now working outside of the more traditional premises of work.

Work-to-family, family-to-work conflict variables

There are three work-family conflict variables used in this study. First, using the following questions: 'How often in the last 12 months, have you …', firstly, 'felt too tired after work to do some of the household jobs which need to be done?' defined here as strain work-to-family conflict (strain WFC); secondly, 'found that your job prevented you from giving the time you wanted to your family?' defined as time work-to-family conflict (time WFC); thirdly, 'found it difficult to concentrate on your job because of your family responsibilities' which indicates mental family-to-work conflict (mental FWC); and finally, 'found that your family responsibilities prevented you from giving the time you should to your job', which indicates time-based family-to-work conflict (time FWC). Respondents could answer: 'Always', 'Most of the time', 'Sometimes', 'Rarely' and 'Never' to these questions. I consider those who indicated 'Always' or 'Most of the time' as those who experience work-to-family and FWC, making a binary variable for each variable, due to the non-normal distribution of the variables. Work-life balance satisfaction is measured through the following question: 'In general, how do your working hours fit in with your family or social commitments outside work?' (work-life fit), where respondents can answer: 'Very well', 'Well', 'Not very well' and 'Not at all well'. This, strictly speaking, does not indicate a more general satisfaction between work and family life, but only measures satisfaction in the balance of working hours with other aspects of one's life. However, due to lack of data we will consider this an indication of work-life balance satisfaction but also being mindful that it is a narrow definition of work-life/working hours fit. I will use this as a continuous variable despite it being, strictly speaking, an ordinal variable.

Spill-over, work during free time variable

To measure mental spill-over, I use the following question: 'How often in the last 12 months, have you …', firstly, 'kept worrying about work problems when you are not working?', which is defined as work-to-family mental spill-over (spill-over), that is, when thoughts about work spill over to other aspects of/family life. Respondents could answer: 'Always', 'Most of the time', 'Sometimes', 'Rarely' and 'Never' to these questions. I consider those who indicated 'Always' or 'Most of the time' as those who experience work-to-family spill-over, making a binary variable for each variable, due to the non-normal distribution of the variables. I also use the question: 'Over the last 12 months, how often have you worked in your free time to meet work demands?', where respondents could answer: 'Daily', 'Several times a week', 'Several times a month', 'Less often' and 'Never'. Those who answered several times a month or more are considered to work frequently during their free time (work free time).

Work-family conflict index for Chapter 9

Here, rather than examine the different types of work-family conflict separately I combined five work-to-family conflict variables into a single index, as done in many previous studies (Kelly et al, 2011; Glavin and Schieman, 2012). In other words, the work-family conflict index combines the extent to which individuals agree with the following five statements: in the past 12 months did you ... 'keep worrying about work problems when you are not working?', 'feel too tired after work to do some of the household jobs which need to be done?', 'found that your job prevented you from giving the time you wanted to your family', 'How often have you worked in your free time to meet work demands?' and finally, 'In general, how do your working hours fit in with your family or social commitments outside work?'. All variables are coded so a higher score entails a higher level of work-family conflict. A principle components analysis of these variables resulted in a one factor solution, indicating that the variables can be considered to represent one underlying latent factor. The Cronbach alpha was 0.70 indicating internal consistency.

Control variables; access to and use of flexible working models

Individual-level characteristics include gender, age of the respondent, whether the worker cohabits with a partner, household income security level (using the question: 'A household may have different sources of income and more than one household member may contribute to it. Thinking of your household's total monthly income, is your household able to make ends meet?', where respondents can respond from: with great difficulty=0, to very easily=5. This variable is used as a continuous variable).

Family demands driven variables include whether the respondent lives with a young child (less than six years old), a primary school-age child (6–11), whether they have other caring responsibilities (of family, friends), has a disability (has a health issue that limits one's daily activity), their health status ('How is your health in general? Would you say it is ...', where respondents can respond from: very bad=0 to very good=4). At the company level, whether an employee representative is present at the workplace, management support ('Your manager helps and supports you'), whether the respondent has a female boss, the gender composition of the workplace (majority women, majority men, or equally represented (reference group)).

Performance goal driven variables include working hours, education level (lower secondary or below, upper secondary (reference category), and tertiary or above), whether the individual is in a supervisory role, whether there is individual performance-related pay, self-managed team, whether the worker has an open-ended contract, job insecurity – that is, whether the respondent feels like they will lose their job in the next six months, occupational level measured through ISCO 1 digit occupational categories.

Structural factors include, company size (1–49, 50–249, and 250 or more employees) (reference category), whether the company is a public company, and sector – based on the NACE R.2 1 digit divisions.

Control variables; work-family conflict models

The models include as control variables factors that have frequently been shown to influence workers' work-family conflict (Michel et al, 2011; Allen et al, 2013), as well as access to flexible working (Golden, 2009; Chung, 2018).

Household characteristics that are included: whether the worker cohabits with a partner, the partner's employment status (employed or not), household income security level, whether the respondent lives with a child (under the age of 18), a young child (less than six years old), and the number of children they have.

Job demands variables include work intensity; that is, whether the respondents need to work at a high speed, on a tight deadline, and their hours worked; and perceived job insecurity.

Job resources variables include career advancement ('My job offers good prospects for career advancement'), whether the worker is in a well-paid job ('Considering all my efforts and achievements in my job, I feel I get paid appropriately'), and management support ('Your manager helps and supports you').

Occupational levels/higher status is measured through ISCO 1 digit occupational categories, and a dummy indicating whether the respondent is in a supervisory role.

Other work characteristics include whether the respondent works in the public sector, whether an employee representative is present at the workplace, whether the respondent has a female boss, the gender composition of the workplace (majority women, majority men, or equally represented (reference group)), whether there is individual performance-related pay, company size and sector – based on the NACE R.2 1 digit divisions.

Other **individual-level characteristics** include gender, age of the respondent and their health status ('How is your health in general? Would you say it is …', where respondents can respond from: very bad=1 to very good=5).

Appendix Figures and Tables

Appendix to Chapter 3

Table A3.1: Explaining company-level provision of flexitime across Europe in 2013

	Flexitime use		% of workers covered	
	beta	Std.err	beta	Std.err
Family-friendly explanations				
% females (standardised)	0.049**	0.017	0.996***	0.309
ER exists	0.187***	0.038	-1.802**	0.690
Work climate	0.119**	0.042	4.411***	0.768
High-performance explanations				
% skilled (standardised)	0.357***	0.020	7.246***	0.307
Performance pay	0.476***	0.033	-1.356*	0.605
Self-managed team work	0.335***	0.044	4.024***	0.691
Structural factors				
Size (ref: 250+)				
10–49	-0.429***	0.054	15.406***	0.865
50–249	-0.301***	0.053	4.060***	0.834
Public company	-0.080	0.061	1.050	1.037
Sector (ref: industry)				
Construction	-0.265***	0.062	0.299	1.224
Commerce and hospitality	-0.127**	0.043	2.518**	0.801
Transport and communication	-0.100	0.062	-1.690	1.144
Financial services and real estate	-0.146+	0.079	9.597***	1.321
Other services	0.193***	0.051	8.367***	0.837
constant	0.221	0.165	41.079***	1.866
Var. country	0.601	0.164	55.052***	15.391
Var. company	3.29		1140.415***	13.305
Log likelihood	-11929.101		-72738.604	

Note: N level 1 = 21582(flexitime use), 14720(% of workers covered – only includes companies that provide flexitime), N level 2=28 countries, *** = $p < 0.001$, ** = $p < 0.01$, *= $p < 0.05$.

Here the proportion of workers covered by flexitime is measured in categories of No workers, 0–20%, 20–40%, 40–60%, 60–80%, 80–99%, ALL workers, which is then transformed into percentages ranging from 0 to 100% and used as a linear continuous variable.

Table A3.2: Explaining individual-level access to flexible working arrangements across Europe in 2015

	Flexitime			Working time autonomy			Teleworking			Working from home		
	B	Std. E	Odds	B	Std. E	Odds	B	Std. E	Odds	B	Std. E	Odds
Female (ref: male)	-0.034	0.047	0.966	0.045	0.084	1.046	-0.217***	0.047	0.805	0.037	0.056	1.038
Age	0.002	0.002	1.002	0.015***	0.004	1.015	-0.006***	0.002	0.994	0.004	0.002	1.004
Has a partner (ref: does not have a partner)	-0.101*	0.043	0.904	0.107	0.080	1.113	-0.035	0.043	0.966	-0.018	0.053	0.982
Household income security (meets household needs with 0=great difficulty, 5=very easily)	0.082***	0.018	1.085	0.290***	0.034	1.336	0.046**	0.017	1.047	0.131***	0.022	1.140
Family demands driven												
Has a preschool child <6	0.173**	0.064	1.189	0.030	0.121	1.031	0.019	0.063	1.020	0.175*	0.078	1.191
Has a young child <12	0.029	0.061	1.029	0.075	0.109	1.077	0.089	0.059	1.093	0.197**	0.072	1.218
Care responsibilities⌐	0.125**	0.046	1.133	0.153+	0.083	1.165	0.202***	0.045	1.224	0.221***	0.056	1.247
Has a disability (ref: no disability)	0.096	0.065	1.101	0.077	0.121	1.080	0.222***	0.065	1.249	0.188*	0.081	1.207
Health condition (0=very bad, 4=very good)	-0.021	0.029	0.979	0.007	0.053	1.007	-0.058*	0.028	0.944	-0.117***	0.036	0.890
Employee representative exists (ref: no ER)	-0.014	0.047	0.986	-0.358***	0.087	0.699	-0.067	0.046	0.935	-0.062	0.058	0.940
Management support	0.162***	0.041	1.176	-0.005	0.074	0.995	-0.076+	0.040	0.927	-0.055	0.050	0.946
Boss woman (ref: boss man)	0.077+	0.045	1.080	-0.074	0.083	0.929	-0.191***	0.045	0.826	-0.184***	0.055	0.832
Gender dominance of job (ref: equal numbers)												
Mostly men with the same job	-0.267***	0.051	0.766	-0.127	0.088	0.881	0.055	0.051	1.056	-0.103	0.064	0.902
Mostly women with the same job	-0.322***	0.050	0.725	-0.577***	0.094	0.561	-0.219***	0.051	0.803	-0.227***	0.061	0.797

Table A3.2: Explaining individual-level access to flexible working arrangements across Europe in 2015 (continued)

	Flexitime			Working time autonomy			Teleworking			Working from home		
	B	Std. E	Odds	B	Std. E	Odds	B	Std. E	Odds	B	Std. E	Odds
Performance goal driven												
Working hours	0.000	0.002	1.000	0.001	0.004	1.001	0.019*	0.002	1.019	0.022***	0.003	1.022
Education (ref: upper secondary)												
Primary or lower secondary	-0.267***	0.069	0.765	-0.124	0.129	0.884	0.005	0.066	1.005	-0.240*	0.107	1.022
Tertiary or above	0.371***	0.047	1.449	0.173	0.087	1.189	0.430***	0.048	1.538	0.565***	0.060	0.787
Supervisory role (ref: not in supervisory role)	0.205***	0.052	1.227	0.634***	0.086	1.885	0.235***	0.051	1.264	0.259***	0.062	1.759
Performance-related pay	0.334***	0.047	1.396	0.356***	0.082	1.427	0.406***	0.048	1.500	0.449***	0.057	1.295
Self-managed team	0.147***	0.041	1.158	-0.500***	0.072	0.607	0.036	0.040	1.036	-0.130**	0.050	1.566
Open-ended contract (ref: not in open-ended)	-0.057	0.057	0.945	-0.390***	0.101	0.677	-0.207***	0.053	0.813	-0.160*	0.071	0.879
Job insecure	-0.189***	0.056	0.827	-0.208+	0.107	0.812	0.119*	0.052	1.126	0.130+	0.067	0.852
Occupational level (ref: service and sales workers)												
Managers	0.856***	0.091	2.355	0.862***	0.145	2.367	0.475***	0.087	1.608	1.439***	0.112	4.217
Professionals	0.822***	0.071	2.275	0.227+	0.131	1.255	0.356***	0.067	1.428	1.318***	0.094	3.737
Associate professionals and technicians	0.735***	0.069	2.086	0.285*	0.126	1.329	0.035	0.068	1.036	0.847***	0.098	2.332
Clerical support workers	0.537***	0.074	1.710	-0.121	0.144	0.886	-0.679***	0.083	0.507	0.211+	0.113	1.235
Crafts and related trades workers	-0.124	0.092	0.884	-0.692***	0.186	0.500	-0.488***	0.089	0.614	0.030	0.135	1.031
Plant and machine operators	-0.353**	0.114	0.703	-0.506*	0.220	0.603	-0.683***	0.106	0.505	-0.055**	0.162	0.946
Elementary occupations	-0.052	0.092	0.950	-0.011	0.161	0.989	-0.301**	0.085	0.740	-0.314**	0.156	0.730

(continued)

Table A3.2: Explaining individual-level access to flexible working arrangements across Europe in 2015 (continued)

	Flexitime			Working time autonomy			Teleworking			Working from home		
	B	Std. E	Odds	B	Std. E	Odds	B	Std. E	Odds	B	Std. E	Odds
Structural												
Establishment size (ref: 250 or more)												
1–49 workers	0.015	0.063	1.015	0.357***	0.110	1.429	0.210***	0.062	1.234	0.174*	0.081	1.190
50–249 workers	-0.237***	0.044	0.789	-0.172*	0.086	0.842	-0.018	0.045	0.982	-0.081	0.055	0.923
Public company	-0.102+	0.053	0.903	-0.468***	0.104	0.627	0.046	0.053	1.047	-0.089	0.065	0.915
Sector (ref: commerce and hospitality)												
Industry	0.056	0.069	1.058	-0.210+	0.121	0.811	-0.309***	0.071	0.734	0.081	0.096	1.084
Transport	-0.194+	0.104	0.824	-0.328+	0.194	0.720	0.381***	0.096	1.464	0.131	0.143	1.140
Financial services	0.272**	0.094	1.313	0.154	0.161	1.166	-0.146	0.106	0.864	0.234***	0.126	1.264
Public admin. and defence	0.583***	0.090	1.791	-0.287	0.196	0.750	0.580***	0.090	1.786	0.516***	0.122	1.675
Education	-0.641***	0.095	0.527	0.109	0.170	1.115	1.047***	0.086	2.849	1.609***	0.110	4.999
Health	-0.441***	0.082	0.643	-0.071	0.149	0.931	-0.265***	0.085	0.768	-0.181	0.115	0.834
Other services	0.395***	0.065	1.484	0.283**	0.108	1.327	0.315***	0.064	1.370	0.683***	0.090	1.980
Constant	-2.483***	0.241	0.083	-4.288***	0.343	0.014	-2.106***	0.190	0.122	-4.391***	0.252	0.012
Log Likelihood	-9572.346			-3608.1001			-9817.457			-67221448		
Variance country level	0.746***	0.208		0.363***	0.112		0.156***	0.046		0.241***	0.070	
Variance individual level	$\pi^2/3$			$\pi^2/3$			$\pi^2/3$			$\pi^2/3$		

Note: N level 1=23408, N level 2=28 countries, *** = $p < 0.001$, ** = $p < 0.010$, * = $p < 0.050$, += $p < 0.100$

£ childcare several times a week or elderly care several times a month

(continued)

201

Appendix to Chapter 4

Table A4.1: Full regression tables showing the association between flexible working and work-to-family (WFC) and family-to-work conflict (FWC)

	Time WFC	Strain WFC	Working time adequacy	Mental FWC	Time FWC
Employer flexibility	-0.123	0.032	-0.010	0.307***	0.345***
Flexitime	-0.067	-0.098+	0.012	0.228***	0.229***
Working time autonomy	0.065	0.183+	0.050*	0.141*	0.137+
Telework	0.361***	0.206***	-0.082***	0.284***	0.365***
Time off work	-0.579***	-0.426***	0.263***	-0.225***	-0.208***
Female (ref: male)	0.287***	0.492***	-0.023*	0.172***	0.099**
Age	-0.018***	-0.010***	0.004***	-0.005**	0.000
Has a partner (ref: does not have a partner)	0.270***	0.119*	-0.015	0.076+	0.076+
Partner employed (ref: not employed)	-0.105+	-0.180***	-0.001	0.077+	0.091*
Health status (very bad=0, very good=4)	-0.395***	-0.530***	0.113***	-0.288***	-0.248***
Household income security (meets household needs with great difficulty=0, very easily=5)	-0.085***	-0.093***	0.039***	-0.128***	-0.100***
Has a child <18	0.520***	0.097	-0.086***	0.519***	0.517***
Has a preschool child <6	0.214**	0.104+	-0.080***	0.179***	0.255***
Number of child(ren) (ref: 3 or more)					
1	-0.125	-0.061	0.033	-0.110	-0.111

(continued)

Table A4.1: Full regression tables showing the association between flexible working and work-to-family (WFC) and family-to-work conflict (FWC) (continued)

	Time WFC	Strain WFC	Working time adequacy	Mental FWC	Time FWC
2	0.046	0.030	0.021	-0.018	-0.030
Elderly care	0.075	0.073	-0.022+	0.314***	0.176***
Education (ref: upper secondary)					
Primary or lower secondary	0.075	0.132*	-0.003	-0.124**	-0.061
Tertiary or above	0.103	0.087+	-0.029*	0.147***	0.112**
Supervisory role (ref: not in supervisory role)	0.350***	0.183**	-0.072***	0.057	0.193***
Working hours	0.051***	0.029***	-0.015***	0.017***	0.015***
Open-ended contract	0.140*	-0.094+	0.034**	0.173***	0.113**
Public company	-0.001	-0.021	0.020	0.005	-0.059
Company size (ref: 250 or more employees)					
1–49	-0.127	-0.161**	0.026+	0.108*	0.192***
50–249	-0.080	-0.051	0.014	0.072*	0.087*
Boss woman (ref: boss man)	-0.098+	0.034	0.009	-0.035	-0.052
Gender dominance of job (ref: equal numbers)					
Mostly men with the same job	0.164*	0.139*	-0.048***	-0.051	0.052
Mostly women with the same job	0.086	0.009	0.017	-0.031	0.026
Performance-related pay	0.069	0.087+	-0.023+	0.158***	0.083
Employee representative exists (ref: no ER)	-0.063	-0.019	0.014	0.081*	0.028
Occupational level (ref: service and sales workers)					
Managers	-0.033	-0.067	0.010	-0.027	0.062

(continued)

Table A4.1: Full regression tables showing the association between flexible working and work-to-family (WFC) and family-to-work conflict (FWC) (continued)

	Time WFC	Strain WFC	Working time adequacy	Mental FWC	Time FWC
Professionals	-0.147	-0.107	0.027	-0.076	0.002
Associate professionals and technicians	-0.390**	-0.404***	0.101***	-0.100	-0.129
Clerical support workers	0.043	0.082	-0.048*	-0.105	-0.067
Crafts and related trades workers	-0.289*	0.058	0.067*	-0.263**	-0.226**
Plant and machine operators	-0.154	-0.018	-0.027	-0.182*	-0.085
Elementary occupations	-0.461**	-0.074	0.079**	-0.436***	-0.307**
Need to work at a high speed	0.137***	0.177***	-0.019***	0.057***	0.067***
Has a tight deadline	0.130***	0.113***	-0.026***	0.075***	0.066***
Job insecurity	0.099***	0.040**	-0.022***	0.087***	0.089***
Management support	-0.317***	-0.230***	0.098***	-0.207***	-0.205***
Well-paid	-0.166***	-0.158***	0.053***	-0.031*	-0.052***
Good prospects for career advancement	-0.107***	-0.113***	0.022***	0.035**	0.099***
Sector (ref: commerce hospitality)					
Industry	-0.123	-0.031	0.030+	-0.028	-0.024
Construction	0.058	0.299**	0.020	-0.035	-0.026
Transport	0.397***	0.271**	-0.095***	-0.051	0.012
Financial services	0.133	0.199+	0.039	0.034	0.168*
Public administration	-0.050	-0.004	0.055*	0.008	0.026

(continued)

Table A4.1: Full regression tables showing the association between flexible working and work-to-family (WFC) and family-to-work conflict (FWC) (continued)

	Time WFC	Strain WFC	Working time adequacy	Mental FWC	Time FWC
Education	0.038	0.271**	0.130***	0.045	0.220**
Health social services	0.096	0.294***	-0.036+	-0.044	-0.013
Other services	0.226**	0.195**	0.011	0.098*	0.092+
Constant	-2.703***	-0.728**	1.810***	-0.094	-0.950***
Log likelihood	-6653.898	-10158.954	-23731.954	-15109.050	-14688.479
Variance country level	0.097 (0.031)	0.236 (0.064)	0.007 (0.002)	0.123 (0.034)	0.092 (0.026)
Variance individual level	π2/3	π2/3	0.426 (0.004)	π2/3	π2/3
N level 1	23717	23818	23888	23725	23656
N level 2	30	30	30	30	30

*** = $p < 0.001$, ** = $p < 0.010$, * = $p < 0.050$, += $p < 0.100$

Appendix to Chapter 6

Table A6.1: Full regression tables showing the association between flexible working and work-to-family spill-over

	Mental spill-over	Work during free time
Employer flex	0.036	0.285***
Flexitime	0.266***	0.484***
Working time autonomy	0.531***	0.719***
Telework	0.623***	1.209***
Time off work	-0.129**	-0.309***
Female (ref: male)	0.172**	-0.051
Age	-0.004*	-0.004+
Has a partner (ref: does not have a partner)	0.088	-0.138*
Partner employed (ref: not employed)	-0.085	0.069
Health status (very bad=0, very good=4)	-0.422***	-0.163***
Household income security (meets household needs with great difficulty=0, very easily=5)	-0.050*	0.022
Has a child <18	0.165	0.345***
Has a preschool child <6	0.017	-0.099
Number of child(ren) (ref: 3 or more)		
1	-0.076	-0.277**
2	-0.064	-0.130
Elderly care	0.151**	0.254***
Education (ref: upper secondary)		
Primary or lower secondary	0.074	-0.085
Tertiary or above	0.111*	0.330***
Supervisory role (ref: not in supervisory role)	0.394***	0.336***
Working hours	0.022***	0.033***
Open-ended contract	0.008	-0.111+
Public company	-0.117+	-0.021
Company size (ref: 250 or more employees)		
1–49	0.015	0.054
50–249	-0.009	0.068
Boss woman (ref: boss man)	0.068	-0.071
Gender dominance of job (ref: equal numbers)		
Mostly men with the same job	0.033	0.030

(continued)

Table A6.1: Full regression tables showing the association between flexible working and work-to-family spill-over (continued)

	Mental spill-over	Work during free time
Mostly women with the same job	-0.014	-0.004
Performance-related pay	0.120*	0.293***
Employee representative exists (ref: no ER)	-0.066	-0.105*
Occupational level (ref: service and sales workers)		
Managers	-0.401***	-0.103
Professionals	-0.663***	-0.516***
Associate professionals and technicians	-0.860***	-0.845***
Clerical support workers	-0.821***	-0.813***
Crafts and related trades workers	-1.096***	-0.862***
Plant and machine operators	-1.217***	-1.030***
Elementary occupations	-1.053***	-1.175***
Need to work at a high speed	0.097***	0.039**
Has a tight deadline	0.142***	0.159***
Job insecurity	0.139***	0.047**
Management support	-0.141**	-0.173***
Well-paid	-0.133***	-0.123***
Good prospects for career advancement	-0.012	0.028+
Sector (ref: commerce hospitality)		
Industry	0.029	-0.096
Construction	0.092	0.057
Transport	0.117	-0.126
Financial services	0.359**	0.212*
Public administration	0.334**	0.023
Education	0.782***	1.205***
Health social services	0.282**	0.189*
Other services	0.194*	0.093
Constant	-1.724***	-2.515***
Log likelihood	-8013.889	-9190.744
Variance country level	0.206 (0.057)	0.072 (0.022)
Variance individual level	$\pi 2/3$	$\pi 2/3$
N level 1	23836	23788
N level 2	30	30

Note: *** = $p < 0.001$, ** = $p < 0.010$, *= $p < 0.050$, += $p < 0.100$

Figure A6.1: The number of workers with schedule control with and without access to flexitime

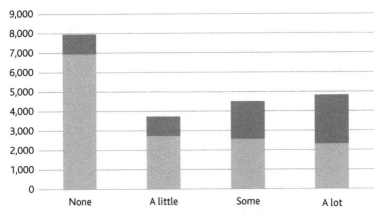

Source: wave 2 (2012) of the Understanding Society data – taken from Chung and van der Horst (2020) Online supplement.

Appendix to Chapter 9

Table A9.1: Summary of the multi-level logistic regression outcomes explaining the use and access to flexible working arrangements in 2015 across 30 (23) European countries

	Flexitime			Working time autonomy		
	all	men	women	all	men	women
Family policy exp. 2015	1.742***	1.693***	1.775***	1.291**	1.275*	1.280**
Child care coverage for 0–3	1.781***	1.675***	1.861***	1.432***	1.413***	1.423***
Collective bargaining coverage 2015	1.605***	1.502***	1.680***	1.505***	1.633***	1.384***
Union density 2015	1.424*	1.314*	1.519**	1.257*	1.320*	1.193+
Unemployment rate 2015	0.629**	0.635**	0.609**	0.797+	0.853	0.740*
Unemployment av. 2010–15	0.582***	0.605***	0.555***	0.731**	0.747*	0.713**
Female emp. rate 2015	1.770***	1.744***	1.808***	1.501***	1.508***	1.489***
Female labour market participation rate 2015	1.617***	1.604***	1.637***	1.430***	1.446***	1.409***
Gender norm 2017	1.907***	1.721***	2.054***	1.501***	1.543***	1.410***
Work centrality norm 2017	0.529***	0.588***	0.488***	0.664***	0.630***	0.727**
GDP/capita 2015	1.162	1.143	1.181	1.221*	1.243+	1.206*

Note: *** p<0.001, ** p<0.01, * p<0.05, + p<0.10

Odds ratios are standardised, meaning the strength of each context variable can be comparable across each group/each dependent variable. For the analysis with gender and work centrality norm, the analysis includes 23 country cases.

Data: EWCS, EUROSTAT, European Value Study, ICTWSS, author's calculation.

Each cell represents the result from one multi-level model (meaning the table represents 66 different analysis results), where only the standardised odds ratio of the context variable is provided. Each model controls for a range of factors, including age and presence of children, young children, individual's health, disability status, care responsibilities, income insecurity, work-related factors such as one's occupation, working hours, their supervisory position, job insecurity, company-level characteristics such as size, sector, gender composition of the workplace, management support and whether there is an employee representative present in the workplace. Detailed results are available upon request.

Table A9.1 Summary of the multi-level logistic regression outcomes explaining the use and access to flexible working arrangements in 2015 across 30 (23) European countries (continued)

	Teleworking			Working from home		
	all	men	women	all	men	women
Family policy exp. 2015	1.215**	1.222**	1.203**	1.252**	1.331***	1.183*
Childcare coverage for 0–3	1.319***	1.325***	1.320***	1.334***	1.389***	1.302***
Collective bargaining coverage 2015	1.259***	1.219**	1.302***	1.282***	1.299***	1.291***
Union density 2015	1.226***	1.215**	1.232***	1.208*	1.226*	1.195*
Unemployment rate 2015	0.945	0.956	0.930	0.812*	0.799+	0.824+
Unemployment av. 2010–15	0.894	0.910	0.878	0.772**	0.761*	0.778*
Female emp. rate 2015	1.209**	1.212**	1.219**	1.340***	1.419***	1.279***
Female labour market participation rate 2015	1.204**	1.216**	1.206**	1.279***	1.358***	1.215*
Gender norm 2017	1.424***	1.439***	1.415***	1.432***	1.532***	1.356***
Work centrality norm 2017	0.737***	0.755***	0.719***	0.721***	0.719***	0.721***
GDP/capita 2015	1.143*	1.139+	1.155*	1.141	1.110	1.152+

Note: *** $p<0.001$, ** $p<0.01$, * $p<0.05$, + $p<0.10$

Odds ratios are standardised, meaning the strength of each context variable can be comparable across each group/each dependent variable. For the analysis with gender and work centrality norm, the analysis includes 23 country cases.

Data: EWCS, EUROSTAT, European Value Study, ICTWSS, author's calculation.

Each cell represents the result from one multi-level model (the table contains results of 66 separate analysis), where only the standardised odds ratio of the context variable is provided. Each model controls for a range of factors, including age and presence of children, young children, individual's health, disability status, care responsibilities, income insecurity, work-related factors such as one's occupation, working hours, their supervisory position, job insecurity, company-level characteristics such as size, sector, gender composition of the workplace, management support and whether there is an employee representative present in the workplace. Detailed results are available upon request.

Table A9.2: Pairwise correlation between different national contexts (2015) and flexibility stigma (2018)

	Flexible working badly perceived by colleagues 2018			Flexible working leads to negative career outcomes 2018		
	all	men	women	all	men	women
Prevalence of flexible working						
Flexible working leads to negative career outcomes 2018	0.70***	0.67***	0.69***	1.00	1.00	1.00
Access to flexitime at the national level 2015	-0.70***	-0.70***	-0.61***	-0.36+	-0.41*	-0.29
Access to working time autonomy at the national level 2015	-0.69***	-0.66***	-0.61***	-0.32	-0.34+	-0.27
Access to schedule control (flexitime + working time autonomy) 2015	-0.71***	-0.71***	-0.62***	-0.36+	-0.40*	-0.29
% of workers teleworking at the national level 2015	-0.41***	-0.40*	-0.38*	-0.13	-0.15	-0.12
% working from home 2015	-0.58***	-0.58***	-0.51**	-0.27	-0.32+	-0.23
National contexts						
Family policy expenditure 2015	-0.43*	-0.55**	-0.25	-0.26	-0.33+	-0.17
Child care coverage for 0–3	-0.39*	-0.44***	-0.29	0.02	-0.01	0.04
Collective bargaining coverage 2015	-0.34+	-0.39*	-0.23	0.10	0.07	0.09
Union density 2015	-0.23	-0.21	-0.19	-0.19	-0.09	-0.27
Unemployment average 2010–15	0.63***	0.62**	0.53**	0.37+	0.39*	0.30
Female labour market participation rate 2015	-0.60***	-0.50**	-0.61***	-0.52**	-0.52**	-0.47*
Gender norm 2017	-0.58**	-0.58**	-0.50*	-0.20	-0.24	-0.14
Work centrality norm 2017	0.57**	0.41+	0.63**	0.18	0.20	0.14
GDP/capita 2015	-0.25	-0.14	-0.31	-0.16	-0.05	-0.22

Note: *** p<0.001, ** p<0.01, * p<0.05, + p<0.10

Data: EWCS, EUROSTAT, European Value Study, ICTWSS, author's calculation.

Detailed results are available upon request.

Table A9.3: Correlation between national level variables

	Collective bargaining coverage as % of total workforce	Union density as % total workforce	Family policy expenditure	Childcare coverage 0–3	Unemployment rate	Unemployment rate average	% flexitime	% working time Auto	% teleworking	% home work	Female labour market participation rate	Gender norms	Working centrality norms	GDP/ capita PPS
Collective bargaining coverage	1.00													
Union density	0.56**	1.00												
Family policy expenditure	0.38*	0.42**	1.00											
Childcare coverage 0–3	0.67***	0.57***	0.55***	1.00										
Unemployment rate 2015	0.01	-0.12	-0.46*	-0.15	1.00									
Unemployment rate ave	-0.17	-0.26	-0.52**	-0.24	0.96***	1.00								
% of flexitime	0.56***	0.56***	0.72***	0.77***	-0.46*	-0.54**	1.00							
% of working time autonomy	0.60***	0.43*	0.44*	0.65***	-0.36	-0.47*	0.78***	1.00						
% of tele working	0.53***	0.59***	0.53***	0.78***	-0.18	-0.29	0.84***	0.75***	1.00					
% of home working	0.53**	0.54**	0.60***	0.75***	-0.41*	-0.49**	0.91***	0.78***	0.94***	1.00				
Female labour market participation rate average 5 years	0.20	0.14	0.38*	0.53**	-0.23	-0.22	0.62***	0.65***	0.52***	0.57***	1.00			
Gender norm (2017)	0.62**	0.68***	0.63***	0.85***	-0.06	-0.17	0.86***	0.69***	0.79***	0.76***	0.71***	1.00		
Work centrality (2017)	-0.46*	-0.21	-0.27	-0.51*	0.09	0.17	-0.66***	-0.68***	-0.64***	-0.62**	-0.66***	-0.61**	1.00	
GDP/capita PPS	0.04	0.18	0.04	0.28	0.01	0.00	0.23	0.44*	0.37*	0.28	0.40*	0.65***	-0.44*	1.00

Note: *** = $p < 0.001$, ** = $p < 0.010$, * = $p < 0.050$

Table A9.4: Flexible working and work-family conflict for those with care responsibilities across 30 European countries in 2015

	Work-family conflict		
Schedule control (ref: fixed schedule)	Model 1.1	Model 1.2	Model 1.3
Employer-oriented flexibility	0.088**	0.070**	0.091*
Flexitime	0.146***	0.087***	0.117***
Working time autonomy	0.170***	0.139***	0.253***
Teleworking	0.490***	0.326***	0.278***
Time off work	-0.526***	-0.297***	-0.324***
Female		0.127***	0.102***
Employer-oriented flexibility*female			-0.033
Flexitime*female			-0.050
Working time autonomy*female			**-0.211*****
Teleworking*female			**0.090*****
Time off work*female			0.046
Controls			
Age		-0.007***	-0.007***
Partner		-0.013	-0.013
Partner in employment		0.006	0.006
Health		-0.224***	-0.223***
Household income security (4=secure, 1=insecure)		-0.059***	-0.059***
Lives with a preschool child (<6)		0.054**	0.054**
Number of children (ref: no children)			
1 child		0.053**	0.053**
2 children		0.094***	0.094***
3 or more		0.135***	0.133***
Caring for a child several time a month or more		0.045*	0.044*
Caring for an elderly/disabled relative several times a month		0.057***	0.057***
Education (ref: upper secondary)			
Lower secondary and below		-0.023	-0.022
Tertiary and above		0.129***	0.128***
Supervisory role		0.146***	0.146***
Working hours		0.022***	0.022***
Permanent contract		0.014	0.015
Public company		-0.025	-0.024
Size of company (ref: 250+)			
Micro company <10		0.002	0.001

(continued)

Table A9.4: Flexible working and work-family conflict for those with care responsibilities across 30 European countries in 2015 (continued)

	Work-family conflict		
SME 10–249		-0.016	-0.017
Direct boss is a woman		-0.013	-0.013
Workforce composition (ref: equal)			
Mostly men in same position		0.052*	0.052**
Mostly women in same position		-0.005	-0.005
Performance-related pay		0.068***	0.068***
Employee representative present		-0.014	-0.015
Work at high speed		0.056***	0.056***
Work with tight deadlines		0.074***	0.074***
Job insecurity		0.157***	0.158***
Management support		-0.155**	-0.154**
Well-paid		-0.083***	-0.083***
Good career prospective		-0.023***	-0.023***
Occupational level (ref: clerical support workers)			
Managers		0.402***	0.397***
Professionals		0.293***	0.291***
Associate professionals and technicians		0.171***	0.170***
Service and sales workers		0.177***	0.177***
Crafts and related trades workers		0.051	0.051
Plant and machine operators		0.084*	0.082*
Elementary occupations		-0.083*	-0.083*
Sector (ref: commerce & hospitality)			
Industry		-0.027	-0.028
Construction		0.057	0.058
Transport		0.088*	0.089*
Financial services		0.080*	0.082*
Public administration		-0.004	-0.002
Education		0.157***	0.152***
Health social svc		0.081**	0.082**
Other services		0.073**	0.073**
Constant	0.203***	-0.072***	-0.050***
Variance level 2	0.033***	0.021***	0.021***
Variance level 1	0.853***	0.629***	0.628***
Log likelihood	- 19060.227	-19088.57	-19060.227

Note: *** = $p < 0.001$, ** = $p < 0.010$, * = $p < 0.050$, + = $p < 0.100$
N level 1= 14,200, N level2=30

Table A9.5: Country-level factors moderating the association between flexitime/working time autonomy and work-family conflict for those with care responsibilities (for men and women) across 30 European countries in 2015

Model	Work-family conflict					
	2.1	2.2	2.3	2.4	2.5	2.6
Model						
Schedule control (ref: fixed schedule)						
Employer-oriented flex	0.067**	0.067**	0.068**	0.066*	0.065*	0.070**
Flexitime	0.098***	0.095***	0.093***	0.110***	0.108***	0.089***
Working time autonomy	0.127***	0.128***	0.129***	0.126***	0.130***	0.196***
Teleworking	0.325***	0.325***	0.326***	0.326***	0.326***	0.326***
Time off work	-0.297***	-0.296***	-0.297***	-0.297***	-0.295***	-0.296***
Female	0.128***	0.128***	0.128***	0.128***	0.128***	0.130***
Childcare coverage	0.069*				0.028	
Female * childcare cov					0.073***	
Flexitime * childcare cov	-0.037*				-0.004	
Flexitime * female					-0.021	
Flexitime*female*chcare cov					-0.059+	
Collective bargaining coverage		0.061*				
Flexitime * CBC		-0.041+				
Union density			0.074**			
Flexitime * union density			-0.031+			

(continued)

Table A9.5: Country-level factors moderating the association between flexitime/working time autonomy and work-family conflict for those with care responsibilities (for men and women) across 30 European countries in 2015 (continued)

Model	Work-family conflict					
	2.1	2.2	2.3	2.4	2.5	2.6
Prevalence of flexitime				-0.039		
Flexitime * prev. flexitime				-0.049**		
Family policy exp.						-0.023
Female*fam policy exp.						0.055***
WTautonomy*family policy exp						0.080+
WTautonomy*female						-0.133+
WTautonomy*female*fam pol exp.						-0.100+
Constant	-0.063	-0.065	-0.068	-0.073	-0.070	-0.066
Var. random slope	0.002	0.003	0.002	0.001	0.002	0.000
Log likelihood [a]	-16892.98	-16893.957	-16892.909	-16894.119	-16881.573	-16886.71
N – level 1	14200					
N – level 2	30					

Note: model controls for a variety of control variables listed in Model 1 of Table 1

*** = $p < 0.001$, ** = $p < 0.01$, * = $p < 0.05$, + = $p < 0.10$, N level 1= 14,200, N level2=30

Table A9.6: Country-level factors moderating the association between teleworking work-family conflict for those with care responsibilities across 30 European countries in 2015

	Work-family conflict			
Model	3.1	3.2	3.3	3.4
Schedule control (ref=fixed schedule)				
Employer-oriented flexibility	0.069**	0.069**	0.068**	0.068**
Flexitime	0.085***	0.084***	0.084***	0.083***
Working time autonomy	0.138***	0.139***	0.138***	0.137***
Teleworking	0.325***	0.286***	0.276***	0.282***
Time off work	-0.297***	-0.296***	-0.294***	-0.294***
Female	0.128***	0.108***	0.108***	0.108***
Union density	0.073***	0.039		
Union density * female		0.057***		
Teleworking * union density	-0.030+	0.005		
Teleworking * female		0.072*		
Teleworking * union density*female		-0.058*		
Collective bargaining coverage			0.013	
Collective bargaining cov* female			0.069***	
Teleworking * collective barg. cov.			0.047+	
Teleworking * female			0.077*	
Teleworking * col. B.C * female			-0.089**	
Childcare coverage 0–3				0.024
Childcare cov * female				0.065***
Teleworking * childcare. cov.				0.032
Teleworking * female				0.068+
Teleworking * childcare cov * female				-0.055+
Constant	-0.070	-0.057	-0.062	-0.052
Var. random slope	0.003	0.003	0.004	0.004
Log likelihood [a]	-16892.731	-16883.374	-16883.007	16883.175
N – level 1	14200			
N – level 2	30			

Note: model controls for a variety of control variables listed in Model 1 in Table 1
*** = $p < 0.001$, ** = $p < 0.01$, *= $p < 0.05$, + = $p < 0.10$, N level 1= 14200, N level 2=30

Appendix to Chapter 10

COVID-19 data sets

There have been so many interesting studies using many data gathered during the COVID-19 pandemic that I would not be able to summarise all studies. However, I thought it would be useful to note a few key studies/ data collection teams that are worth looking into.

UK

Along with colleagues at Kent – Hyojin Seo, and the University of Birmingham – Sarah Forbes, Holly Birkett, we collected data mostly of dual-earning heterosexual couples with children under 18 during the first lockdown in the UK:

• Chung, H., Seo, H., Forbes, S., et al (2020b) Working from home during the COVID-19 lockdown: Changing preferences and the future of work. Canterbury, UK: University of Kent. For more information see: https:// wafproject.org/Covidwfh/

We also collected data from managers during July and August.

• Forbes, S., Birkett, H., Evans, L., Chung, H. and Whiteman, J. (2020) Managing employees during the COVID-19 pandemic: Flexible working and the future of work. Birmingham: University of Birmingham and the University of Kent.

Similarly, Understanding Society – the UK Household Panel Survey gathered several waves of data (every month from April to July, and bimonthly afterwards) during the COVID-19 period of their panel members www. understandingsociety.ac.uk/topic/Covid-19

US

In the US, Petts, Carlson and Pipin gathered data focusing on parents:

• Carlson, D.L., Petts, R.J. and Pepin, J.R. (2020) Changes in parents' domestic labor during the COVID-19 pandemic. *SocArXiv https://doi. org/10.31235/osf.io/jy8fn*
• Petts, R.J., Carlson, D.L. and Pepin, J.R. (2020) A gendered pandemic: Childcare, homeschooling, and parents' employment during COVID-19. *Gender, Work & Organization* 28(S2): 515–34.

Zamarro, Prados and colleagues captured work-family and gendered outcomes of the pandemic in the US longitudinally using the Understanding America Study (UAS):

- Zamarro, G., Perez-Arce, F. and Prados, M.J. (2020) Gender differences in the impact of COVID-19. Working Paper. https://ktla.com/wp-content/uploads/sites/4/2020/06/ZamarroGenderDiffImpactCOVID-19_061820-2.pdf
- Prados, M. and Zamarro, G. (2020) Gender differences in couples' division of childcare, work and mental health during COVID-19. *CESR-Schaeffer Working Paper.*

Canada

Schieman, S., Badawy, P.J., Milkie, M. and Bierman, A. (2021) Work-life conflict during the COVID-19 pandemic, gathered two waves of data using C-QWELS. *Socius: Sociological Research for a Dynamic World* 7.

Australia

Craig, L. and Churchill, B. (2020) Dual-earner parent couples' work and care during COVID-19. *Gender, Work & Organization* 28(S1): 66–79.

The Netherlands

Yerkes and colleagues gathered data across the lockdown over three periods using the LISS panel administered by Tilburg University:

- Yerkes, M.A., André, S., Beckers, D.G., et al (2020) 'Intelligent' lockdown, intelligent effects? Results from a survey on gender (in)equality in paid work, the division of childcare and household work, and quality of life among parents in the Netherlands during the COVID-19 lockdown. *PloS One* 15(11): e0242249. https://journals.plos.org/plosone/article?id=10.1371/journal.pone.0242249

Germany

Both the German SOEP www.eui.eu/Research/Library/ResearchGuides/Economics/Statistics/DataPortal/GSOEP and the GESIS Panel www.gesis.org/gesis-panel/coronavirus-outbreak gathered data around COVID-19 and the impact it had on families/workers.

Cross-European

Finally, the European Foundation gathered three waves of data using online surveys across all EU member states www.eurofound.europa.eu/data/Covid-19

References

Abrahamson, P. (2004) Review essay liquid modernity: Bauman on contemporary welfare society. *Acta Sociologica* 47(2): 171–9.

ACAS (2016) The right to request flexible working. www.acas.org.uk/index.aspx?articleid=1616

Acker, J. (1990) Hierarchies, jobs, bodies: A theory of gendered organizations. *Gender & Society* 4(2): 139–58.

Adler, M.A. (1993) Gender differences in job autonomy. *The Sociological Quarterly* 34(3): 449–65.

Alexander, A., Cracknell, R., De Smet, A., Langstaff, M., Mysore, M. and Ravid, D. (2021) What employees are saying about the future of remote work. www.mckinsey.com/business-functions/people-and-organizational-performance/our-insights/what-employees-are-saying-about-the-future-of-remote-work

Allen, T.D., Johnson, R.C., Kiburz, K.M. and Shockley, K.M. (2013) Work–family conflict and flexible work arrangements: Deconstructing flexibility. *Personnel Psychology* 66(2): 345–76.

Allen, T.D., Golden, T.D. and Shockley, K.M. (2015) How effective is telecommuting? Assessing the status of our scientific findings. *Psychological Science in the Public Interest* 16(2): 40–68.

Ambrose, J. (2021) BP to tell 25,000 office staff to work from home two days a week. *The Guardian.*

Andersen, S.H. (2018) Paternity leave and the motherhood penalty: New causal evidence. *Journal of Marriage and Family* 80(5): 1125–43.

Andrew, A., Cattan, S., Dias, M.C., Farquharson, C., Kraftman, L., Krutikova, S., et al (2020) How are mothers and fathers balancing work and family under lockdown? *Institute for Fiscal Studies.*

Anker, R. (1997) Theories of occupational segregation by sex: An overview. *International Labour Review* 136(3): 315–40.

Appelbaum, E., Bailey, T., Berg, P.B. and Kalleberg, A.L. (2000) *Manufacturing advantage: Why high-performance work systems pay off.* Ithaca, NY: Cornell University Press.

Armstrong, C. (2018) *The mother of all jobs.* London: Green Tree.

Arthur, M.B. (1994) The boundaryless career: A new perspective for organizational inquiry. *Journal of Organizational Behavior* 15(4): 295–306.

Aryee, S., Luk, V. and Stone, R. (1998) Family-responsive variables and retention-relevant outcomes among employed parents. *Human Relations* 51(1): 73–87.

Ashforth, B.E., Kreiner, G.E. and Fugate, M. (2000) All in a day's work: Boundaries and micro role transitions. *Academy of Management Review* 25(3): 472–91.

Avendano, M. and Panico, L. (2018) Do flexible work policies improve parents' health? A natural experiment based on the UK Millennium Cohort Study. *Journal of Epidemiology & Community Health* 72: 244–51.

Bakker, A.B. and Geurts, S.A.E. (2004) Toward a dual-process model of work-home interference. *Work and Occupations* 31(3): 345–66.

Bakker, A.B. and Demerouti, E. (2007) The job demands-resources model: State of the art. *Journal of Managerial Psychology* 22: 309–28.

Bakker, A.B., Demerouti, E., De Boer, E. and Schaufeli, W.B. (2003) Job demands and job resources as predictors of absence duration and frequency. *Journal of Vocational Behavior* 62(2): 341–56.

Bank of Korea (2020) 코로나19 사태로 인한 재택근무 확산: 쟁점과 평가. Seoul, Korea: Bank of Korea (한국은행).

Banks, J. and Xu, X. (2020) The mental health effects of the first two months of lockdown and social distancing during the COVID-19 pandemic in the UK. *IFS Working Papers*.

Bardoel, E.A., Moss, S.A., Smyrnios, K.X. and Tharenou, P. (1999) Employee characteristics associated with the provision of work-family policies and programs. *International Journal of Manpower* 20: 563–77.

Barrett, P. (2019) Digital wellbeing: Caring for employees in an 'always on' culture. *HR Zone*.

Bathini, D.R. and Kandathil, G.M. (2019) An orchestrated negotiated exchange: Trading home-based telework for intensified work. *Journal of Business Ethics* 154: 411–23.

Batt, R. and Valcour, M. (2003) Human resources practices as predictors of work family outcomes and employee turnover. *Industrial Relations: A Journal of Economy and Society* 42(2): 189–220.

Bauman, Z. (2013) *Liquid modernity*. Cambridge: Polity Press.

BBC (2021) We're travelling on a one-way road to freedom – PM. *BBC*.

Beauregard, T.A. and Henry, L.C. (2009) Making the link between work-life balance practices and organizational performance. *Human Resource Management Review* 19(1): 9–22.

Beauregard, T.A., Basile, K. and Canonico, E. (2013) Home is where the work is: A new study of homeworking in Acas – and beyond. *ACAS Research Paper* 10: 1–99.

Beck, U. (1992) *Risk society: Towards a new modernity*. London: Sage Publications.

Becker, G.S. (1964) *Human capital*. New York: Columbia University Press.

Been, W.M., van der Lippe, T., den Dulk, L., Das Dores Horta Guerreiro, M., Mrčela, A.K. and Niemistö, C. (2017) European top managers' support for work-life arrangements. *Social Science Research* 65: 60–74.

Bellezza, S., Paharia, N. and Keinan, A. (2017) Conspicuous consumption of time: When busyness and lack of leisure time become a status symbol. *Journal of Consumer Research* 44(1): 118–38.

Benzeval, M., Borkowska, M., Burton, J., Crossley, T.F., Fumagalli, L., Jäckle, A., et al (2020) Understanding Society COVID-19 Survey April Briefing Note: Home schooling. *Understanding Society Working Paper No 12/2020*. ISER, University of Essex.

Berdahl, J.L., Cooper, M., Glick, P., Livingston, R.W. and Williams, J.C. (2018) Work as a masculinity contest. *Journal of Social Issues* 74(3): 422–48.

Berg, P., Appelbaum, E., Bailey, T. and Kalleberg, A.L. (2004) Contesting time: International comparisons of employee control of working time. *Industrial & Labor Relations Review* 57(3): 331–49.

Berg, P., Kossek, E.E., Baird, M. and Block, R.N. (2013) Collective bargaining and public policy: Pathways to work-family policy adoption in Australia and the United States. *European Management Journal* 31(5): 495–504.

Berg, P., Kossek, E.E., Misra, K. and Belman, D. (2014) Work-life flexibility policies: Do unions affect employee access and use? *ILR Review* 67(1): 111–37.

Berman, E.M., West, J.P., Richter, J. and Maurice, N. (2002) Workplace relations: Friendship patterns and consequences (according to managers). *Public Administration Review* 62(2): 217–30.

Bettio, F. and Plantenga, J. (2004) Comparing care regimes in Europe. *Feminist Economics* 10(1): 85–113.

Bianchi, S.M., Milkie, M.A., Sayer, L.C. and Robinson, J.P. (2000) Is anyone doing the housework? Trends in the gender division of household labor. *Social Forces* 79(1): 191–228.

Bianchi, S.M., Sayer, L.C., Milkie, M.A. and Robinson, J.P. (2012) Housework: Who did, does or will do it, and how much does it matter? *Social Forces* 91(1): 55–63.

Blair-Loy, M. (2009) *Competing devotions: Career and family among women executives*. Cambridge, MA: Harvard University Press.

Bloom, N., Liang, J., Roberts, J. and Ying, Z.J. (2015) Does working from home work? Evidence from a Chinese experiment. *The Quarterly Journal of Economics* 130: 165–218.

Boltz, M., Cockx, B., Diaz, A.M. and Salas, L.M. (2020) How does working-time flexibility affect workers' productivity in a routine job? Evidence from a field experiment. Ghent University, Faculty of Economics and Business Administration.

Booth, R. (2019) Four-day week: Trial finds lower stress and increased productivity. *The Guardian*.

Bothwell, E. (2018) Work-life balance survey 2018: Long hours take their toll on academics. *Times Higher Education*.

Bowlby, J. (1979) The Bowlby-Ainsworth attachment theory. *Behavioral and Brain Sciences* 2(4): 637–8.

Brandth, B. and Kvande, E. (1998) Masculinity and child care: The reconstruction of fathering. *The Sociological Review* 46(2): 293–313.

Brescoll, V.L., Glass, J. and Sedlovskaya, A. (2013) Ask and ye shall receive? The dynamics of employer-provided flexible work options and the need for public policy. *Journal of Social Issues* 69(2): 367–88.

Brines, J. (1993) The exchange value of housework. *Rationality and Society* 5(3): 302–40.

Brines, J. (1994) Economic dependency, gender, and the division of labor at home. *American Journal of Sociology* 100(3): 652–88.

Bröckling, U. (2015) *The entrepreneurial self: Fabricating a new type of subject.* London: Sage.

Budd, J.W. and Mumford, K. (2004) Trade unions and family-friendly policies in Britain. *Industrial and Labor Relations Review* 57(2): 204–22.

Budig, M.J. and England, P. (2001) The wage penalty for motherhood. *American Sociological Review* 66(2): 204–25.

Budig, M.J. and Hodges, M.J. (2010) Differences in disadvantage: Variation in the motherhood penalty across white women's earnings distribution. *American Sociological Review* 75(5): 705–28.

Budig, M.J., Misra, J. and Boeckmann, I. (2012) The motherhood penalty in cross-national perspective: The importance of work-family policies and cultural attitudes. *Social Politics: International Studies in Gender, State & Society* 19(2): 163–93.

Buffer (2020) The 2020 state of remote work. https://lp.buffer.com/state-of-remote-work-2020

Buffer (2021) The 2021 state of remote work. https://buffer.com/2021-state-of-remote-work

Bünning, M. (2015) What happens after the 'daddy months'? Fathers' involvement in paid work, childcare, and housework after taking parental leave in Germany. *European Sociological Review* 31(6): 738–48.

Burgess, A. and Goldman, R. (2021) Lockdown fathers: The untold story (full report). *Contemporary Fathers in the UK series.* London: Fatherhood Institute.

Byron, K. (2005) A meta-analytic review of work-family conflict and its antecedents. *Journal of Vocational Behavior* 67: 169–98.

Cano, T., Perales, F. and Baxter, J. (2018) A matter of time: Father involvement and child cognitive outcomes. *Journal of Marriage and Family* 81(1): 164–84.

Carlson, D.L., Petts, R.J. and Pepin, J.R. (2020) Changes in parents' domestic labor during the COVID-19 pandemic. *SocArXiv.* https://doi.org/10.31235/osf.io/jy8fn

Caruso, C.C., Bushnell, T., Eggerth, D., Heitmann, A., Kojola, B., Newman, K., et al (2006) Long working hours, safety, and health: Toward a national research agenda. *American Journal of Industrial Medicine* 49(11): 930–42.

Casalicchio, E. (2021) UK should seize pandemic 'opportunity' to work more flexibly, says review chief. *Politico.*

Cech, E.A. and Blair-Loy, M. (2014) Consequences of flexibility stigma among academic scientists and engineers. *Work and Occupations* 41(1): 86–110.

Cha, Y. (2013) Overwork and the persistence of gender segregation in occupations. *Gender & Society* 27(2): 158–84.

Cha, Y. and Weeden, K.A. (2014) Overwork and the slow convergence in the gender gap in wages. *American Sociological Review* 79(3): 457–84.

Chan, T.F. (2018) South Korea has limited a working week to 52 hours, in order to stop overwork. *Business Insider*.

Chandola, T., Booker, C.L., Kumari, M. and Benzeval, M. (2019) Are flexible work arrangements associated with lower levels of chronic stress-related biomarkers? A study of 6025 employees in the UK Household Longitudinal Study. *Sociology* 53(4): 779–99.

Chung, H. (2008) Provision of work-life balance arrangements in European companies: Public vs. private. In: Keune, M., Leschke, J. and Watt, A. (eds) *Privatisation and marketisation of services: Social and economic impacts on employment, labour markets and trade unions.* Brussels: ETUI-REHS, pp 285–319.

Chung, H. (2009) *Flexibility for whom? Working time flexibility practices of European companies.* Ridderkerk: Ridderprint.

Chung, H. (2011) Work-family conflict across 28 European countries: A multi-level approach. In: Drobnič, S. and Guillén, A. (eds) *Work-life balance in Europe: The role of job quality.* Hampshire: Palgrave Macmillan, pp 42–68.

Chung, H. (2014) Explaining the provision of flexitime in companies across Europe (in the pre- and post-crisis Europe): Role of national contexts. *WAF working paper 1.* Canterbury: University of Kent.

Chung, H. (2017) Work autonomy, flexibility and work-life balance final report. Canterbury: University of Kent.

Chung, H. (2018) Dualization and the access to occupational family-friendly working-time arrangements across Europe. *Social Policy and Administration* 52(2): 491–507.

Chung, H. (2019a) National-level family policies and the access to schedule control in a European comparative perspective: Crowding out or in, and for whom? *Journal of Comparative Policy Analysis* 21(1): 23–40.

Chung, H. (2019b) Part-time working women's access to other types of flexible working-time arrangements across Europe. In: Nicolaisen, H., Heidi, K. and Cecilie, H. (eds) *Dualisation of part-time work: The development of labour market insiders and outsiders.* Bristol: Policy Press, pp 109–32.

Chung, H. (2019c) 'Women's work penalty' in the access to flexible working arrangements across Europe. *European Journal of Industrial Relations* 25(1): 23–40.

Chung, H. (2020a) Company-level family policies: Who has access to it and what are some of its outcomes. In: Nieuwenhuis, R. and van Lanker, W. (eds) *Handbook on family policy*. Hampshire: Palgrave Macmillan, pp 535–73.

Chung, H. (2020b) Gender, flexibility stigma, and the perceived negative consequences of flexible working in the UK. *Social Indicators Research* 151: 521–45.

Chung, H. (2020c) Institutions versus market forces: Explaining the employment insecurity of European individuals eight years after the 2008 financial crisis. In: Laenen, T., Meuleman, B. and Van Oorschot, W. (eds) *Welfare state legitimacy in times of crisis and austerity*. Cheltenham: Edward Elgar Publishing, pp 222–48.

Chung, H. (2020d) Return of the 1950s housewife? How to stop coronavirus lockdown reinforcing sexist gender roles. *The Conversation*.

Chung, H. (2021a) How do within-family caring arrangements impact wellbeing and outcomes? Literature review. *Research report for the UK Government Equalities Office*. London: UK Cabinet Office, Government Equalities Office.

Chung, H. (2021b) How to be a great academic. In: Laenen, T., Meuleman, B., Otto, A., Roosma, F. and Van Lanker, W. (eds) *Leading social policy analysis from the front*. Leuven: KU Leuven, pp 11–20.

Chung, H. (2021c) National contexts moderating the association between flexible working and work-family conflict among caregivers across 30 European countries. *SocArxiv*.

Chung, H. (forthcoming/2022) A social policy case for a four-day week. *Journal of Social Policy*. Online first.

Chung, H. and van Oorschot, W. (2011) Institutions versus market forces: Explaining the employment insecurity of European individuals during (the beginning of) the financial crisis. *Journal of European Social Policy* 21(4): 287–301.

Chung, H. and Tijdens, K. (2013) Working time flexibility components and working time regimes in Europe: Using company level data across 21 countries. *International Journal of Human Resource Management* 24(7): 1418–34.

Chung, H. and Mau, S. (2014) Subjective insecurity and the role of institutions. *Journal of European Social Policy* 24(4): 303–18.

Chung, H. and van der Horst, M. (2018) Women's employment patterns after childbirth and the perceived access to and use of flexitime and teleworking. *Human Relations* 71(1): 47–72.

Chung, H. and Schober, P. (2019) Multidimensionality of gender ideology and relationships with gendered practices: An exploratory analysis across Europe in 2002 and 2012. SSRN. https://ssrn.com/abstract=3505948 or http://dx.doi.org/10.2139/ssrn.3505948

Chung, H. and van der Horst, M. (2020) Flexible working and unpaid overtime in the UK: The role of gender, parental and occupational status. *Social Indicators Research* 151(2): 495–520.

Chung, H. and van der Lippe, T. (2020) Flexible working work life balance and gender equality: Introduction. *Social Indicators Research* 151 (2): 365–81.

Chung, H. and Booker, C. (forthcoming) Flexible working and division of housework and childcare: Examining the divisions across occupational lines.

Chung, H., Kerkhofs, M. and Ester, P. (2007) Working time flexibility in European companies. *Establishment Survey on Working Time 2004–2005*. Luxembourg: European Foundation for the Improvement of Living and Working Conditions.

Chung, H., Bekker, S. and Houwing, H. (2012) Young people and the post-recession labour market in the context of Europe 2020. *Transfer: European Review of Labour and Research* 18(3): 301–17.

Chung, H., Birkett, H., Forbes, S. and Seo, H. (2020a) Working from home and the division of housework and childcare among dual earner couples during the pandemic in the UK. *SocArXiv*.

Chung, H., Seo, H., Forbes, S. and Birkett, H. (2020b) Working from home during the COVID-19 lockdown: Changing preferences and the future of work. Canterbury: University of Kent.

Chung, H., Birkett, H., Forbes, S. and Seo, H. (2021) COVID-19, flexible working, and implications for gender equality in the United Kingdom. *Gender & Society* 35(2): 218–32.

CIPD (2020) Embedding new ways of working: Implications for the post-pandemic workplace. London: Chartered Institute of Personnel and Development.

CIPD (2021) Flexible working: Lessons from the pandemic. London: Chartered Institute of Personnel and Development.

Clarence-Smith, L. (2021) Half of staff would quit if denied flexible working. *The Times*.

Clark, S.C. (2000) Work/family border theory: A new theory of work/family balance. *Human Relations* 53(6): 747–70.

Clawson, D. and Gerstel, N. (2014) *Unequal time: Gender, class, and family in employment schedules*. New York: Russell Sage Foundation.

CMI (2020) Management transformed: Managing in a marathon crisis. London: Chartered Management Institute.

Cohen, G.A. (1979) The labor theory of value and the concept of exploitation. *Philosophy & Public Affairs* 8(4): 338–60.

Collins, C., Landivar, L.C., Ruppanner, L. and Scarborough, W.J. (2020) COVID-19 and the gender gap in work hours. *Gender, Work & Organization* 28(S1): 101–12.

Collins, C., Ruppanner, L., Landivar, L.C. and Scarborough, W.J. (2021) The gendered consequences of a weak infrastructure of care: School reopening plans and parents' employment during the COVID-19 pandemic. *Gender & Society* 35(2): 180–93.

Coltrane, S., Miller, E.C., DeHaan, T. and Stewart, L. (2013) Fathers and the flexibility stigma. *Journal of Social Issues* 69(2): 279–302.

Connolly, R. (2020) The pandemic has taken surveillance of workers to the next level. *The Guardian*.

Connolly, S. and Gregory, M. (2008) Moving down: Women's part-time work and occupational change in Britain 1991–2001. *The Economic Journal* 118(526): F52–76.

Connolly, S. and Gregory, M. (2009) The part-time pay penalty: Earnings trajectories of British women. *Oxford Economic Papers* 61.

Cooper, R. and Baird, M. (2015) Bringing the 'right to request' flexible working arrangements to life: From policies to practices. *Employee Relations* 37(5): 568–81.

Coote, A., Harper, A. and Stirling, A. (2020) *The case for a four day week*. Cambridge: Polity Press.

Correll, S.J., Benard, S. and Paik, I. (2007) Getting a job: Is there a motherhood penalty? *American Journal of Sociology* 112(5): 1297–338.

Coser, M. (1974) *Greedy institutions*. New York: Free Press.

Costa Dias, M., Joyce, R. and Parodi, F. (2018a) The gender pay gap in the UK: Children and experience in work. London: Institute for Fiscal Studies.

Costa Dias, M., Robert, J. and Parodi, F. (2018b) Wage progression and the gender wage gap: The causal impact of hours of work. London: Institute for Fiscal Studies.

Costa Dias, M., Joyce, R. and Keiller, A.N. (2020) COVID-19 and the career prospects of young people. London: Institute for Fiscal Studies.

Craig, L. and Mullan, K. (2011) How mothers and fathers share childcare: A cross-national time-use comparison. *American Sociological Review* 76(6): 834–61.

Craig, L. and Powell, A. (2012) Dual-earner parents' work-family time: The effects of atypical work patterns and non-parental childcare. *Journal of Population Research* 29(3): 229–47.

Craig, L. and Brown, J.E. (2017) Feeling rushed: Gendered time quality, work hours, nonstandard work schedules, and spousal crossover. *Journal of Marriage and Family* 79(1): 225–42.

Craig, L. and Churchill, B. (2020) Dual-earner parent couples' work and care during COVID-19. *Gender, Work & Organization* 28(S1): 66–79.

Cristea, I.C. and Leonardi, P.M. (2019) Get noticed and die trying: Signals, sacrifice, and the production of face time in distributed work. *Organization Science* 30(3): 552–72.

Cunningham, M. (2001) Parental influences on the gendered division of housework. *American Sociological Review* 66(2): 184–203.

Curtice, J., Clery, E., Perry, J., Phillips, M. and Rahim, N. (2019) *British Social Attitudes: The 36th Report.* London: The National Centre for Social Research.

Dale, G. (2020) *Flexible working: How to implement flexibility in the workplace to improve employee and business performance.* London: Kogan Page.

Davis, A.E. and Kalleberg, A.L. (2006) Family-friendly organizations? Work and family programs in the 1990s. *Work and Occupations* 33(2): 191–223.

de Menezes, L.M. and Kelliher, C. (2011) Flexible working and performance: A systematic review of the evidence for a business case. *International Journal of Management Reviews* 13(4): 452–74.

Deloitte (2018) Deloitte Millennial Survey. www2.deloitte.com/global/en/pages/about-deloitte/articles/millennialsurvey.html

Dembe, A.E., Erickson, J.B., Delbos, R.G. and Banks, S.M. (2005) The impact of overtime and long work hours on occupational injuries and illnesses: New evidence from the United States. *Occupational & Environmental Medicine* 62(9): 588–97.

Demerouti, E., Bakker, A.B., Nachreiner, F. and Schaufeli, W.B. (2001) The job demands-resources model of burnout. *Journal of Applied Psychology* 86(3): 499–512.

den Dulk, L., Peters, P. and Poutsma, E. (2012) Variations in adoption of workplace work-family arrangements in Europe: The influence of welfare-state regime and organizational characteristics. *The International Journal of Human Resource Management* 23(12): 2785–808.

den Dulk, L., Groeneveld, S., Ollier-Malaterre, A. and Valcour, M. (2013) National context in work-life research: A multi-level cross-national analysis of the adoption of workplace work-life arrangements in Europe. *European Management Journal* 31: 478–94.

Dex, S. and Scheibl, F. (2001) Flexible and family-friendly working arrangements in UK-based SMEs: Business Cases. *British Journal of Industrial Relations* 39(3): 411–31.

Dex, S. and Smith, C. (2002) *The nature and pattern of family-friendly employment policies in Britain.* Bristol: Policy Press.

Dias, M., Joyce, R. and Keiller, A. (2020) *COVID-19 and the career prospects of young people.* London: Institute for Fiscal Studies.

DiMaggio, P.J. and Powell, W.W. (1983) The iron cage revisited: Institutional isomorphism and collective rationality in organizational fields. *American Sociological Review* 48(2): 147–60.

Dotti Sani, G.M. and Treas, J. (2016) Educational gradients in parents' child-care time across countries, 1965–2012. *Journal of Marriage and Family* 78(4): 1083–96.

Douglas, J. and Hannon, P. (2021) U.K. economy suffers biggest slump in 300 years amid Covid-19 lockdowns. *Wall Street Journal*. www.wsj.com/articles/u-k-economy-suffers-biggest-slump-in-300-years-amid-covid-19-lockdowns-11613118912

Drago, R.W., Black, D. and Wooden, M. (2005) The existence and persistence of long work hours. *IZA Discussion Paper No. 1720*.

Drobnič, S. and Guillén Rodríguez, A.M. (2011) Tensions between work and home: Job quality and working conditions in the institutional contexts of Germany and Spain. *Social Politics* 18: 232–68.

Dunatchik, A. and Speight, S. (2020) Re-examining how partner co-presence and multitasking affect parents' enjoyment of childcare and housework. *Sociological Science* 7: 268–90.

Dunatchik, A., Gerson, K., Glass, J., Jacobs, J.A. and Stritzel, H. (2021) Gender, parenting, and the rise of remote work during the pandemic: Implications for domestic inequality in the United States. *Gender & Society* 35(2): 194–205.

Durbin, S. and Tomlinson, J. (2010) Female part-time managers: Networks and career mobility. *Work, Employment and Society* 24(4): 621–40.

Duxbury, L., Higgins, C. and Lee, C. (1994) Work-family conflict. *Journal of Family Issues* 15(3): 449–66.

Eaton, S.C. (2003) If you can use them: Flexibility policies, organizational commitment, and perceived performance. *Industrial Relations: A Journal of Economy and Society* 42(2): 145–67.

ELENA (2018) Toolkit for the implementation of flexible working arrangements in private companies. Rome: Department of Equal Opportunities, Italy.

Elliott, K. (2016) Caring masculinities: Theorizing an emerging concept. *Men and Masculinities* 19(3): 240–59.

Epstein, C.F., Seron, C., Oglensky, B. and Sauté, R. (1999) *The part-time paradox: Time norms, professional life, family and gender*. New York: Routledge.

Erickson, J.J., Martinengo, G. and Hill, E.J. (2010) Putting work and family experiences in context: Differences by family life stage. *Human Relations* 63(7): 955–79.

Esping-Andersen, G. (1990) *The three worlds of welfare capitalism*. Princeton: Princeton University Press.

ETUC (2015) ETUC position on the first-stage consultation of the EU social partners on a 'new start' for work-life balance. Brussels: European Trade Union Confederation.

Eurofound (2020) Living, working and COVID-19. *COVID-19 series*. Luxembourg: Publications Office of the European Union.

Eurofound and the International Labour Office (2017) *Working anytime, anywhere: The effects on the world of work*. Geneva: Publications Office of the European Union, Luxembourg, and the International Labour Office.

European Parliament (2021) Parliament wants to ensure the right to disconnect from work. Brussels: European Parliament.

Eurostat (2016) Percentage of part-time employment by sex, age groups and household composition. http://appsso.eurostat.ec.europa.eu/nui/show.do?dataset= lfst_hhptety

Evans, J.M. (2001) The firm's contribution to the reconciliation between work and family life. *Labour Market and Social Policy Occasional Paper.* Paris: OECD.

Falk, A. and Kosfeld, M. (2006) The hidden costs of control. *American Economic Review* 96(5): 1611–30.

Felstead, A. and Henseke, G. (2017) Assessing the growth of remote working and its consequences for effort, well-being and work-life balance. *New Technology, Work and Employment* 32(3): 195–212.

Felstead, A., Jewson, N. and Walters, S. (2003) Managerial control of employees working at home. *British Journal of Industrial Relations* 41(2): 241–64.

Ferragina, E. and Seeleib-Kaiser, M. (2015) Determinants of a silent (r)evolution: Understanding the expansion of family policy in rich OECD countries. *Social Politics: International Studies in Gender, State & Society* 22(1): 1–37.

Filer, R.K. (1985) Male-female wage differences: The importance of compensating differentials. *ILR Review* 38(3): 426–37.

Fleckenstein, T. and Seeleib-Kaiser, M. (2011) Business, skills and the welfare state: The political economy of employment-oriented family policy in Britain and Germany. *Journal of European Social Policy* 21(2): 136–49.

Fleetwood, S. (2007) Re-thinking work-life balance: Editor's introduction. *The International Journal of Human Resource Management* 18(3): 351–9.

Folbre, N. (2006) Measuring care: Gender, empowerment, and the care economy. *Journal of Human Development* 7(2): 183–99.

Forbes, S., Birkett, H., Evans, L., Chung, H. and Whiteman, J. (2020) Managing employees during the COVID-19 pandemic: Flexible working and the future of work. Birmingham: University of Birmingham and the University of Kent.

Fouarge, D. and Muffels, R. (2009) Working part-time in the British, German and Dutch labour market: Scarring for the wage career? *Schmollers Jahrbuch* 129(2): 217–26.

Foucault, M. (2010) *The birth of biopolitics: Lectures at the Collège de France, 1978–1979.* New York: Palgrave Macmillan.

Franklin, N. (2018) Quarter of UK workforce have turned down a job for not offering flexible working. *Workplace Insight.*

Franklin, N. (2019) Flexible working seen as top workplace benefit by workers. *Workplace Insight.* https://workplaceinsight.net/flexible-working-seen-as-top-workplace-benefit-by-workers/

Fraser, N. (1994) After the family wage: Gender equity and the welfare state. *Political theory* 22(4): 591–618.

Frayne, D. (2015) *The refusal of work: The theory and practice of resistance to work*. London: Zed Books Ltd.

Friedman, A. (2020) Proof our work-life balance is in danger (but there's still hope). *Atlassian*.

Fuller, S. and Hirsh, C.E. (2018) 'Family-friendly' jobs and motherhood pay penalties: The impact of flexible work arrangements across the educational spectrum. *Work and Occupations* 46(1): 3–44.

Fuller, S. and Qian, Y. (2021) COVID-19 and the gender gap in employment among parents of young children in Canada. *Gender & Society* 35(2): 206–17.

Gajendran, R.S. and Harrison, D.A. (2007) The good, the bad, and the unknown about telecommuting: Meta-analysis of psychological mediators and individual consequences. *Journal of Applied Psychology* 92(6): 1524–41.

Gascoigne, C. and Kelliher, C. (2018) The transition to part-time: How professionals negotiate 'reduced time and workload' i-deals and craft their jobs. *Human Relations* 71(1): 103–25.

Gershuny, J. (2005) Busyness as the badge of honor for the new superordinate working class. *Social Research* 72: 287–314.

Gerstel, N. and Clawson, D. (2018) Control over time: Employers, workers, and families shaping work schedules. *Annual Review of Sociology* 44: 77–97.

Gibson, M. (2014) Here's a radical way to end vacation email overload. *Time*.

Glass, J., Simon, R.W. and Andersson, M.A. (2016) Parenthood and happiness: Effects of work-family reconciliation policies in 22 OECD countries. *American Journal of Sociology* 122(3): 886–929.

Glass, J.L. (1990) The impact of occupational segregation on working conditions. *Social Forces* 68(3): 779–96.

Glass, J.L and Finley, A. (2002) Coverage and effectiveness of family-responsive workplace policies. *Human Resource Management Review* 12(3): 313–37.

Glass, J.L and Noonan, M.C. (2016) Telecommuting and earnings trajectories among American women and men 1989–2008. *Social Forces* 95(1): 217–50.

Glauber, R. (2011) Limited access: Gender, occupational composition, and flexible work scheduling. *The Sociological Quarterly* 52(3): 472–94.

Glauber, R. (2012) Women's work and working conditions: Are mothers compensated for lost wages? *Work and Occupations* 39(2): 115–38.

Glavin, P. and Schieman, S. (2012) Work-family role blurring and work-family conflict: The moderating influence of job resources and job demands. *Work and Occupations* 39(1): 71–98.

Goffman, E. (1990) *Stigma: Notes on the management of spoiled identity*. New Jersey: Penguin Books.

Golden, L. (2001) Flexible work schedules: Which workers get them? *American Behavioral Scientist* 44(7): 1157–78.

Golden, L. (2009) Flexible daily work schedules in US jobs: Formal introductions needed? *Industrial Relations: A Journal of Economy and Society* 48(1): 27–54.

Golden, T.D., Veiga, J.F. and Simsek, Z. (2006) Telecommuting's differential impact on work-family conflict: Is there no place like home? *Journal of Applied Psychology* 91(6): 1340–50.

Goldin, C. (2014) A grand gender convergence: Its last chapter. *The American Economic Review* 104(4): 1091–119.

Goodstein, J.D. (1994) Institutional pressures and strategic responsiveness: Employer involvement in work-family issues. *Academy of Management Journal* 37(2): 350–82.

Gornick, J.C., Meyers, M.K. and Ross, K.E. (1997) Supporting the employment of mothers: Policy variation across fourteen welfare states. *Journal of European Social Policy* 7(1): 45–70.

Grönlund, A. and Öun, I. (2010) Rethinking work-family conflict: Dual earner policies, role conflict and role expansion in Western Europe. *Journal of European Social Policy* 20(3): 179–95.

Hackman, J.R. and Oldham, G.R. (1975) Development of the job diagnostic survey. *Journal of Applied Psychology* 60(2): 159–70.

Haisken-DeNew, J.P. and Frick, J.R. (2005) DTC Desktop Companion to the German Socio-Economic Panel (SOEP). Version 8.0-Dec 2005, Updated to Wave 21 (U). Berlin: DWI Berlin.

Hall, D.T. and Richter, J. (1988) Balancing work life and home life: What can organizations do to help? *The Academy of Management Executive* 2(3): 213–23.

Hall, P.A. and Soskice, D.W. (2001) *Varieties of capitalism: The institutional foundations of comparative advantage.* New York: Oxford University Press.

Hammer, L.B., Kossek, E.E., Yragui, N.L., Bodner, T.E. and Hanson, G.C. (2009) Development and validation of a multidimensional measure of family supportive supervisor behaviors (FSSB). *Journal of Management* 35(4): 837–56.

Hangyoreh (2019) 탄력근로제 최장 6개월"…노사정, 사회적 대화 첫 합의. *Hangyoreh.* Seoul.

Hannah, F. (2019) The firm with 900 staff and no office. *BBC.*

Haraldsson, G.D. and Kellam, J. (2021) *Going public: Iceland's journey to a shorter working week.* London: Autonomy.

Hardt, M. and Negri, A. (2001) *Empire.* Cambridge, MA: Harvard University Press.

Harris, L. (2003) Home-based teleworking and the employment relationship: Managerial challenges and dilemmas. *Personnel Review* 32(4): 422–37.

Harris, M. (2017) *Kids these days: Human capital and the making of millennials.* London: Little, Brown.

Hays, S. (1998) *The cultural contradictions of motherhood.* New Haven: Yale University Press.

He, G., Pan, Y. and Tanaka, T. (2020) The short-term impacts of COVID-19 lockdown on urban air pollution in China. *Nature Sustainability* 3: 1005–11.

Health and Safety Executive (2019) Work-related stress, anxiety or depression statistics in Great Britain, 2019. *Annual Statistics.* London: HSE.

Henshaw, C. (2019) Teachers work more unpaid overtime than anyone else. *TES.*

Henz, U. (2006) Informal caregiving at working age: Effects of job characteristics and family configuration. *Journal of Marriage and Family* 68(2): 411–29.

Hilbrecht, M., Shaw, S.M., Johnson, L.C. and Andrey, J. (2008) 'I'm home for the kids': Contradictory implications for work-life balance of teleworking mothers. *Gender, Work & Organization* 15(5): 454–76.

Hilbrecht, M., Shaw, S.M., Johnson, L.C. and Andrey, J. (2013) Remixing work, family and leisure: Teleworkers' experiences of everyday life. *New Technology, Work and Employment* 28(2): 130–44.

Hill, A. (2020) Parents worried by lack of UK summer camp options due to COVID-19. *The Guardian.*

Hipp, L. and Bünning, M. (2020) Parenthood as a driver of increased gender inequality during COVID-19? Exploratory evidence from Germany. *European Societies* (S1): 1–16.

Hobson, B. (2011) The agency gap in work-life balance: Applying Sen's capabilities framework within European contexts. *Social Politics* 18(2): 147–67.

Hobson, B. (2013) *Worklife balance: The agency and capabilities gap.* Oxford: Oxford University Press.

Hobson, B. and Fahlén, S. (2009) Competing scenarios for European fathers: Applying Sen's capabilities and agency framework to work-family balance. *The Annals of the American Academy of Political and Social Science* 624(1): 214–33.

Hochschild, A.R. (2001) *The time bind: When work becomes home and home becomes work.* New York: Holt Paperbacks.

Hochschild, A.R. and Machung, A. (1989) *The second shift: Working parents and the revolution at home.* New York: Viking.

Hodges, M.J. and Budig, M.J. (2010) Who gets the daddy bonus? Organizational hegemonic masculinity and the impact of fatherhood on earnings. *Gender & Society* 24(6): 717–45.

Hofstede, G., Hofstede, G.J. and Minkov, M. (1991) *Cultures and organizations: Software for the mind.* London and New York: McGraw-Hill.

Hook, A., Sovacool, B.K. and Sorrell, S. (2020) A systematic review of the energy and climate impacts of teleworking. *Environmental Research Letters* 15: 093003.

Hook. J.L. (2006) Care in context: Men's unpaid work in 20 countries, 1965–2003. *American Sociological Review* 71(4): 639–60.

Hook, J.L. (2010) Gender inequality in the welfare state: Sex segregation in housework, 1965–2003. *American Journal of Sociology* 115(5): 1480–523.

Horowitz, J. and Graf, N. (2019) Most US teens see anxiety and depression as a major problem among their peers. *Pew Research Trends.* Washington DC: Pew Research Center.

Huws, U., Robinson, W.B. and Robinson, S. (1990) *Telework towards the elusive office.* New York: John Wiley & Sons, Inc.

Jaffee, D. (1989) Gender inequality in workplace autonomy and authority. *Social Science Quarterly* 70(2): 375–90.

Javornik, J. and Kurowska, A. (2017) Work and care opportunities under different parental leave systems: Gender and class inequalities in Northern Europe. *Social Policy & Administration* 51(4): 617–37.

Jolly, D. (2000) A critical evaluation of the contradictions for disabled workers arising from the emergence of the flexible labour market in Britain. *Disability & Society* 15(5): 795–810.

Jones, M. and Wass, V. (2013) Understanding changing disability-related employment gaps in Britain 1998–2011. *Work, Employment and Society* 27(6): 982–1003.

Jones, M.K. (2008) Disability and the labour market: A review of the empirical evidence. *Journal of Economic Studies* 35(5): 405–24.

Joyce, R. and Keiller, A. (2018) The 'gender commuting gap' widens considerably in the first decade after childbirth. *Institute for Fiscal studies* 7.

Jung, S-J. (2021)) [코로나가 바꾼 대한민국] ② 절반이 맛본 재택근무의 달콤함… "집에서 일하고 싶어요."[코로나가 바꾼 대한민국] ② 절반이 맛본 재택근무의 달콤함… "집에서 일하고 싶어요. *Aju business daily.* Aju.

Kalmijn, M. (1991) Status homogamy in the United States. *American Journal of Sociology* 97(2): 496–523.

Karasek, R.A.Jr. (1979) Job demands, job decision latitude, and mental strain: Implications for job redesign. *Administrative Science Quarterly* 24(2): 285–308.

Kassinis, G.I. and Stavrou, E.T. (2013) Non-standard work arrangements and national context. *European Management Journal* 31(5): 464–77.

Kelliher, C. and Anderson, D. (2010) Doing more with less? Flexible working practices and the intensification of work. *Human Relations* 63(1): 83–106.

Kelliher, C. and de Menezes, L.M. (2019) *Flexible working in organisations: A research overview.* Abingdon: Routledge.

Kelliher, C., Richardson, J. and Boiarintseva, G. (2019) All of work? All of life? Reconceptualising work-life balance for the 21st century. *Human Resource Management Journal* 79(2): 97–112.

Kelly, E.L. and Kalev, A. (2006) Managing flexible work arrangements in US organizations: Formalized discretion or 'a right to ask'. *Socio-Economic Review* 4(3): 379–416.

Kelly, E.L. and Moen, P. (2020) *Overload: How good jobs went bad and what we can do about it.* Princeton: Princeton University Press.

Kelly, E.L., Moen, P. and Tranby, E. (2011) Changing workplaces to reduce work-family conflict schedule control in a white-collar organization. *American Sociological Review* 76(2): 265–90.

Kelly, E.L., Moen, P., Oakes, J.M., Fan, W., Okechukwu, C., Davis, K.D., et al (2014) Changing work and work-family conflict: Evidence from the work, family, and health network. *American Sociological Review* 79(3): 485–516.

Kerkhofs, M., Chung, H. and Ester, P. (2008) Working time flexibility across Europe: A typology using firm-level data. *Industrial Relations Journal* 39(6): 569–85.

Kim, J. (2020) Workplace flexibility and parent-child interactions among working parents in the U.S. *Social Indicators Research* 151(2): 427–69.

Kim, J.Y., Campbell, T.H., Shepherd, S. and Kay, A.C. (2020) Understanding contemporary forms of exploitation: Attributions of passion serve to legitimize the poor treatment of workers. *Journal of Personality and Social Psychology* 118(1): 121–48.

King, B. (2020) Unemployment rate: How many people are out of work? *BBC.*

Knight, C.R. and Brinton, M.C. (2017) One egalitarianism or several? Two decades of gender-role attitude change in Europe. *American Journal of Sociology* 122(5): 1485–532.

Knight, K.W., Rosa, E.A. and Schor, J.B. (2013) Could working less reduce pressures on the environment? A cross-national panel analysis of OECD countries, 1970–2007. *Global Environmental Change* 23(4): 691–700.

Korean Ministry of Employment and Labor (2018) 유연근로시간제 가이드. Seoul: 고용노동부.

Korpi, W. (1989) Power, politics, and state autonomy in the development of social citizenship: Social rights during sickness in eighteen OECD countries since 1930. *American Sociological Review* 54: 309–28.

Korpi, W., Ferrarini, T. and Englund, S. (2013) Women's opportunities under different family policy constellations: Gender, class, and inequality tradeoffs in western countries re-examined. *Social Politics: International Studies in Gender, State & Society* 20(1): 1–40.

Kossek, E.E. and Lautsch, B.A. (2008) *CEO of me: Creating a life that works in the flexible job age.* New Jersey: Wharton School Publishing.

Kossek, E.E. and Lautsch, B.A. (2018) Work-life flexibility for whom? Occupational status and work-life inequality in upper, middle, and lower level jobs. *Academy of Management Annals* 12(1): 5–36.

Kossek, E.E. and Ollier-Malaterre, A. (2019) Desperately seeking sustainable careers: Redesigning professional jobs for the collaborative crafting of reduced-load work. *Journal of Vocational Behavior* 117: 1–15.

Kossek, E.E., Lautsch, B.A. and Eaton, S.C. (2005) Flexibility enactment theory: Implications of flexibility type, control, and boundary management for work-family effectiveness. In: Kossek, E.E. and Lambert, S.J. (eds) *Work and life integration: Organizational, cultural, and individual perspectives.* Mahwah, NJ: Lawrence Erlbaum Associates Publishers, pp 243–61.

Kossek, E.E., Lautsch, B.A. and Eaton, S.C. (2006) Telecommuting, control, and boundary management: Correlates of policy use and practice, job control, and work-family effectiveness. *Journal of Vocational Behavior* 68(2): 347–67.

Kossek, E.E., Rosokha, L.M. and Leana, C. (2019) Work schedule patching in health care: Exploring implementation approaches. *Work and Occupations* 47(2): 228–61.

Kossek, E.E., Hammer, L.B., Kelly, E.L. and Moen, P. (2014) Designing work, family & health organizational change initiatives. *Organizational Dynamics* 43(1): 53–63.

Kunda, G. (1992) *Engineering culture: Control and commitment in a high-tech corporation.* Philadelphia, PA: Temple University Press.

Künemund, H. and Rein, M. (1999) There is more to receiving than needing: Theoretical arguments and empirical explorations of crowding in and crowding out. *Ageing & Society* 19(1): 93–121.

Künn-Nelen, A., De Grip, A. and Fouarge, D. (2013) Is part-time employment beneficial for firm productivity? *ILR Review* 66(5): 1172–91.

Kurowska, A. (2020) Gendered effects of home-based work on parents' capability to balance work with nonwork: Two countries with different models of division of labour compared. *Social Indicators Research* 151: 405–25.

Lambert, S.J. and Haley-Lock, A. (2004) The organizational stratification of opportunities for work-life balance: Addressing issues of equality and social justice in the workplace. *Community, Work & Family* 7: 179–95.

Lee, Y. (2020) 코로나19에 국내기업 절반 재택근무 도입…근로자 91% "만족. *Yonhap News.* Seoul.

Leslie, L.M., Manchester, C.F., Park, T-Y. and Mehng, S.A. (2012) Flexible work practices: A source of career premiums or penalties? *Academy of Management Journal* 55(6): 1407–28.

Lewis, J., Knijn, T., Martin, C. and Ostner, I. (2008) Patterns of development in work/family reconciliation policies for parents in France, Germany, the Netherlands, and the UK in the 2000s. *Social Politics: International Studies in Gender, State & Society* 15(3): 261–86.

Lott, Y. (2015) Working-time flexibility and autonomy: A European perspective on time adequacy. *European Journal of Industrial Relations* 21(3): 259–74.

Lott, Y. (2019) Weniger Arbeit, mehr Freizeit? Wofür Mütter und Väter flexible Arbeitsarrangements nutzen. Dusseldorf, Germany: WSI-HBF.

Lott, Y. (2020) Does flexibility help employees switch off from work? Flexible working-time arrangements and cognitive work-to-home spillover for women and men in Germany. *Social Indicators Research* 151: 471–94.

Lott, Y. and Chung, H. (2016) Gender discrepancies in the outcomes of schedule control on overtime hours and income in Germany. *European Sociological Review* 32(6): 752–65.

Lott, Y. and Klenner, C. (2018) Are the ideal worker and ideal parent norms about to change? The acceptance of part-time and parental leave at German workplaces. *Community, Work & Family* 21(5): 564–80.

Lyness, K.S., Gornick, J.C., Stone, P. and Grotto, A.R. (2012) It's all about control: Worker control over schedule and hours in cross-national context. *American Sociological Review* 77(6): 1023–49.

Lyonette, C. and Crompton, R. (2015) Sharing the load? Partners' relative earnings and the division of domestic labour. *Work, Employment and Society* 29(1): 23–40.

Lyonette, C., Anderson, D., Lewis, S., Payne, N. and Wood, S. (2016) Work-life balance and austerity: Implications of new ways of working in British public sector organisations. *Political Science.*

Macpherson, D.A. and Hirsch, B.T. (1995) Wages and gender composition: Why do women's jobs pay less? *Journal of Labor Economics* 13(3): 426–71.

Magnusson, C. (2019) Flexible time – but is the time owned? Family-friendly and family-unfriendly work arrangements, occupational gender composition and wages: A test of the mother-friendly job hypothesis in Sweden. *Community, Work & Family* 24(3): 291–314.

Makortoff, K. (2020) Nearly 75% of City firms reviewing office space provision. *The Guardian.*

Makortoff, K. and Farrer, M. (2021) HSBC to slash post-Covid office space by 40% as profits drop by a third. *The Guardian.*

Masuda, A.D., Poelmans, S.A., Allen, T.D., Spector, P.E., Lapierre, L.M., Cooper, C.L., et al (2012) Flexible work arrangements availability and their relationship with work-to-family conflict, job satisfaction, and turnover intentions: A comparison of three country clusters. *Applied Psychology* 61(1): 1–29.

Mazmanian, M., Orlikowski, W.J. and Yates, J. (2013) The autonomy paradox: The implications of mobile email devices for knowledge professionals. *Organization Science* 24(5): 1337–57.

McGinn, K.L., Ruiz Castro, M. and Lingo, E.L. (2019) Learning from mum: Cross-national evidence linking maternal employment and adult children's outcomes. *Work, Employment and Society* 33(3): 375–400.

McKinsey (2020a) *How COVID-19 has pushed companies over the technology tipping point – and transformed business forever.* London: McKinsey.

McKinsey (2020b) Women in the workplace 2020. https://wiw-report. s3.amazonaws.com/Women_in_the_Workplace_2020.pdf

McRae, S. (2003) Constraints and choices in mothers' employment careers: A consideration of Hakim's preference theory. *The British Journal of Sociology* 54(3): 317–38.

Meakin, L. (2021) Remote working's longer hours are new normal for many. *Bloomberg.*

Miani, C. and Hoorens, S. (2014) Parents at work: Men and women participating in the labour force. *Short statistical report No.2 Prepared for the European Commission Directorate General – Justice and Fundamental Rights.* RAND Europe.

Michel, J.S., Kotrba, L.M., Mitchelson, J.K., Clark, M.A. and Baltes, B.B. (2011) Antecedents of work-family conflict: A meta analytic review. *Journal of Organizational Behavior* 32(5): 689–725.

Mills, M. and Täht, K. (2010) Nonstandard work schedules and partnership quality: Quantitative and qualitative findings. *Journal of Marriage and Family* 72(4): 860–75.

Mincer, J. (1962) On-the-job training: Costs, returns, and some implications. *The Journal of Political Economy* 70(5): 50–79.

Minnotte, K.L., Cook, A. and Minnotte, M.C. (2010) Occupation and industry sex segregation, gender, and workplace support: The use of flexible scheduling policies. *Journal of Family Issues* 31(5): 656–80.

Misra, J., Budig, M. and Boeckmann, I. (2011) Work-family policies and the effects of children on women's employment hours and wages. *Community, Work & Family* 14: 139–57.

Moen, P. and Yu, Y. (2000) Effective work/life strategies: Working couples, work conditions, gender, and life quality. *Social Problems* 47(3): 291–326.

Moen, P., Kelly, E.L., Fan, W., Lee, S.-R., Almeida, D., Kossek, E.E., et al (2016) Does a flexibility/support organizational initiative improve high-tech employees' well-being? Evidence from the work, family, and health network. *American Sociological Review* 81: 134–64.

Moen, P., Kelly, E.L., Lee, S-R., Oakes, J.M., Fan, W., Bray, J., et al (2017) Can a flexibility/support initiative reduce turnover intentions and exits? Results from the work, family, and health network. *Social Problems* 64(1): 53–85.

Morning Consult and The New York Times (2020) National Tracking Poll #200424 9–10 April 2020. https://assets.morningconsult.com/wp-uploads/2020/05/19175645/200424_crosstabs_NYT_Adults_v5_JB.pdf

Morris, N. (2020) Mums are doing majority of homeschooling in lockdown as teaching still considered 'women's work'. *Metro.*

Moss, J. (2019) When passion leads to burnout. *Harvard Business Review.*

Munsch, C.L. (2016) Flexible work, flexible penalties: The effect of gender, childcare, and type of request on the flexibility bias. *Social Forces* 94(4): 1567–91.

Muro, M., Liu, S., Whiton, J. and Kulkarni, S. (2017) Digitalization and the American workforce. Washington DC: Brookings Institute.

Nagar, V. (2002) Delegation and incentive compensation. *The Accounting Review* 77(2): 379–95.

Nair, P. (2018) Revealed: How Britain's always-on culture is really affecting employees. *Business Advice.*

Nelson, E. (2020) Britain's new record: A recession worse than in Europe and North America. *The New York Times.*

Nepomnyaschy, L. and Waldfogel, J. (2007) Paternity leave and fathers' involvement with their young children: Evidence from the American ECLS-B. *Community, Work and Family* 10(4): 427–53.

Newport, C. (2016) *Deep work: Rules for focused success in a distracted world.* New York and Boston: Grand Central Publishing.

Nicolaisen, H., Kavli, H.C. and Jensen, R.S. (2019) *Dualisation of part-time work: The development of labour market insiders and outsiders.* Bristol: Policy Press.

Nolsoe, E. (2021) One in four businesses intend to allow all workers to work from home at least some of the time. London: YouGov.

Noonan, M.C. and Glass, J.L. (2012) The hard truth about telecommuting. *Monthly Labour Review* 135: 38–45.

Noonan, M.C., Estes, S.B. and Glass, J.L. (2007) Do workplace flexibility policies influence time spent in domestic labor? *Journal of Family Issues* 28(2): 263–88.

Nordenmark, M. (2004) Multiple social roles and well-being: A longitudinal test of the role stress theory and the role expansion theory. *Acta Sociologica* 47(2): 115–26.

Norman, H. (2019) Does paternal involvement in childcare influence mothers' employment trajectories during the early stages of parenthood in the UK? *Sociology* 54(2): 329–45.

Norman, H., Elliot, M. and Fagan, C. (2014) Which fathers are the most involved in taking care of their toddlers in the UK? An investigation of the predictors of paternal involvement. *Community, Work & Family* 17(2): 163–80.

OECD (2020) Family database. www.oecd.org/els/family/database.htm

Ojala, S. (2011) Supplemental work at home among Finnish wage earners: Involuntary overtime or taking the advantage of flexibility? *Nordic Journal of Working Life Studies* 1(2): 77–97.

ONS (2019) Families and the labour market, UK: 2019. London: Office for National Statistics.

ONS (2020a) Coronavirus and homeworking in the UK labour market: 2019. London: Office for National Statistics.

ONS (2020b) Coronavirus and homeschooling in Great Britain: April to June 2020. London: Office for National Statistics.

ONS (2020c) Coronavirus and homeworking in the UK labour market: 2019. London: Office for National Statistics.

ONS (2020d) Coronavirus and homeworking in the UK: April 2020. *Statistical Bulletin*. London: Office for National Statistics.

ONS (2020e) Coronavirus and how people spent their time under lockdown: 28 March to 26 April 2020. London: Office for National Statistics.

ONS (2020f) GDP first quarterly estimate, UK: April to June 2020. www.ons.gov.uk/releases/gdpfirstquarterlyestimateukapriltojune2020

ONS (2020g) Parenting in lockdown: Coronavirus and the effects on work-life balance. London: Office for National Statistics.

ONS (2021a) Coronavirus (COVID-19) and the different effects on men and women in the UK, March 2020 to February 2021. London: Office for National Statistics.

ONS (2021b) Female employment rate (aged 16 to 64, seasonally adjusted) March 2021. *Labour market statistics time series (LMS)*. London: Office for National Statistics.

Ortega, J. (2009) Why do employers give discretion? Family versus performance concerns. *Industrial Relations: A Journal of Economy and Society* 48(1): 1–26.

Osborne, H. (2021) Home workers putting in more hours since Covid, research shows. *The Guardian*.

Osterman, P. (1995) Work/family programs and the employment relationship. *Administrative Science Quarterly* 40: 681–700.

Oxford University (2021) Parental mental health worsens under new national COVID-19 restrictions. www.ox.ac.uk/news/2021-01-19-parental-mental-health-worsens-under-new-national-covid-19-restrictions

Pang, A.S-K. (2017) *Rest: Why you get more done when you work less.* London: Penguin.

Pang, A.S-K. (2019) *Shorter: How working less will revolutionise the way your company gets things done.* London: Penguin.

Park, A., Bryson, C., Clery, E., Curtice, J. and Phillips, M. (2013) *British Social Attitudes: the 30th Report.* London: NatCen Social Research

Parkinson, C.N. and Osborn, R.C. (1957) *Parkinson's law, and other studies in administration.* Boston: Houghton Mifflin Boston.

Paul, K. (2019) Microsoft Japan tested a four-day work week and productivity jumped by 40%. *The Guardian*.

Pencavel, J. (2014) The productivity of working hours. *The Economic Journal* 125(589): 2052–76.

Peters, P., Tijdens, K.G. and Wetzels, C. (2004) Employees' opportunities, preferences, and practices in telecommuting adoption. *Information & Management* 41(4): 469–82.

Peters, P., Den Dulk, L. and van der Lippe, T. (2009) The effects of time-spatial flexibility and new working conditions on employees' work–life balance: The Dutch case. *Community, Work & Family* 12(3): 279–97.

Petersen, A.H. (2019) How millennials became the burnout generation. *Buzz Feed News*.

Pettigrew, T.F. (1998) Intergroup contact theory. *Annual Review of Psychology* 49(1): 65–85.

Petts, R.J., Carlson, D.L. and Pepin, J.R. (2020) A gendered pandemic: Childcare, homeschooling, and parents' employment during COVID-19. *Gender, Work & Organization* 28(S2): 515–34.

Pongratz, H.J. and Voß, G.G. (2003) From employee to 'entreployee': Towards a 'self-entrepreneurial' work force? *Concepts and Transformation* 8(3): 239–54.

Powell, A. and Craig, L. (2015) Gender differences in working at home and time use patterns: Evidence from Australia. *Work, Employment and Society* 29(4): 571–89.

Prados, M. and Zamarro, G. (2020) Gender differences in couples' division of childcare, work and mental health during COVID-19. *CESR-Schaeffer Working Paper*.

Präg, P. and Mills, M. (2014) Family-related working schedule flexibility across Europe. Short Statistical Report no. 6. Cambridge: RAND Europe. www.rand.org/pubs/research_reports/RR365.html

Presser, H.B. (1988) Shift work and child care among young dual-earner American parents. *Journal of Marriage and the Family* 50(1): 133–48.

Putnam, L.L., Myers, K.K. and Gailliard, B.M. (2014) Examining the tensions in workplace flexibility and exploring options for new directions. *Human Relations* 67(4): 413–40.

Radcliffe, L.S. and Cassell, C. (2014) Flexible working, work-family conflict, and maternal gatekeeping: The daily experiences of dual-earner couples. *Journal of Occupational and Organizational Psychology* 88(4): 835–55.

Rapoport, R., Bailyn, L., Fletcher, J.K. and Pruitt, P.H. (2002) *Beyond work-family balance: Advancing gender equity and work performance.* San Francisco: John Wiley & Sons.

Regan, M. (1994) Beware the work/family culture shock. *Personnel Journal* 73(1): 35–6.

Reid, E.M. (2011) Passing as superman: The ideal worker and men's professional identities. *Academy of Management Proceedings* 1: 1–6.

Resolution Foundation (2020) Covid has created a U-shaped crisis as majority of young adults and pensioners stopped working. London: Resolution Foundation.

Riedmann, A., Bielenski, H., Szczurowska, T. and Wagner, A. (2006) Working time and work-life balance in European companies: Establishment survey on working time 2004–2005. Luxembourg: European Foundation for the Improvement of Living and Working Conditions.

Riva, E., Lucchini, M., den Dulk, L. and Ollier-Malaterre, A. (2018) The skill profile of the employees and the provision of flexible working hours in the workplace: A multilevel analysis across European countries. *Industrial Relations Journal* 49(2): 128–52.

Rose, N. (1999) *Powers of freedom: Reframing political thought.* Cambridge: Cambridge University Press.

Roy, K.M., Tubbs, C.Y. and Burton, L.M. (2004) Don't have no time: Daily rhythms and the organization of time for low-income families. *Family relations* 53(2): 168–78.

RSPH (2021) Disparity begins at home: How home working is impacting the public's health. London: Royal Society for Public Health.

Rudman, L.A. and Mescher, K. (2013) Penalizing men who request a family leave: Is flexibility stigma a femininity stigma? *Journal of Social Issues* 69(2): 322–40.

Ruppanner, L., Lee, R. and Huffman, M. (2018a) Do mothers benefit from flexible work? Cross-national evidence for work time, job quality, and satisfaction. *International Journal of Sociology* 48(2): 170–87.

Ruppanner, L., Perales, F. and Baxter, J. (2018b) Harried and unhealthy? Parenthood, time pressure, and mental health. *Journal of Marriage and Family* 81(2): 308–26.

Ryan, F. (2021) Remote working has been life-changing for disabled people, don't take it away now. *The Guardian.*

Ryan, R.M. and Deci, E.L. (2000) Self-determination theory and the facilitation of intrinsic motivation, social development, and well-being. *American Psychologist* 55(1): 68–78.

Schaufeli, W.B., Bakker, A.B. and Van Rhenen, W. (2009) How changes in job demands and resources predict burnout, work engagement, and sickness absenteeism. *Journal of Organizational Behavior: The International Journal of Industrial, Occupational and Organizational Psychology and Behavior* 30(7): 893–917.

Schawbel, D. (2018) Why work friendships are critical for long-term happiness. *CNBC*. Online.

Schieman, S. and Glavin, P. (2008) Trouble at the border?: Gender, flexibility at work, and the work-home interface. *Social Problems* 55(4): 590–611.

Schieman, S. and Young, M. (2010) Is there a downside to schedule control for the work-family interface? *Journal of Family Issues* 31(10): 1391–414.

Schieman, S., Glavin, P. and Milkie, M.A. (2009) When work interferes with life: Work-nonwork interference and the influence of work-related demands and resources. *American Sociological Review* 74(6): 966–88.

Schieman, S., Schafer, M.H. and McIvor, M. (2013) The rewards of authority in the workplace: Do gender and age matter? *Sociological Perspectives* 56(1): 75–96.

Schieman, S., Badawy, P.J., Milkie, M. and Bierman, A. (2020) Work-life conflict during the COVID-19 pandemic. *Socius: Sociological Research for a Dynamic World* 7: 1–19.

Schober, P.S. (2013) The parenthood effect on gender inequality: Explaining the change in paid and domestic work when British couples become parents. *European Sociological Review* 29(1): 74–85.

Schober, P.S. and Schmitt, C. (2013) Day-care expansion and parental subjective well-being: Evidence from Germany. *SOEP papers on Multidisciplinary Panel Data Research No. 602*. Berlin: DIW/The Open Access Publication Server of the ZBW – Leibniz Information Centre for Economics.

Schor, J. (2008) *The overworked American: The unexpected decline of leisure.* New York: Basic Books.

Schulte, B. (2015) *Overwhelmed: How to work, love, and play when no one has the time.* London: Bloomsbury.

Scott, J. and Clery, E. (2013) Gender roles: An incomplete revolution? *British Social Attitude 30.* London: NatCen.

Seal, R. (2021) *Solo: How to work alone (and not lose your mind).* New York: Simon and Schuster.

Sears, D.O., Lau, R.R., Tyler, T.R. and Allen, H.M., Jr. (1980) Self-interest vs. symbolic politics in policy attitudes and presidential voting. *American Political Science Review* 74(3): 670–84.

Seeleib-Kaiser, M. and Fleckenstein, T. (2009) The political economy of occupational family policies: Comparing workplaces in Britain and Germany. *British Journal of Industrial Relations* 47(4): 741–64.

Sennett, R. (1998) *The corrosion of character: The personal consequences of work in the new capitalism.* New York: WW Norton & Company.

Shanafelt, T.D., Boone, S., Tan, L., Dyrbye, L.N., Sotile, W., Satele, D., et al (2012) Burnout and satisfaction with work-life balance among US physicians relative to the general US population. *Archives of Internal Medicine* 172(18): 1377–85.

Singley, S.G. and Hynes, K. (2005) Transitions to parenthood work-family policies, gender, and the couple context. *Gender & Society* 19(3): 376–97.

Skinner, N. and Pocock, B. (2011) Flexibility and work-life interference in Australia. *Journal of Industrial Relations* 53(1): 65–82.

Smith, M. (2020) Most workers want to work from home after COVID-19. London: YouGov.

Sonnentag, S. (2003) Recovery, work engagement, and proactive behavior: A new look at the interface between nonwork and work. *Journal of Applied Psychology* 88(3): 518–28.

Sonnentag, S. (2012) Psychological detachment from work during leisure time: The benefits of mentally disengaging from work. *Current Directions in Psychological Science* 21(2): 114–18.

Sonnentag, S. and Bayer, U.-V. (2005) Switching off mentally: Predictors and consequences of psychological detachment from work during off-job time. *Journal of Occupational Health Psychology* 10(4): 393–414.

Stanczyk, A.B., Henly, J.R. and Lambert, S.J. (2017) Enough time for housework? Low-wage work and desired housework time adjustments. *Journal of Marriage and Family* 79(1): 243–60.

Standing, G. (2011) *The precariat: The new dangerous class.* London: Bloomsbury Publishing.

Stewart, E. and Bivand, P. (2016) *How flexible hiring could improve business performance and living standards.* London: Joseph Rowntree Foundation.

Stewart, H. (2021) Labour says it will make flexible working the 'new normal'. *The Guardian.*

Stier, H., Lewin-Epstein, N. and Braun, M. (2001) Welfare regimes, family-supportive policies, and women's employment along the life-course. *American Journal of Sociology* 106(6): 1731–60.

Stone, P. and Hernandez, L.A. (2013) The all-or-nothing workplace: Flexibility stigma and 'opting out' among professional-managerial women. *Journal of Social Issues* 69(2): 235–56.

Stronge, W., Harper, A. and Guizzo, D. (2019) The shorter working week: A radical and pragmatic proposal. *Autonomy and Four Day Week Campaign.* https://autonomy.work/portfolio/the-shorter-working-week-a-report-from-autonomy-in-collaboration-with-members-of-the-4-day-week-campaign/

Sullivan, C. and Lewis, S. (2001) Home-based telework, gender, and the synchronization of work and family: Perspectives of teleworkers and their co-residents. *Gender, Work & Organization* 8(2): 123–145.

Summers, H. (2020) UK society regressing back to 1950s for many women, warn experts. *The Guardian.*

Swanberg, J.E., Pitt-Catsouphes, M. and Drescher-Burke, K. (2005) A question of justice disparities in employees' access to flexible schedule arrangements. *Journal of Family Issues* 26(6): 866–95.

Tanaka, S. and Waldfogel, J. (2007) Effects of parental leave and work hours on fathers' involvement with their babies: Evidence from the millennium cohort study. *Community, Work and Family* 10(4): 409–26.

Taylor, E.A. and Scott, J. (2018) Gender: New consensus or continuing battleground? In: Phillips, D., Curtice, J., Phillips, M. and Perry, J. (eds) *British Social Attitudes: The 35th Report.* London: The National Centre for Social Research, pp 56–85.

Thomas, D. (2021) Employers aim for hybrid working after COVID-19 pandemic. *Financial Times.*

Thornthwaite, L. and Sheldon, P. (2004) Employee self-rostering for work-family balance: Leading examples in Austria. *Employee Relations* 26(3): 238–54.

Timm, J. (2016) The plight of the overworked nonprofit employee. *The Atlantic.*

Tipping, S., Chanfreau, J., Perry, J. and Tait, C. (2012) The fourth work-life balance employee survey. *Employment Relations Research Series 122.* London: Department for Business and Innovation.

Tomlinson, J. (2006) Women's work-life balance trajectories in the UK: Reformulating choice and constraint in transitions through part-time work across the life-course. *British Journal of Guidance & Counselling* 34(3): 365–82.

Topping, A. (2020) Pandemic could lead to profound shift in parenting roles, say experts. *The Guardian.*

Tubbs, C.Y., Roy, K.M. and Burton, L.M. (2005) Family ties: Constructing family time in low-income families. *Family Process* 44(1): 77–91.

TUC (2017) Better jobs for mums and dads. London: Trades Union Congress.

TUC (2020) Young workers are most at risk from job losses due to the coronavirus crisis. London: Trades Union Congress.

TUC (2021a) Workers in the UK put in more than £35 billion worth of unpaid overtime last year – TUC analysis. London: Trades Union Congress.

TUC (2021b) Denied and discriminated against: The reality of flexible working for working mums. London: Trades Union Congress.

University of Essex (2015) Understanding Society: Waves 1–5, 2009–2014. [data collection]. 7th Edition. UK Data Service. SN: 6614, http://dx.doi.org/10.5255/UKDA-SN-6614-7. Institute for Social and Economic Research, NatCen Social Research.

Vallerand, R.J., Paquet, Y., Philippe, F.L. and Charest, J. (2010) On the role of passion for work in burnout: A process model. *Journal of Personality* 78(1): 289–312.

van der Lippe, T. and Lippényi, Z. (2020) Beyond formal access: Organizational context, working from home, and work-family conflict of men and women in European workplaces. *Social Indicators Research* 151: 383–402.

van der Lippe, T. and Lippényi, Z. (2021) *Investments in a sustainable workforce in Europe.* Abingdon, Oxon: Taylor & Francis.

van der Lippe, T., De Ruijter, J., De Ruijter, E. and Raub, W. (2010) Persistent inequalities in time use between men and women: A detailed look at the influence of economic circumstances, policies, and culture. *European Sociological Review* 27(2): 164–79.

van der Lippe, T., Treas, J. and Norbutas, L. (2018) Unemployment and the division of housework in Europe. *Work, Employment and Society* 32(4): 650–69.

van der Lippe, T., Van Breeschoten, L. and Van Hek, M. (2019) Organizational work-life policies and the gender wage gap in European workplaces. *Work and Occupations* 46(2): 111–48.

van Oorschot, W. (2006) Making the difference in social Europe: Deservingness perceptions among citizens of European welfare states. *Journal of European Social Policy* 16(1): 23–42.

van Oorschot, W. and Arts, W. (2005) The social capital of European welfare states: The crowding out hypothesis revisited. *Journal of European Social Policy* 15(1): 5–26.

van Oorschot, W. and Chung, H. (2015) Feelings of dual-insecurity among European workers: A multi-level analysis. *European Journal of Industrial Relations* 21(1): 23–37.

Viale, V. (2018) Smart working in Italy: How a new law is introducing flexibility. *Work Life Hub*.

Voß, G.G. and Pongratz, H.J. (1998) Der Arbeitskraftunternehmer. Eine neue Grundform der Ware Arbeitskraft? *Kolner Zeitschrift fur Soziologie und Sozialpsychologie* 50(1): 131–58.

Vouchercloud (2016) How many productive hours in a work day? Just 2 hours, 23 minutes... London: Vouchercloud.

Voydanoff, P. (2005) Work demands and work-to-family and family-to-work conflict: Direct and indirect relationships. *Journal of Family Issues* 26(6): 707–26.

Wall, G. (2010) Mothers' experiences with intensive parenting and brain development discourse. *Women's Studies International Forum* 33(3): 253–63.

Walrave, M. and De Bie, M. (2005) *Mijn kantoor is waar mijn laptop staat: mythe en realiteit van telewerk*: Fac. Politieke en Sociale Wetenschappen, Univ. Antwerpen.

Walter, N. (2021) Guilt and fury: How Covid brought mothers to breaking point. *The Guardian*. https://www.theguardian.com/lifeandstyle/2021/feb/28/mums-women-coronavirus-covid-home-schooling-inequality

Walthery, P. and Chung, H. (2021) *Sharing of childcare and well-being outcomes: An empirical analysis*. London: Government Equalities Office.

Wanrooy, B.v., Bewley, H., Bryson, A., Forth, J., Freeth, S., Stokes, L., et al (2013) The 2011 workplace employment relations study: First findings. Report for the UK Department for Business, Energy and Industrial Strategies. https://www.gov.uk/government/publications/the-2011-workplace-employment-relations-study-wers

Warmate, Z., Eldaly, M.K. and Elamer, A.A. (2021) Offering flexible working opportunities to people with mental disabilities: The missing link between sustainable development goals and financial implications. *Business Strategy and the Environment* 30(4): 1563–79.

West, C. and Zimmerman, D.H. (1987) Doing gender. *Gender & Society* 1(2): 125–51.

Wheatley, D. (2012) Good to be home? Time-use and satisfaction levels among home-based teleworkers. *New Technology, Work and Employment* 27(3): 224–41.

Wilder, S. (2014) Effects of parental involvement on academic achievement: A meta-synthesis. *Educational Review* 66(3): 377–97.

Williams, J. (1999) *Unbending gender: Why family and work conflict and what to do about it.* New York: Oxford University Press.

Williams, J. (2010) *Reshaping the work-family debate: Why men and class matter.* Cambridge, MA: Harvard University Press.

Williams, J., Blair-Loy, M. and Berdahl, J.L. (2013) Cultural schemas, social class, and the flexibility stigma. *Journal of Social Issues* 69(2): 209–34.

Wilthagen, T. and Tros, F. (2004) The concept of 'flexicurity': A new approach to regulating employment and labour markets. *Transfer* 10(2): 166–86.

Wishart, R., Dunatchik, A., Mayer, M. and Speight, S. (2019) Changing patterns in parental time use in the UK. https://natcen.ac.uk/media/1722408/Parental_time_use_report.pdf

Wiß, T. (2017) Paths towards family-friendly working time arrangements: Comparing workplaces in different countries and industries. *Social Policy & Administration* 51(7): 1406–30.

Wood, S.J. and De Menezes, L.M. (2010) Family-friendly management, organizational performance and social legitimacy. *The International Journal of Human Resource Management* 21(10): 1575–97.

Wood, S.J., De Menezes, L.M. and Lasaosa, A. (2003) Family-friendly management in Great Britain: Testing various perspectives. *Industrial Relations: A Journal of Economy and Society* 42(2): 221–50.

Wood, Z. (2021) UK workers take fewer sick days in 2020 despite coronavirus. *The Guardian.*

Working Families (2017) Modern Family Index 2017. London: Working Families.

Working Families (2021) Modern Families Index 2020. London: Working Families.

Workingmums (2016) Mums forced out due to lack of flexible jobs. *Workingmums blog.*

World Economic Forum (2020) Global Gender Gap Report 2020. Geneva: World Economic Forum.

Yamauchi, C. (2010) The availability of child care centers, perceived search costs and parental life satisfaction. *Review of Economics of the Household* 8(2): 231–53.

Yanofsky, D. (2012) That friend who says he works 75 hours a week? He's probably only clocking 50. *Quartz.*

Yerkes, M. and Javornik, J. (2019) *Social policy and the capability approach: Concepts, measurements and application.* Bristol: Policy Press.

Yerkes, M.A., André, S., Besamusca, J.W., Kruyen, P.M., Remery, C.L.H.S., Zwan, R.v.d., et al (2020) 'Intelligent' lockdown, intelligent effects? Results from a survey on gender (in)equality in paid work, the division of childcare and household work, and quality of life among parents in the Netherlands during the COVID-19 lockdown. *PloS One* 15(11): e0242249. https://journals.plos.org/plosone/article?id=10.1371/journal.pone.0242249

Young, Z. (2018) *Women's work: How mothers manage flexible working in careers and family life*. Bristol: Bristol University Press.

YTN (2019) 민주노총 총파업… 탄력 근로 확대 법안 철회 요구. Seoul: YTN.

Yucel, D. and Chung, H. (2021) Working from home, work–family conflict, and the role of gender and gender role attitudes. *Community, Work & Family*. Online first. 1–32.

Zamarro, G., Perez-Arce, F. and Prados, M.J. (2020) Gender differences in the impact of COVID-19. Working Paper. https://ktla.com/wp-content/uploads/sites/4/2020/06/ZamarroGenderDiffImpactCOVID-19_061820-2.pdf

Zwolinski, M. and Wertheimer, A. (2017) Exploitation. In: Zalta, E.N. (ed) *The Stanford encyclopedia of philosophy* (Summer 2017 Edition). https://plato.stanford.edu/archives/sum2017/entries/exploitation/

Index

References to figures appear in *italic* type; those in
bold type refer to tables. References to endnotes
show both the page number and the note number (231n3).